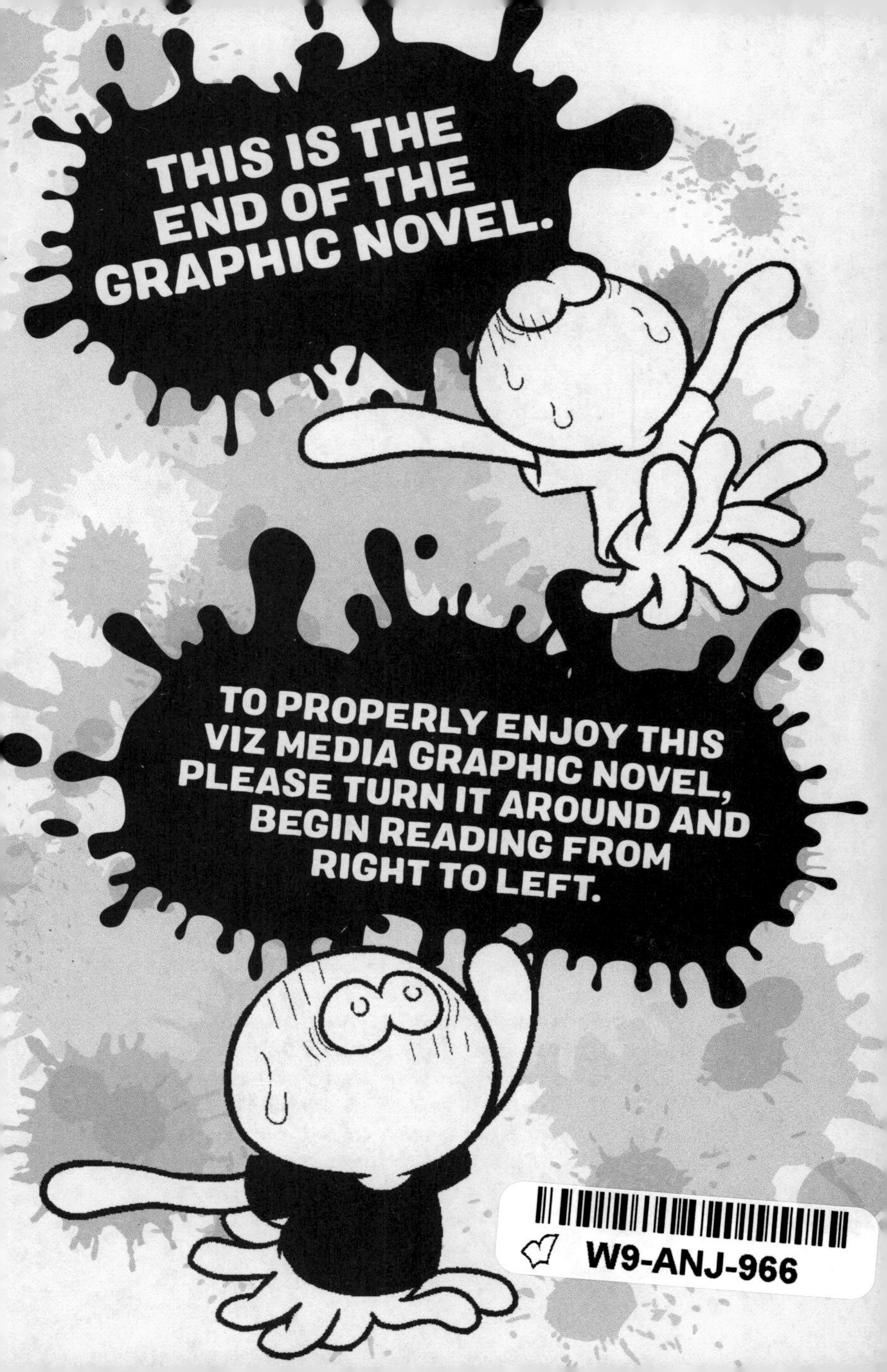
THIS IS THE END OF THE GRAPHIC NOVEL.
TO PROPERLY ENJOY THIS VIZ MEDIA GRAPHIC NOVEL, PLEASE TURN IT AROUND AND BEGIN READING FROM RIGHT TO LEFT.

Splatoon
SQUID KIDS COMEDY SHOW
3

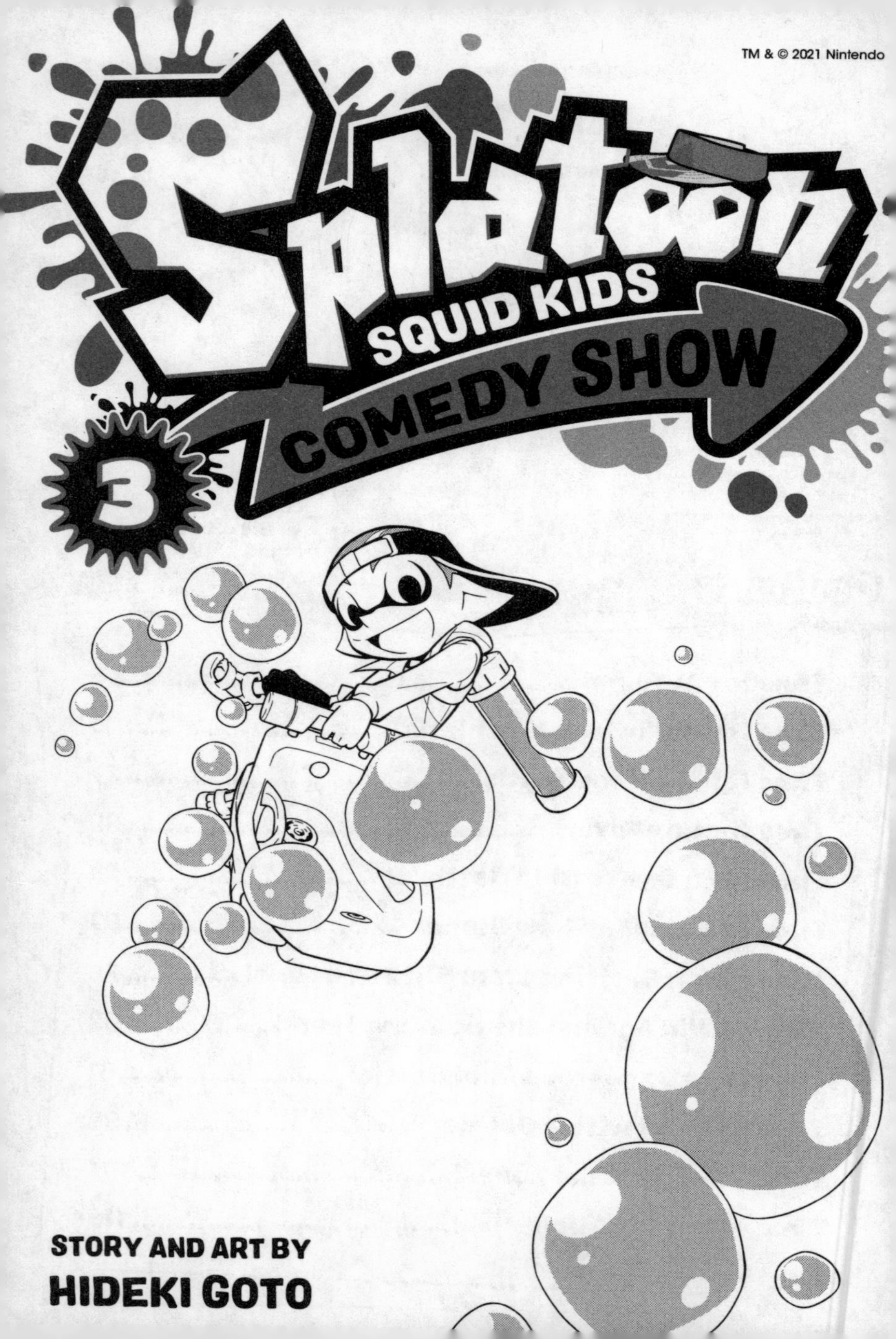

STORY AND ART BY
HIDEKI GOTO

Maika
A city girl who
uses Dualies.

Characters

Kou
An elite boy with three
big advantages going
for him—he's tall, rich
and smart.

Hit
A boy from the
countryside who came
to the city to be a cool
squid kid!

Contents

TIME FOR AUTUMN!

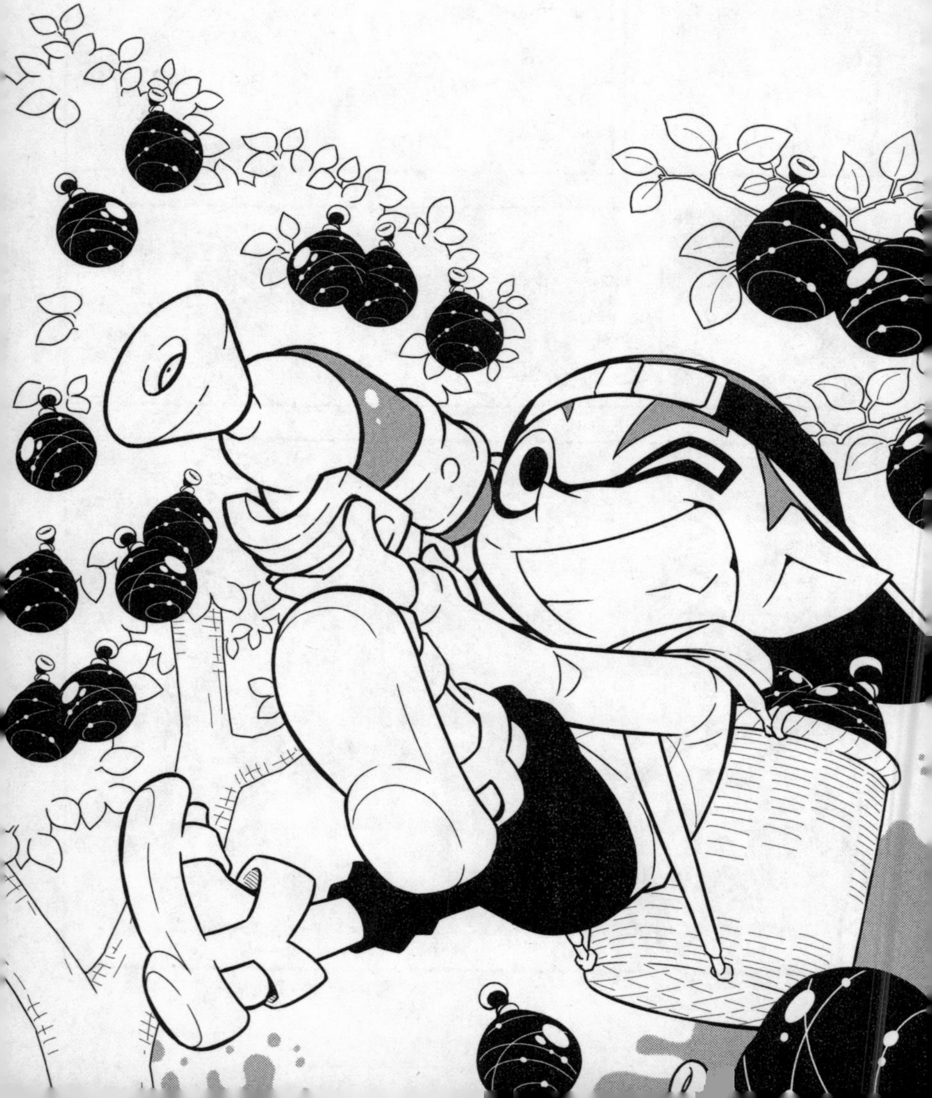

AUTUMN LEAVES

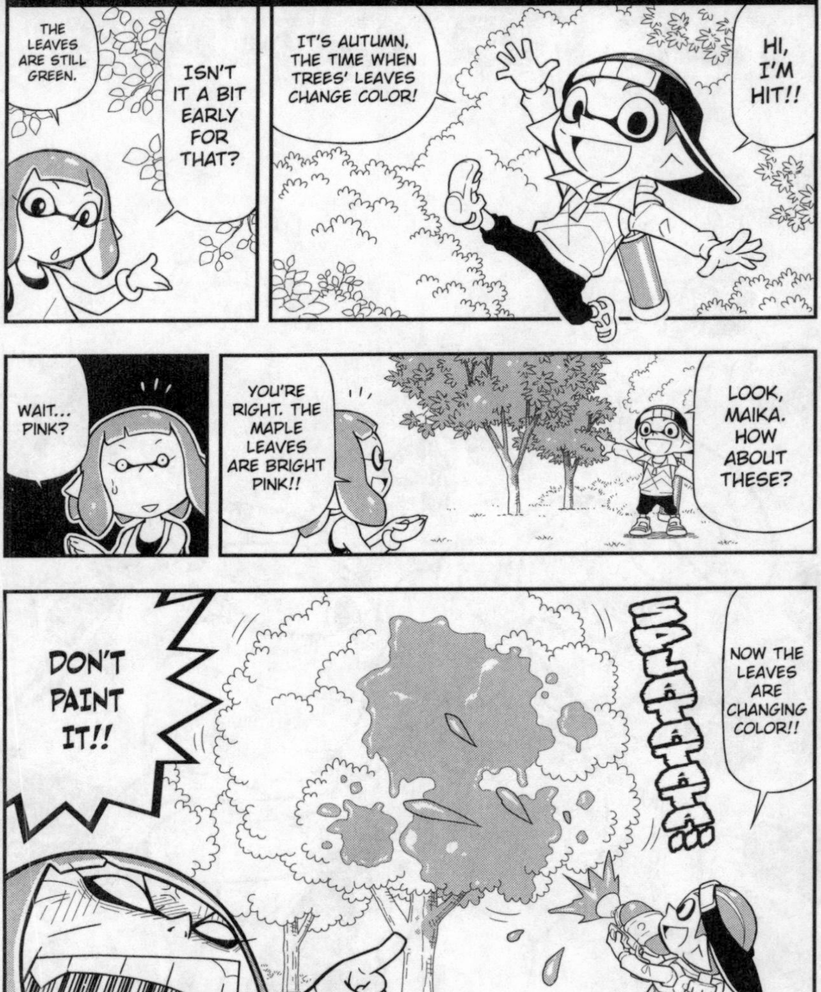
HI, I'M HIT!!
IT'S AUTUMN, THE TIME WHEN TREES' LEAVES CHANGE COLOR!
ISN'T IT A BIT EARLY FOR THAT?
THE LEAVES ARE STILL GREEN.
LOOK, MAIKA. HOW ABOUT THESE?
YOU'RE RIGHT. THE MAPLE LEAVES ARE BRIGHT PINK!!
WAIT... PINK?
NOW THE LEAVES ARE CHANGING COLOR!!
SPLATATATA!!
DON'T PAINT IT!!
*Don't try this at home, everyone!!

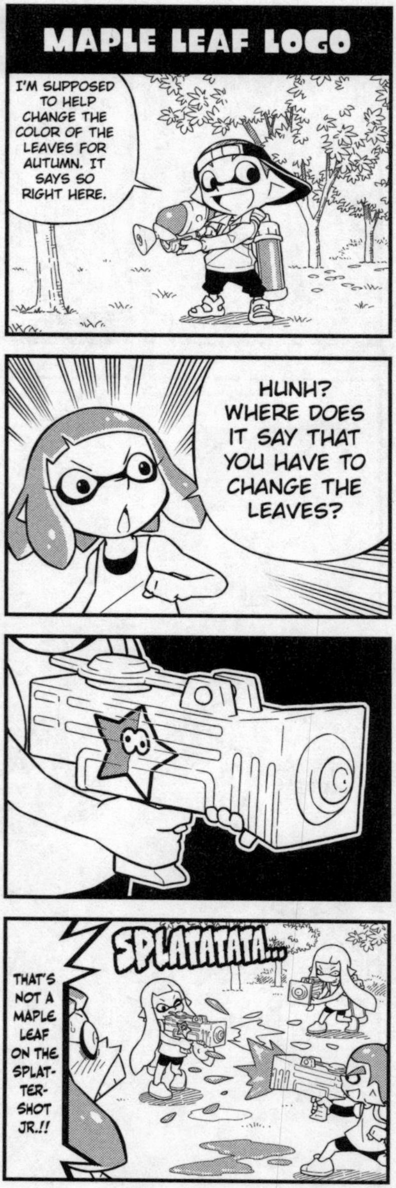
MAPLE LEAF LOGO
I'M SUPPOSED TO HELP CHANGE THE COLOR OF THE LEAVES FOR AUTUMN. IT SAYS SO RIGHT HERE.
HUNH? WHERE DOES IT SAY THAT YOU HAVE TO CHANGE THE LEAVES?
SPLATATATA...
THAT'S NOT A MAPLE LEAF ON THE SPLATTERSHOT JR.!!

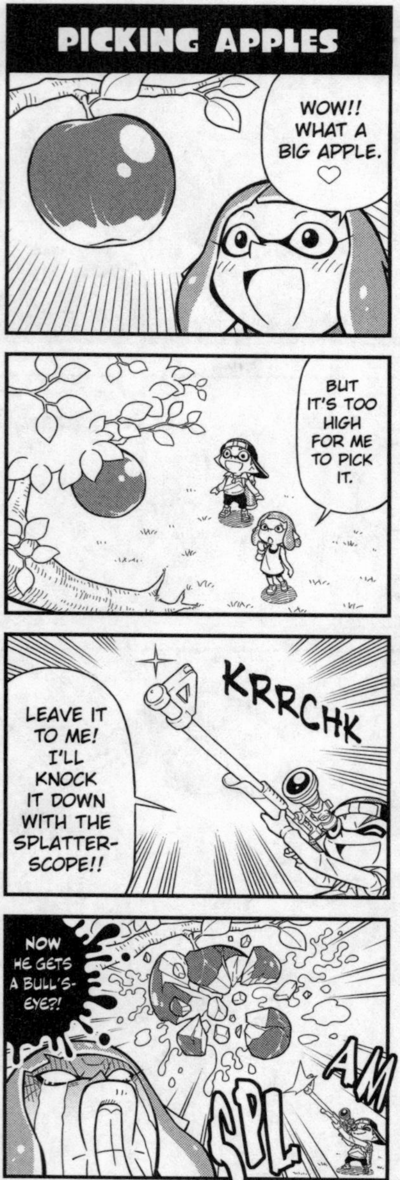
PICKING APPLES
WOW!! WHAT A BIG APPLE. ♡
BUT IT'S TOO HIGH FOR ME TO PICK IT.
KRRCHK
LEAVE IT TO ME! I'LL KNOCK IT DOWN WITH THE SPLATTERSCOPE!!
NOW HE GETS A BULL'S-EYE?!
SPLAM

GRAPE PICKING

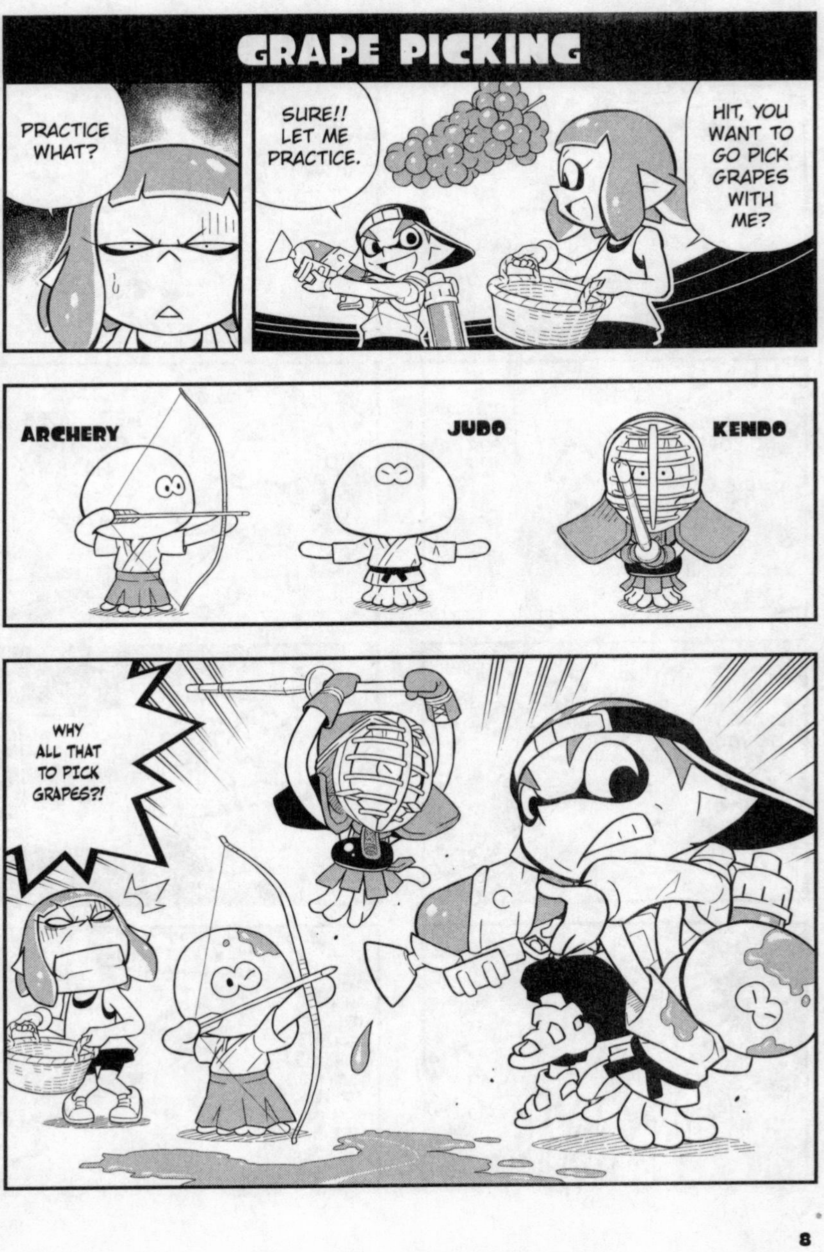

HIT, YOU WANT TO GO PICK GRAPES WITH ME?
SURE!! LET ME PRACTICE.
PRACTICE WHAT?
KENDO
JUDO
ARCHERY
WHY ALL THAT TO PICK GRAPES?!

MUSHROOM PICKING

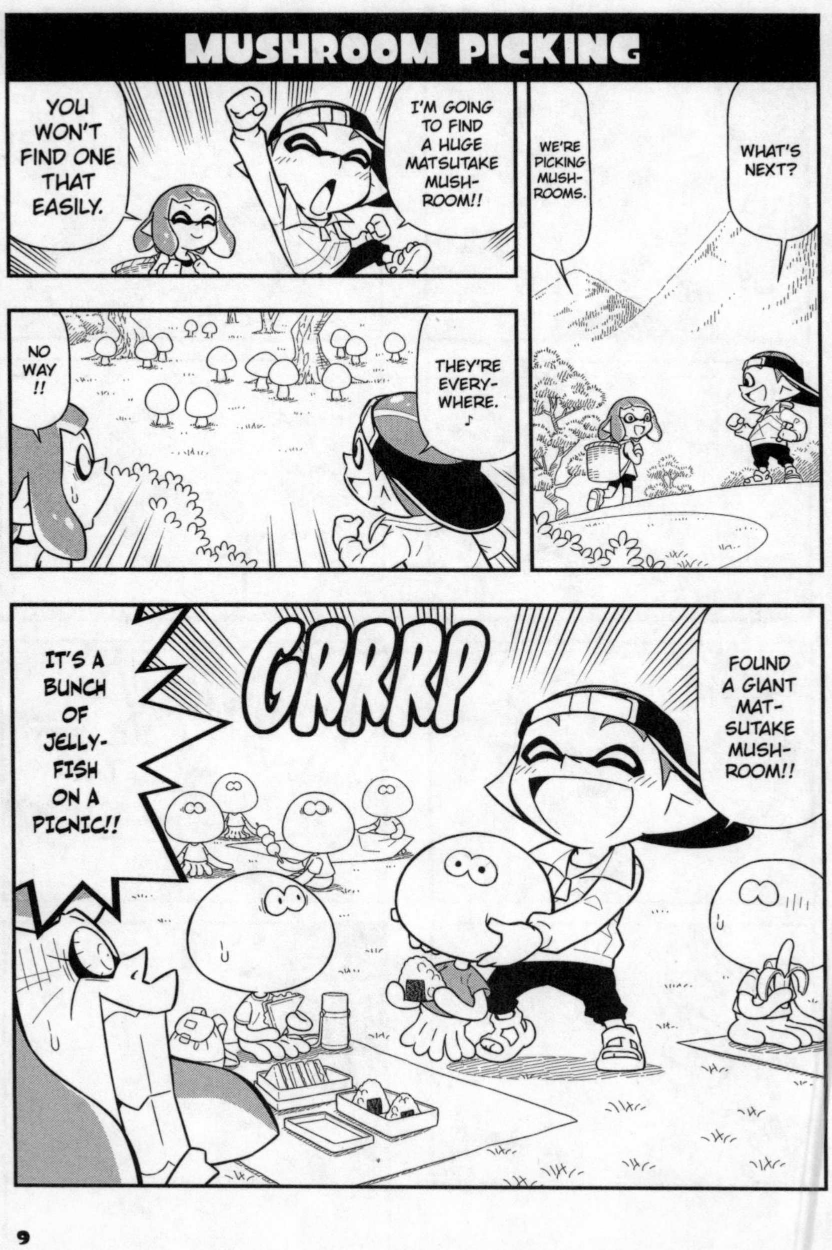
WHAT'S NEXT?
WE'RE PICKING MUSHROOMS.
I'M GOING TO FIND A HUGE MATSUTAKE MUSHROOM!!
YOU WON'T FIND ONE THAT EASILY.
THEY'RE EVERYWHERE. ♪
NO WAY!!
FOUND A GIANT MATSUTAKE MUSHROOM!!
GRRRP
IT'S A BUNCH OF JELLYFISH ON A PICNIC!!

POTATO DIGGING

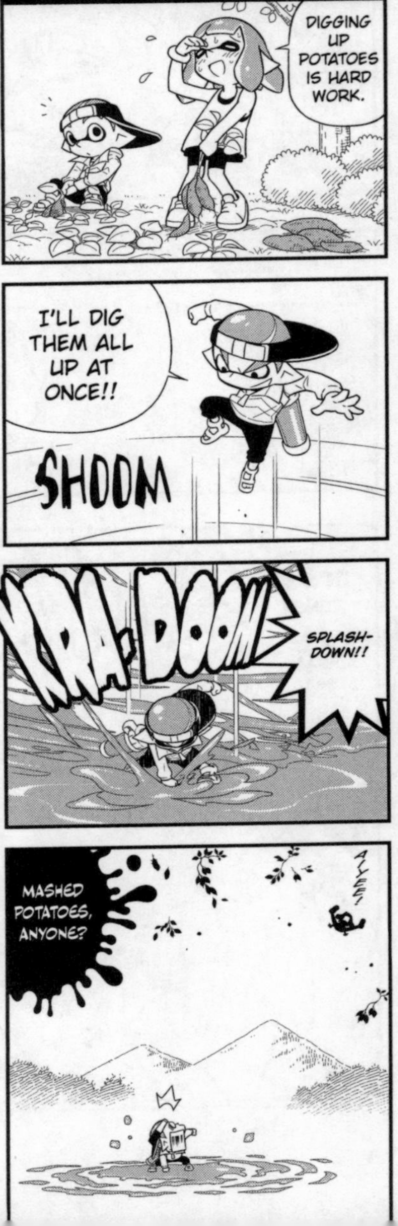
DIGGING UP POTATOES IS HARD WORK.
I'LL DIG THEM ALL UP AT ONCE!!
SHOOM
KRA-DOOM
SPLASH-DOWN!!
AIYEE!
MASHED POTATOES, ANYONE?

CHESTNUT PICKING

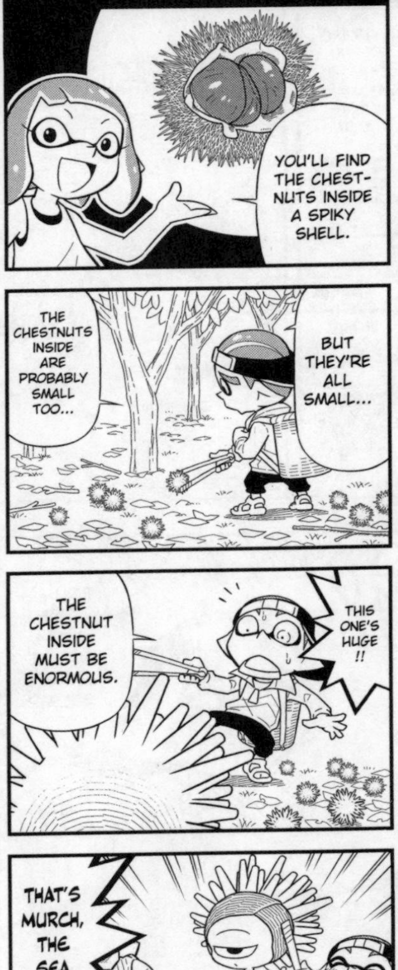
YOU'LL FIND THE CHESTNUTS INSIDE A SPIKY SHELL.
BUT THEY'RE ALL SMALL...
THE CHESTNUTS INSIDE ARE PROBABLY SMALL TOO...
THIS ONE'S HUGE!!
THE CHESTNUT INSIDE MUST BE ENORMOUS.
THAT'S MURCH, THE SEA URCHIN!!

MANDARIN ORANGE PICKING AREA

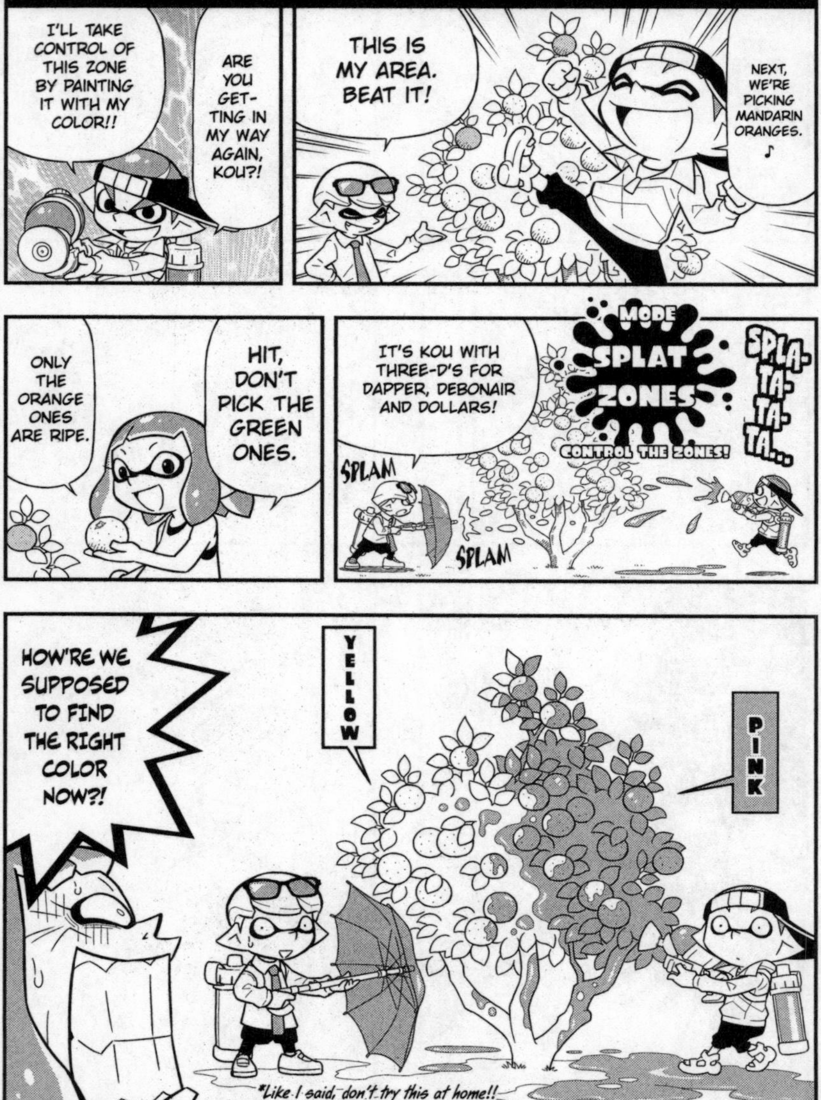
NEXT, WE'RE PICKING MANDARIN ORANGES. ♪
THIS IS MY AREA. BEAT IT!
ARE YOU GET-TING IN MY WAY AGAIN, KOU?!
I'LL TAKE CONTROL OF THIS ZONE BY PAINTING IT WITH MY COLOR!!
SPLA-TA-TA-TA...
MODE
SPLAT ZONES
CONTROL THE ZONES!
IT'S KOU WITH THREE-D'S FOR DAPPER, DEBONAIR AND DOLLARS!
SPLAM
SPLAM
HIT, DON'T PICK THE GREEN ONES.
ONLY THE ORANGE ONES ARE RIPE.
PINK
YELLOW
HOW'RE WE SUPPOSED TO FIND THE RIGHT COLOR NOW?!
*Like I said, don't try this at home!!

AUTUMN FEAST

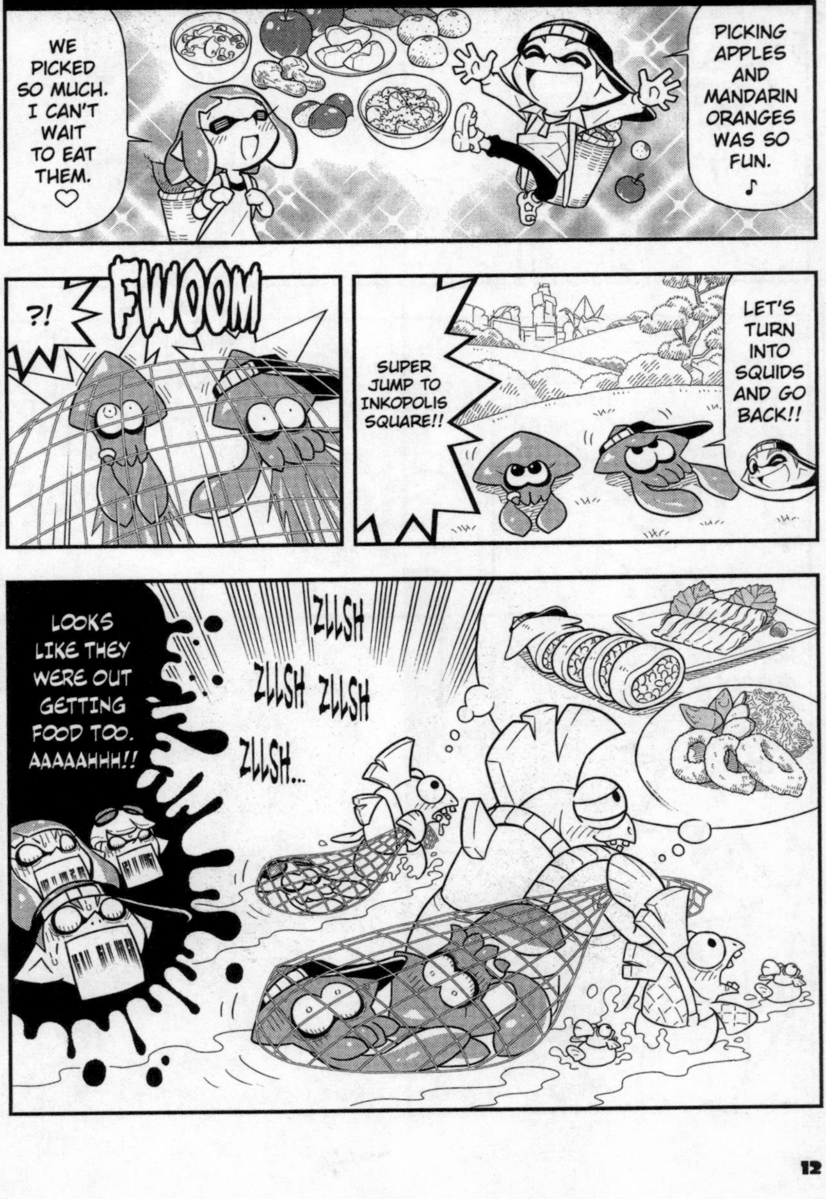
PICKING APPLES AND MANDARIN ORANGES WAS SO FUN. ♪
WE PICKED SO MUCH. I CAN'T WAIT TO EAT THEM. ♡
LET'S TURN INTO SQUIDS AND GO BACK!!
SUPER JUMP TO INKOPOLIS SQUARE!!
FWOOM
?!
ZLLSH
ZLLSH ZLLSH
ZLLSH...
LOOKS LIKE THEY WERE OUT GETTING FOOD TOO. AAAAAHHH!!

SPLOOSH-O-MATIC

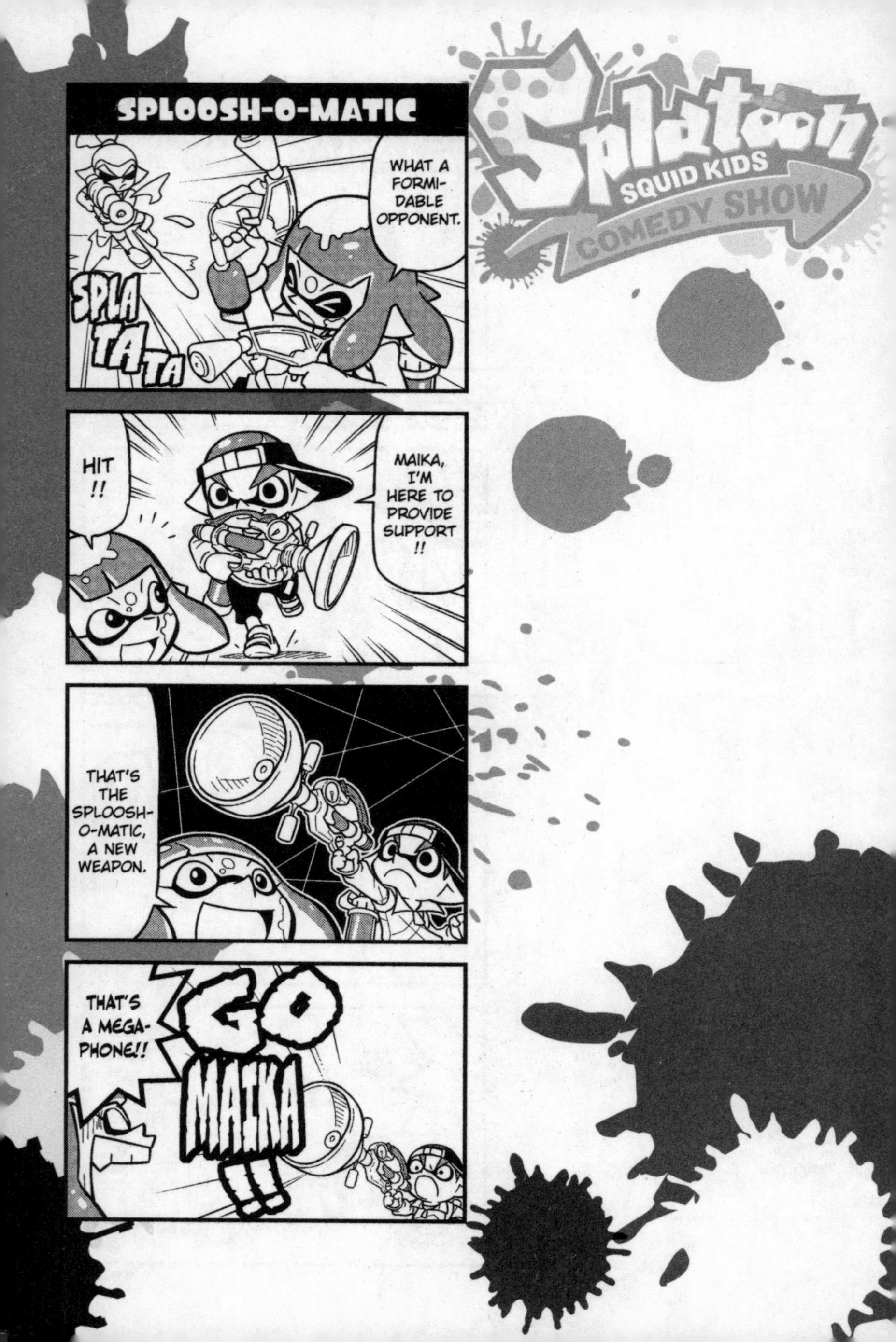
WHAT A FORMIDABLE OPPONENT.
SPLA TA TA
MAIKA, I'M HERE TO PROVIDE SUPPORT!!
HIT!!
THAT'S THE SPLOOSH-O-MATIC, A NEW WEAPON.
GO MAIKA
THAT'S A MEGAPHONE!!

Splatoon
SQUID KIDS
COMEDY SHOW

SPLAT BRELLA
EEEEK!!
DASH
I'LL PROTECT YOU!!
SWIP
THE SPLAT BRELLA WILL BLOCK ANY ATTACK !!
SKRRRRCH
THUN
GKT
AIYEEEEE!!

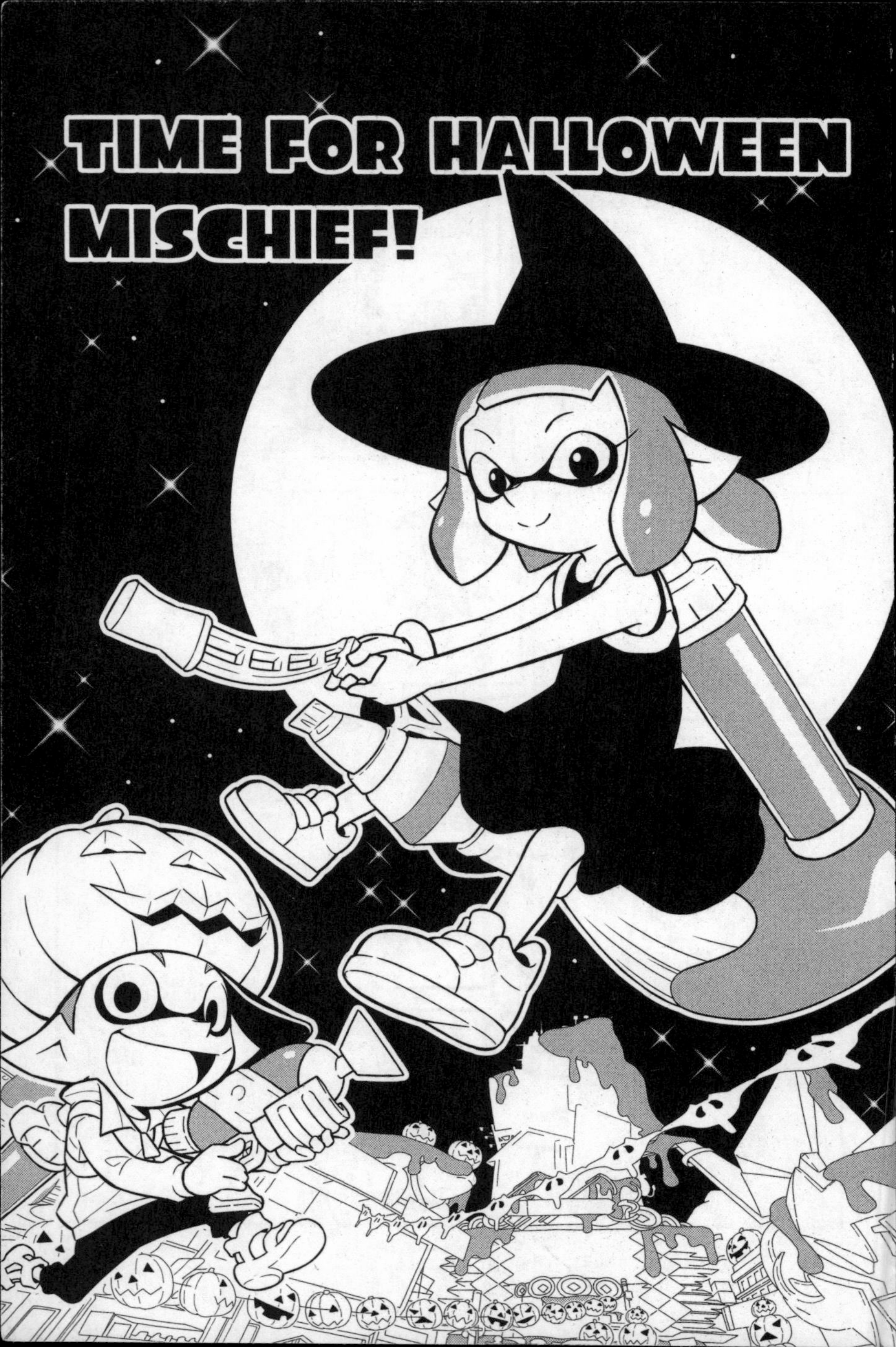
TIME FOR HALLOWEEN MISCHIEF!

HALLOWEEN SPLATFEST

HI, I'M HIT!!
THE HALLOWEEN SPLATFEST IS TODAY!
HIT? THAT'S A JACK-O'-LANTERN COSTUME.
YOU'RE DRESSED UP AS A WITCH, MAIKA!!
MY MAGIC BROOMSTICK IS THE INKBRUSH, SO I CAN PAINT TOO.
TMP TMP TMP
I'VE GOT A WEAPON TOO!!
WHAT?! WHERE?
FIRE!!
BWOOOSH
TENTA MISSILES... KINDA!!

HALLOWEEN DECORATION

THE TOWN'S COVERED IN HALLOWEEN DECORATIONS.
SPLUB
WHAT THE ...?!
I CAN TEST MY WEAPON OUT AS MUCH AS I WANT TO.
SPLUB
THEY AREN'T TARGETS !!
SPLATATATA...

TRICK OR TREAT

TRICK OR TREAT !!
WE'RE GONNA TRICK YOU IF YOU DON'T GIVE US TREATS!!
HERE YOU GO!!
SO MANY BAGS FILLED WITH TREATS !!
YOU'RE SO GENEROUS, SHELDON.
SPLAM
THESE ARE BURST BOMBS!!

SMALLFRY SNACKS

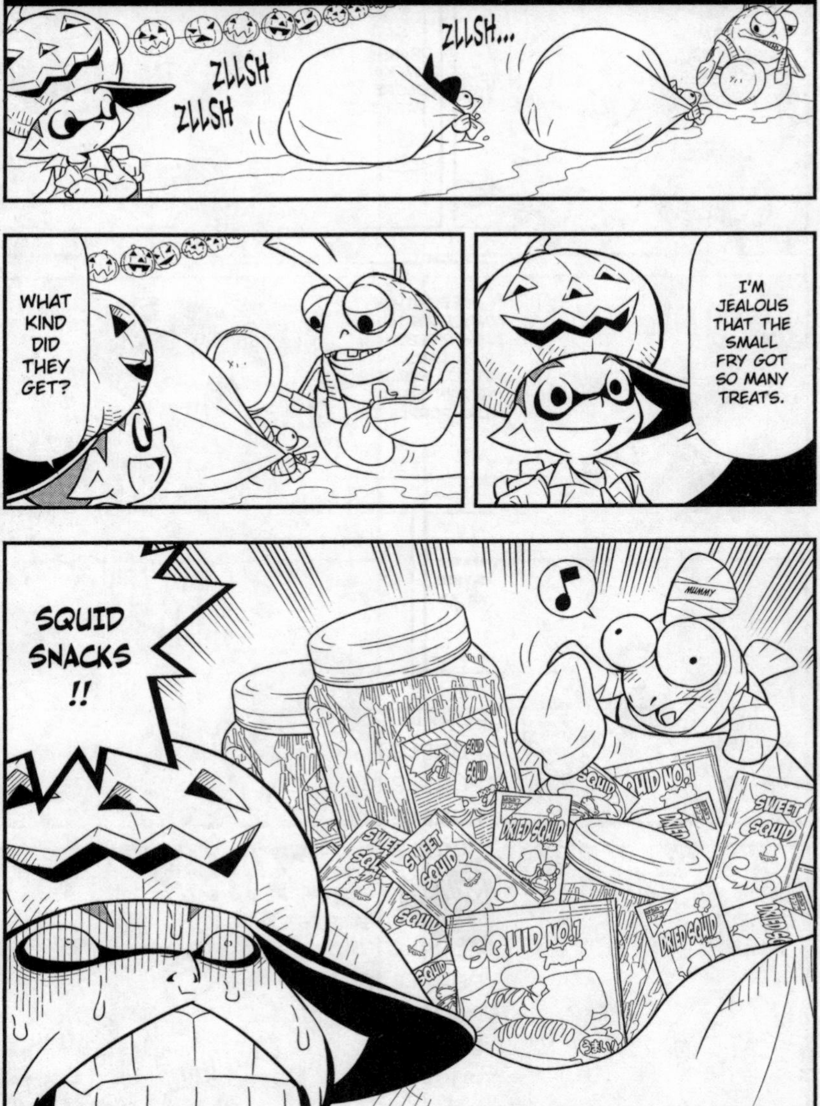
ZLLSH...
ZLLSH
ZLLSH
I'M JEALOUS THAT THE SMALL FRY GOT SO MANY TREATS.
WHAT KIND DID THEY GET?
MUMMY
SQUID SNACKS !!
SQUID NO.1
SWEET SQUID
DRIED SQUID
SWEET SQUID
DRIED SQUID
SQUID NO.1
DRIED SQUID
うまい!

PURPLE...I THINK...

THIS IS OUR TURF. STAY OUT!!

AN ORANGE PUMPKIN-COLORED PATH!!

I'LL CREATE A PATH FOR THE HALLOWEEN PARADE!!

THE GRAPHIC NOVEL'S IN BLACK AND WHITE, SO I CAN'T TELL WHAT COLOR IT IS!!

IT GOES WITH MY *THREE-D'S* FOR DAPPER, DEBONAIR AND DOLLARS!! AND CAN'T YOU SEE THAT I'VE PAINTED THIS TURF PURPLE?!

KOU, YOU'RE DRACULA?

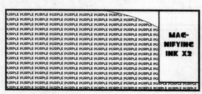

MAG-NIFYING INK X2

LOOK CLOSER!!

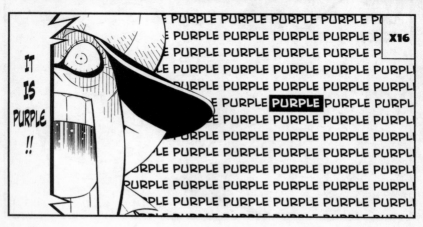

IT IS PURPLE!!

X16

PURPLE **PURPLE** PURPLE PURPLE PURPLE PURPLE PURPLE PURPLE PURPLE PURPLE PURPLE PURPLE PURPLE PURPLE PURPLE PURPLE PURPLE PURPLE PURPLE

ORANGE ARMY

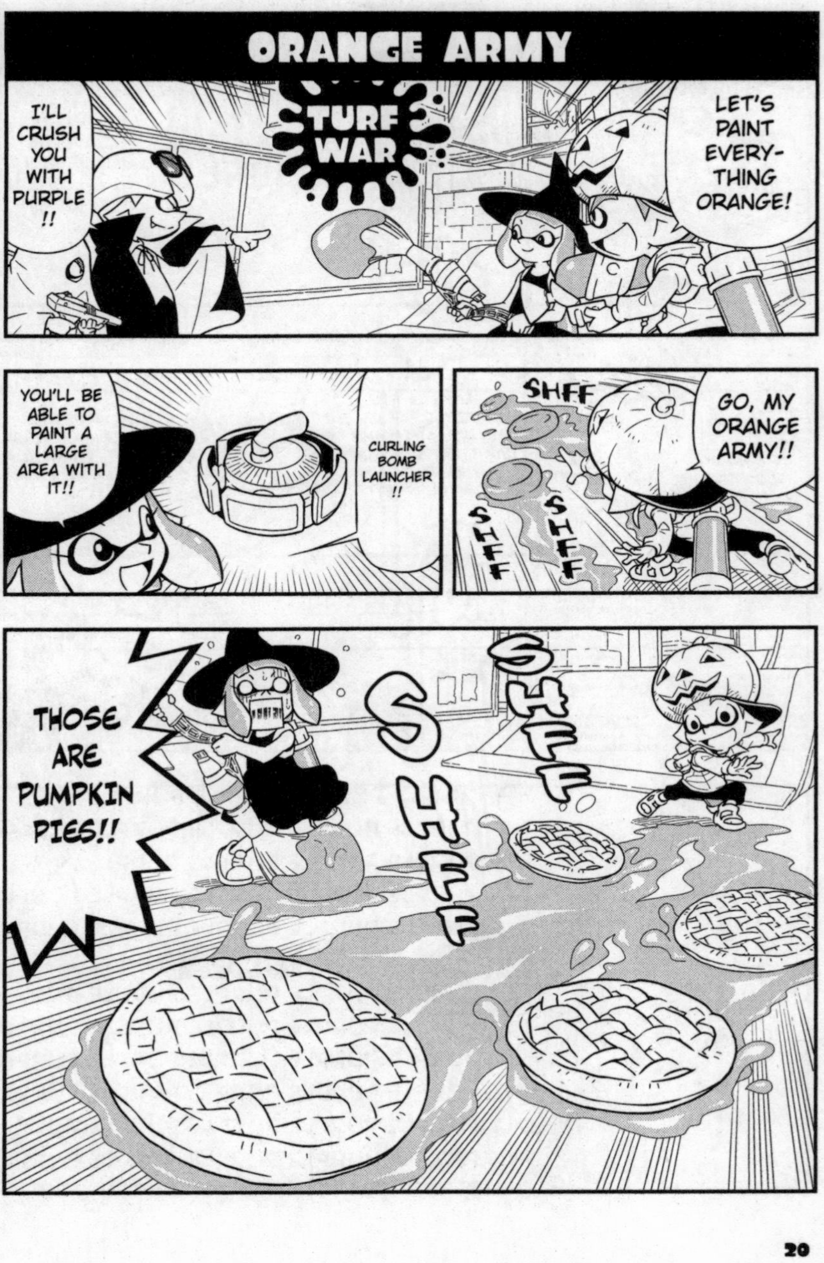
LET'S PAINT EVERYTHING ORANGE!
TURF WAR
I'LL CRUSH YOU WITH PURPLE!!
GO, MY ORANGE ARMY!!
SHFF
SHFF
SHFF
CURLING BOMB LAUNCHER!!
YOU'LL BE ABLE TO PAINT A LARGE AREA WITH IT!!
SHFF
SHFF
THOSE ARE PUMPKIN PIES!!

HALLOWEEN BALLER

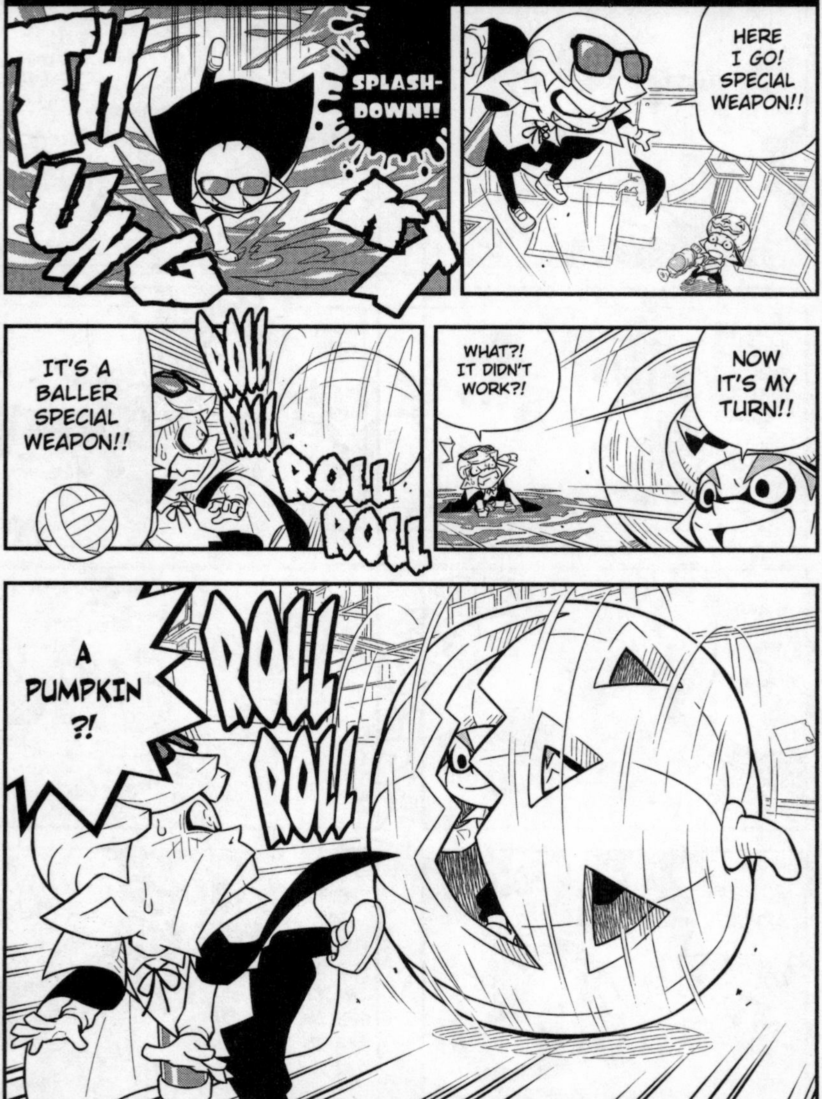
HERE I GO! SPECIAL WEAPON!!
SPLASH-DOWN!!
THUNGK
NOW IT'S MY TURN!!
WHAT?! IT DIDN'T WORK?!
ROLL ROLL
ROLL ROLL
IT'S A BALLER SPECIAL WEAPON!!
ROLL ROLL
A PUMPKIN ?!

FLYING GHOSTS

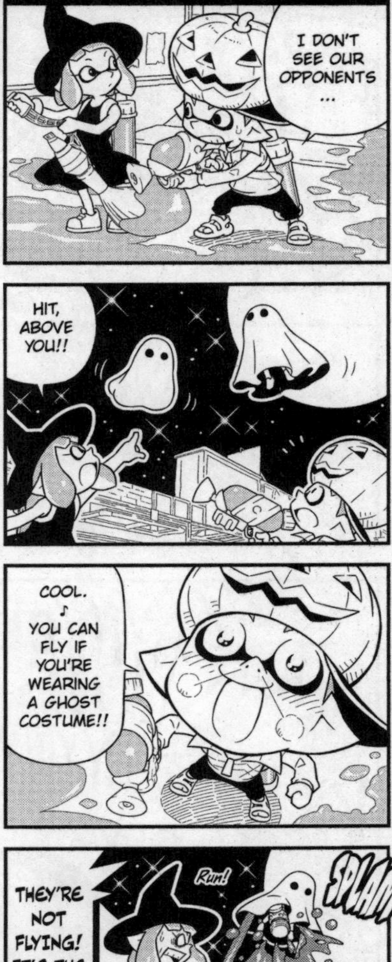
I DON'T SEE OUR OPPONENTS ...
HIT, ABOVE YOU!!
COOL. ♪ YOU CAN FLY IF YOU'RE WEARING A GHOST COSTUME!!
SPLAM
Run!
THEY'RE NOT FLYING! IT'S THE INKJET SPECIAL WEAPON !!

WITCH BOMB

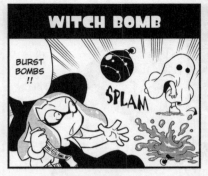

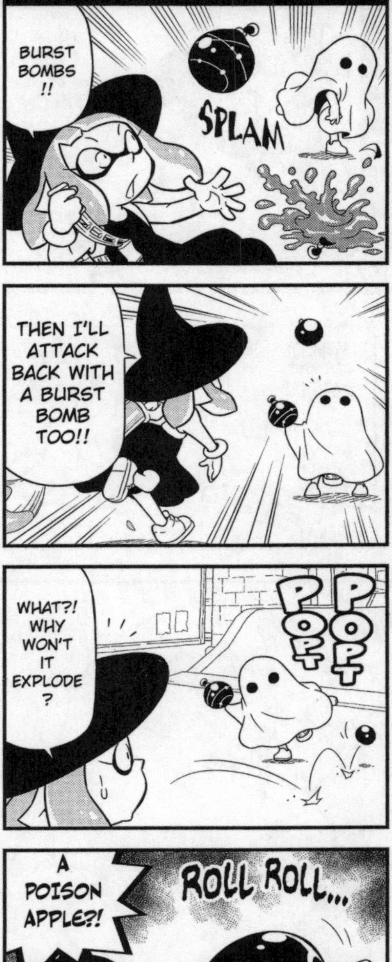
BURST BOMBS !!
SPLAM
THEN I'LL ATTACK BACK WITH A BURST BOMB TOO!!
POP POP
WHAT?! WHY WON'T IT EXPLODE ?
ROLL ROLL...
A POISON APPLE?!

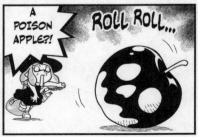

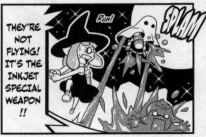

WEAKNESS

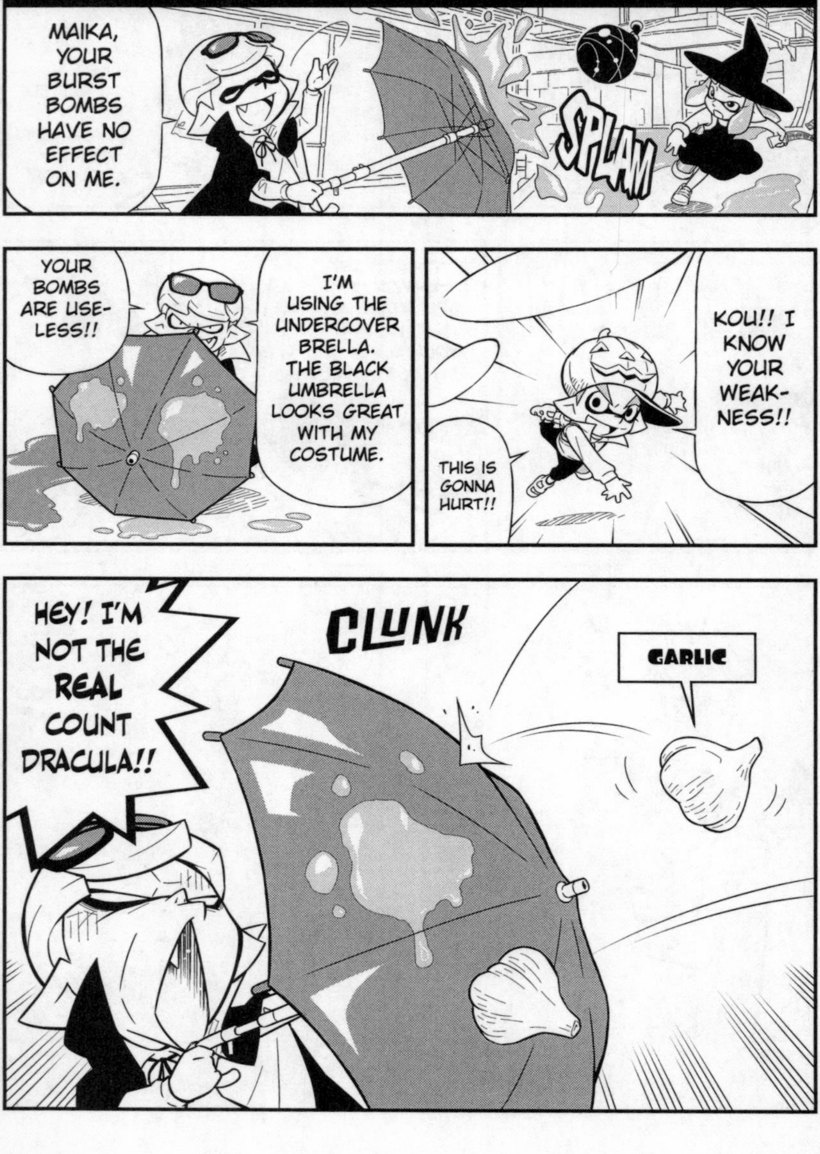
SPLAM
MAIKA, YOUR BURST BOMBS HAVE NO EFFECT ON ME.
KOU!! I KNOW YOUR WEAKNESS!!
THIS IS GONNA HURT!!
I'M USING THE UNDERCOVER BRELLA. THE BLACK UMBRELLA LOOKS GREAT WITH MY COSTUME.
YOUR BOMBS ARE USELESS!!
GARLIC
CLUNK
HEY! I'M NOT THE REAL COUNT DRACULA!!

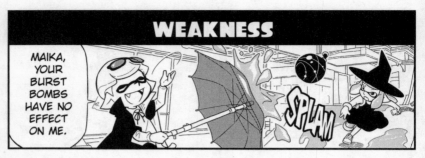

HALLOWEEN ARMOR

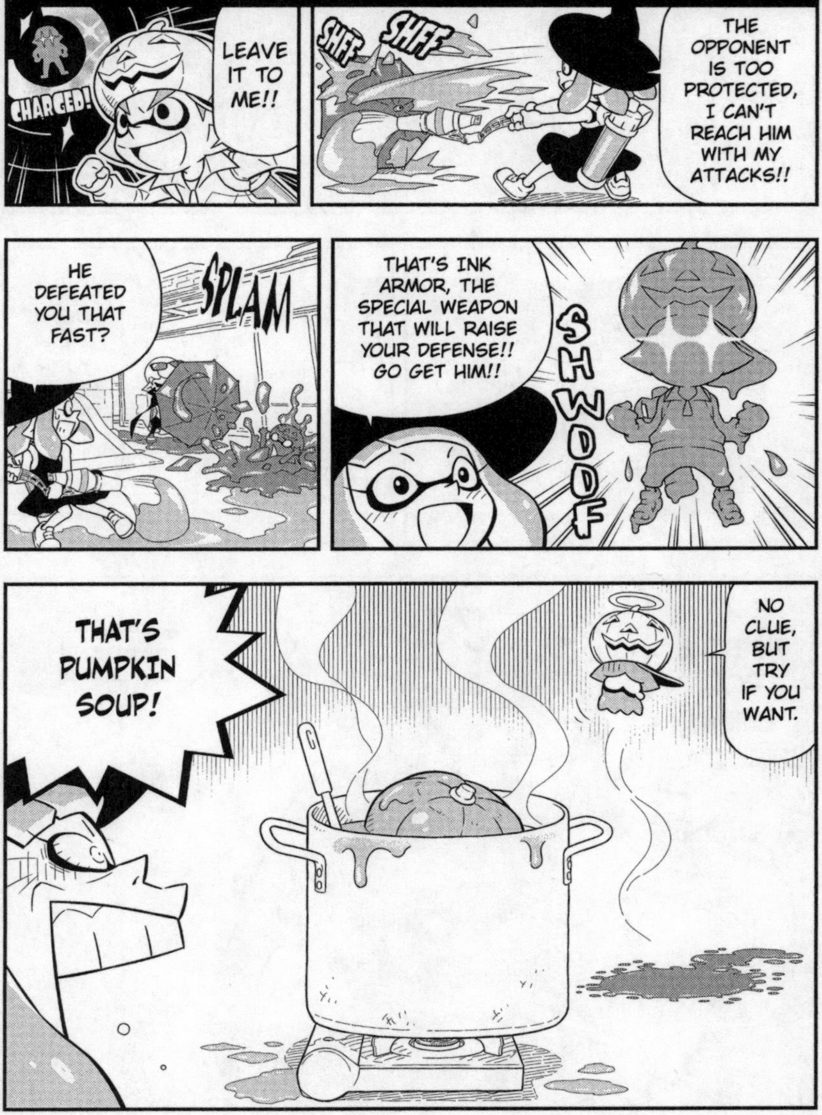

THE OPPONENT IS TOO PROTECTED, I CAN'T REACH HIM WITH MY ATTACKS!!
SHFF
SHFF
LEAVE IT TO ME!!
CHARGED!
THAT'S INK ARMOR, THE SPECIAL WEAPON THAT WILL RAISE YOUR DEFENSE!! GO GET HIM!!
SHWDDF
HE DEFEATED YOU THAT FAST?
SPLAM
NO CLUE, BUT TRY IF YOU WANT.
THAT'S PUMPKIN SOUP!

THE END OF HALLOWEEN

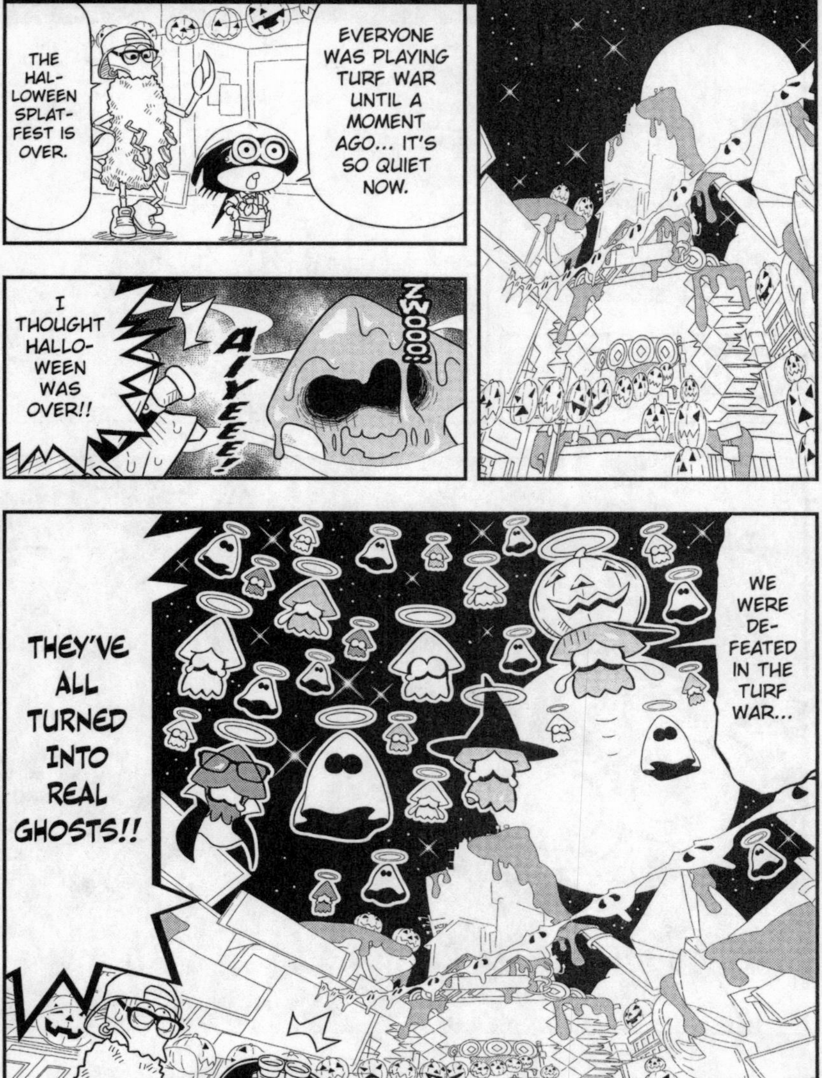
EVERYONE WAS PLAYING TURF WAR UNTIL A MOMENT AGO... IT'S SO QUIET NOW.
THE HALLOWEEN SPLATFEST IS OVER.
ZWOOO!!
AIYEEEE!
I THOUGHT HALLOWEEN WAS OVER!!
WE WERE DEFEATED IN THE TURF WAR...
THEY'VE ALL TURNED INTO REAL GHOSTS!!

CHRISTMAS ILLUMINATION

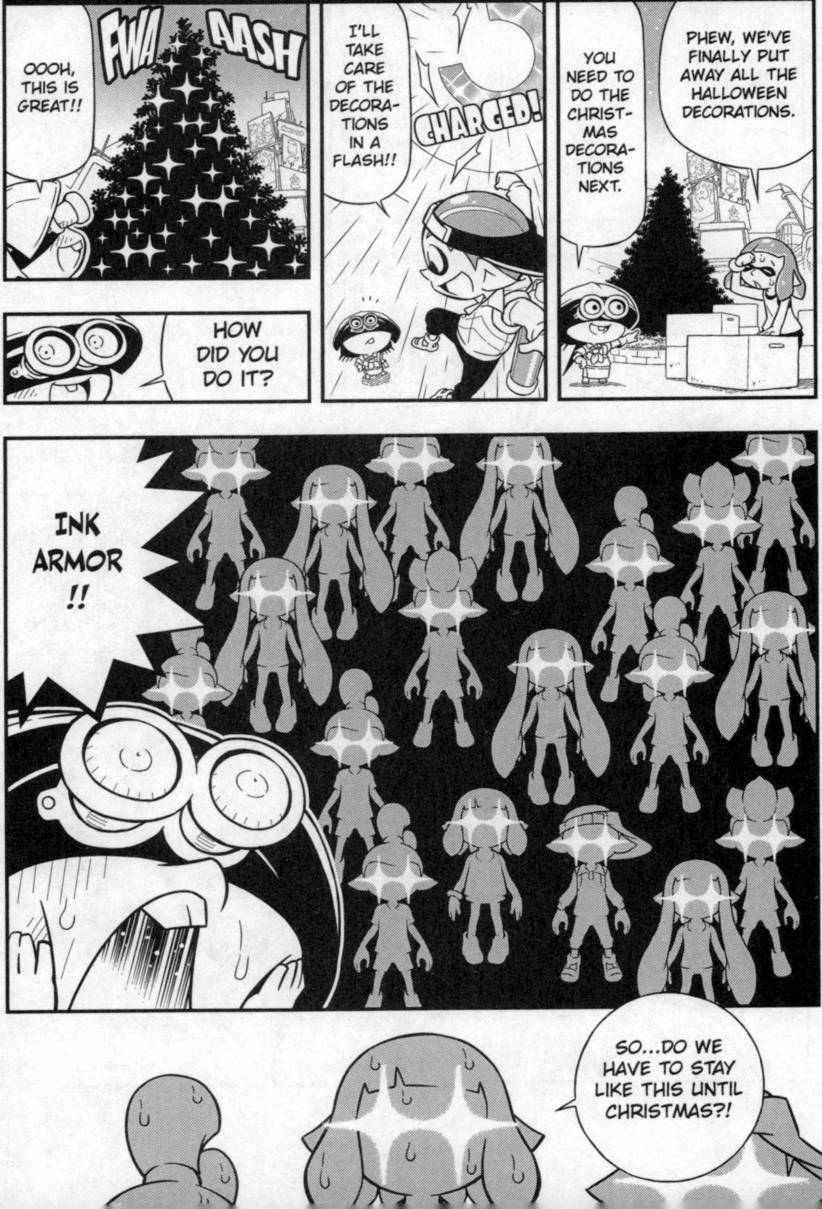
PHEW, WE'VE FINALLY PUT AWAY ALL THE HALLOWEEN DECORATIONS.
YOU NEED TO DO THE CHRIST-MAS DECORA-TIONS NEXT.
I'LL TAKE CARE OF THE DECORA-TIONS IN A FLASH!!
CHARGED!
FWAAASH
OOOH, THIS IS GREAT!!
HOW DID YOU DO IT?
INK ARMOR!!
SO...DO WE HAVE TO STAY LIKE THIS UNTIL CHRISTMAS?!

TIME FOR SPLATOON CARDS!

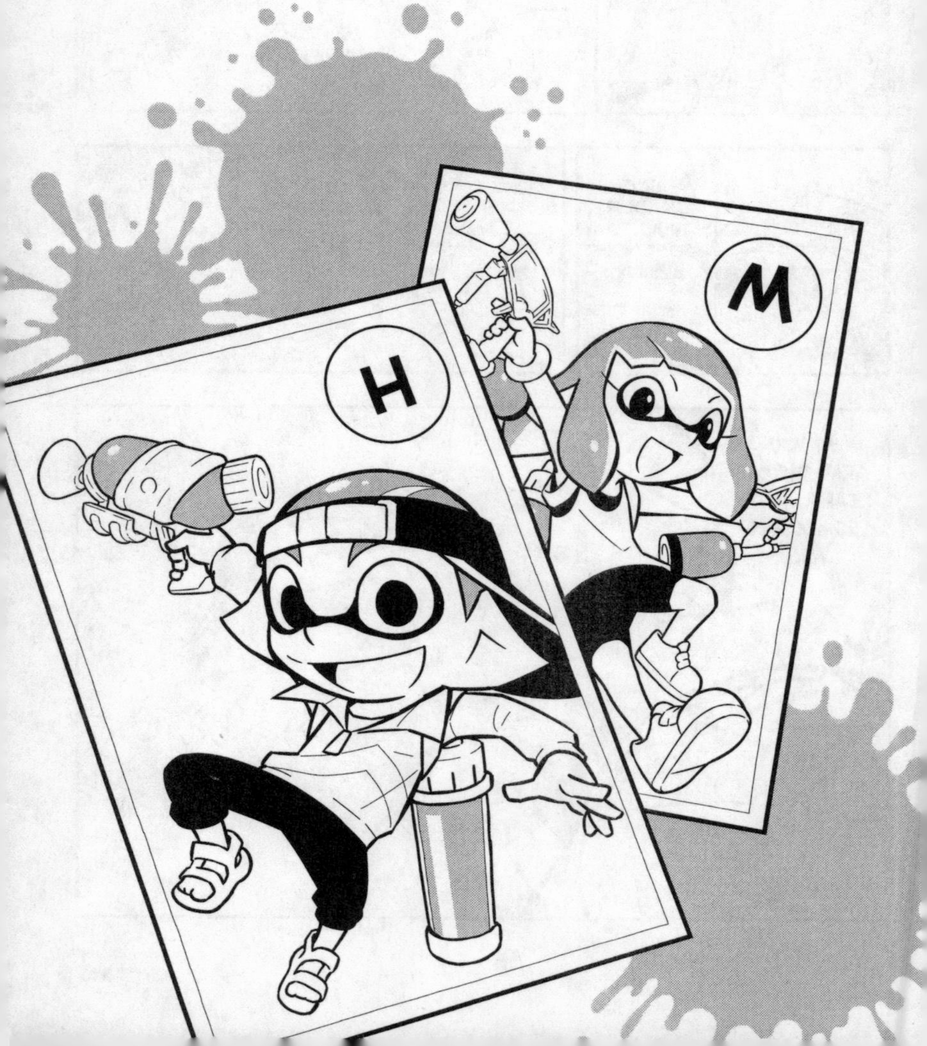

H
M

CARD GAME

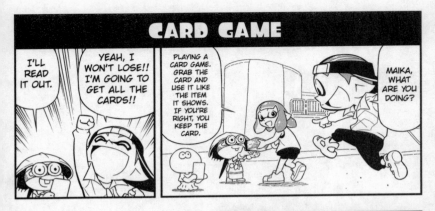

MAIKA, WHAT ARE YOU DOING?
PLAYING A CARD GAME. GRAB THE CARD AND USE IT LIKE THE ITEM IT SHOWS. IF YOU'RE RIGHT, YOU KEEP THE CARD.
YEAH, I WON'T LOSE!! I'M GOING TO GET ALL THE CARDS!!
I'LL READ IT OUT.
ZZTZZT...
READY, SHELDON.
WEAR ONE ON YOUR HEAD TO BOOST YOUR ABILITY.
I'VE COLLECTED SO MANY!!
W! YOU GRAB THE "W" CARD...NOT SOMEONE'S WIG!

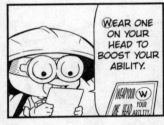

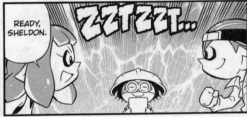

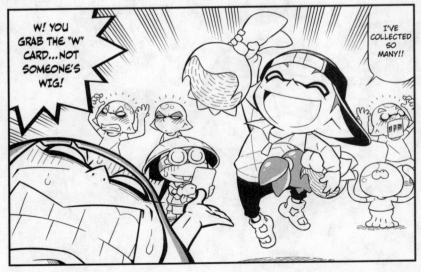

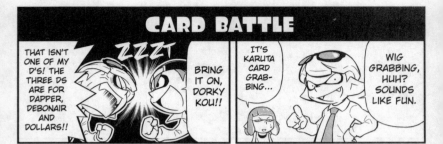

CARD BATTLE

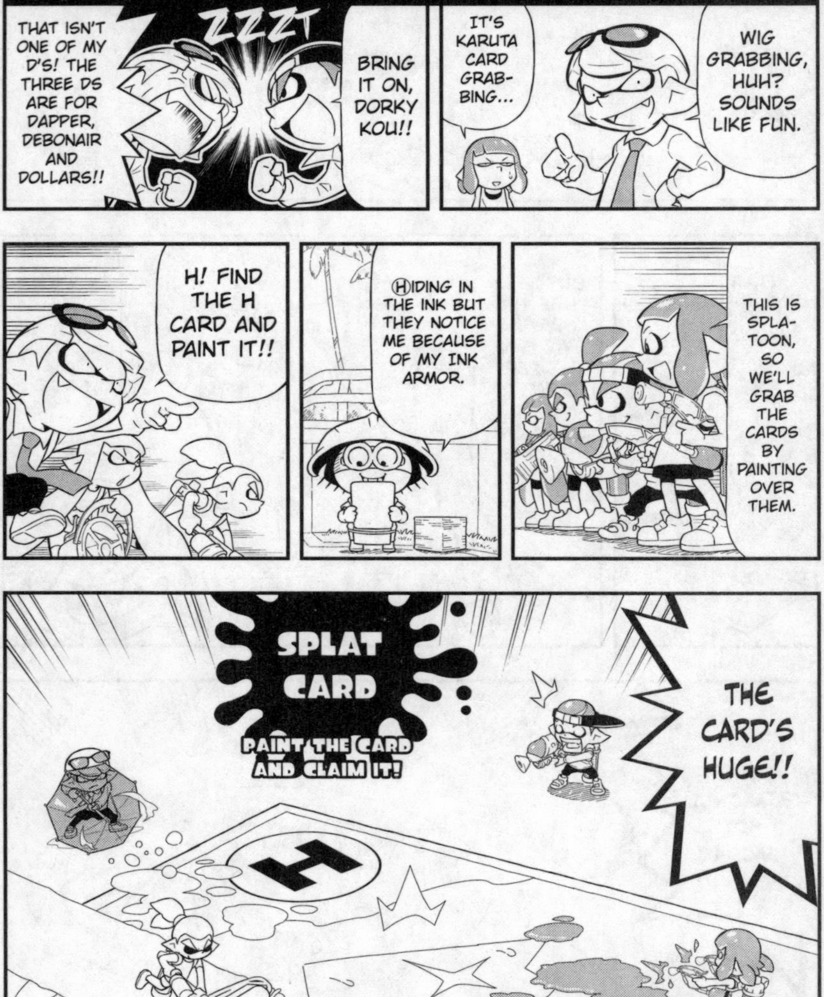
WIG GRABBING, HUH? SOUNDS LIKE FUN.
IT'S KARUTA CARD GRAB-BING...
BRING IT ON, DORKY KOU!!
ZZZZT
THAT ISN'T ONE OF MY D'S! THE THREE DS ARE FOR DAPPER, DEBONAIR AND DOLLARS!!
THIS IS SPLA-TOON, SO WE'LL GRAB THE CARDS BY PAINTING OVER THEM.
ⒽIDING IN THE INK BUT THEY NOTICE ME BECAUSE OF MY INK ARMOR.
H! FIND THE H CARD AND PAINT IT!!
SPLAT CARD
PAINT THE CARD AND CLAIM IT!
THE CARD'S HUGE!!

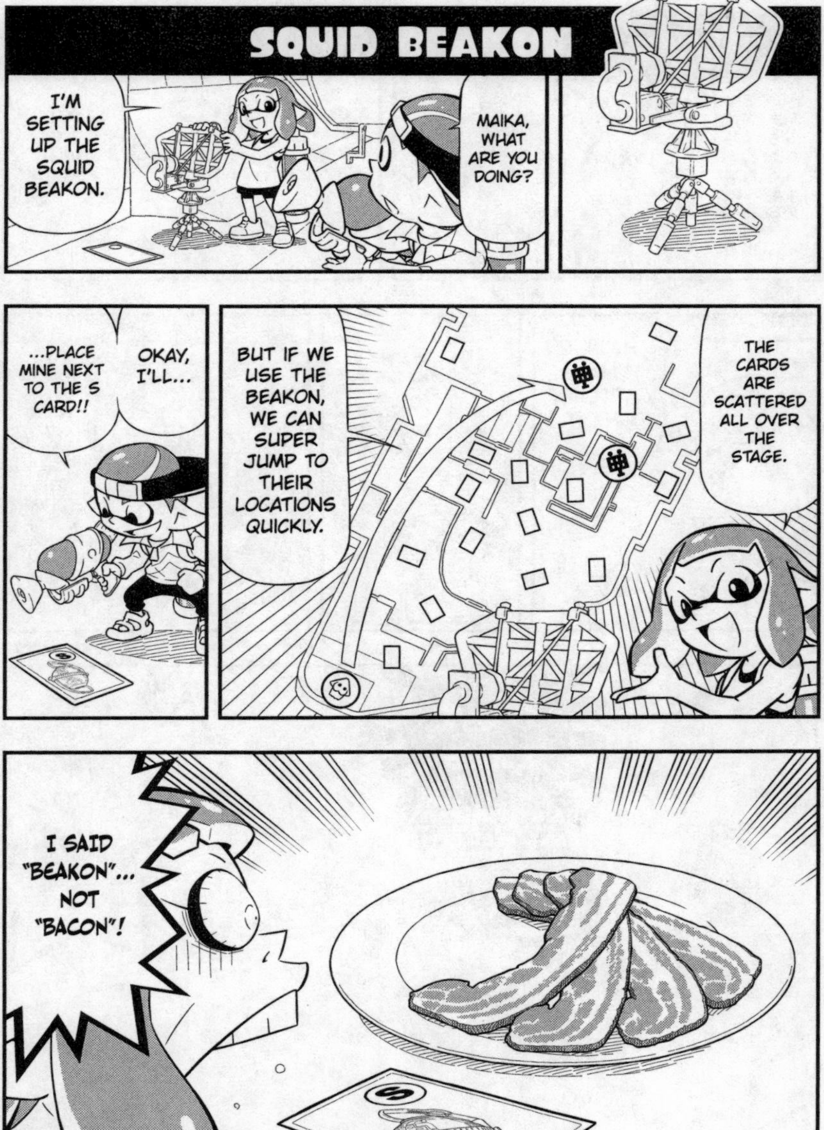
SQUID BEAKON
MAIKA, WHAT ARE YOU DOING?
I'M SETTING UP THE SQUID BEAKON.
THE CARDS ARE SCATTERED ALL OVER THE STAGE.
BUT IF WE USE THE BEAKON, WE CAN SUPER JUMP TO THEIR LOCATIONS QUICKLY.
OKAY, I'LL...
...PLACE MINE NEXT TO THE S CARD!!
I SAID "BEAKON"... NOT "BACON"!

SCOPE

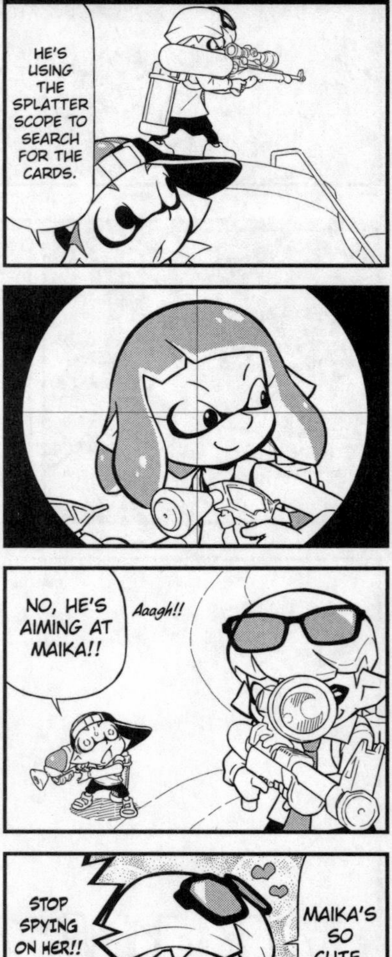
HE'S USING THE SPLATTER SCOPE TO SEARCH FOR THE CARDS.
NO, HE'S AIMING AT MAIKA!!
Aaagh!!
MAIKA'S SO CUTE. ♥
STOP SPYING ON HER!!

STAMP EVERYTHING

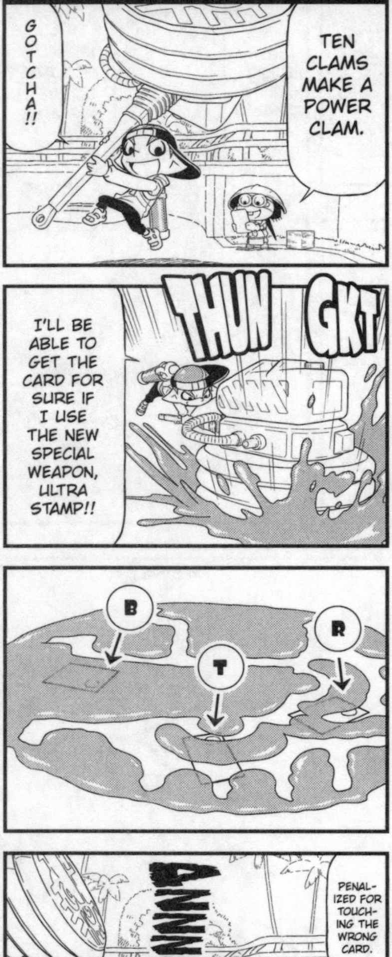
TEN CLAMS MAKE A POWER CLAM.
GOTCHA!!
THUN
GKT
I'LL BE ABLE TO GET THE CARD FOR SURE IF I USE THE NEW SPECIAL WEAPON, ULTRA STAMP!!
B
R
T
PENALIZED FOR TOUCHING THE WRONG CARD.

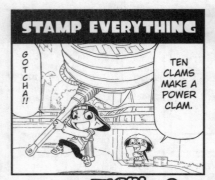

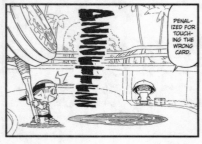

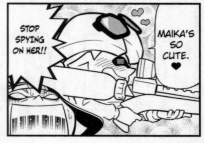

WINTER INK STORM

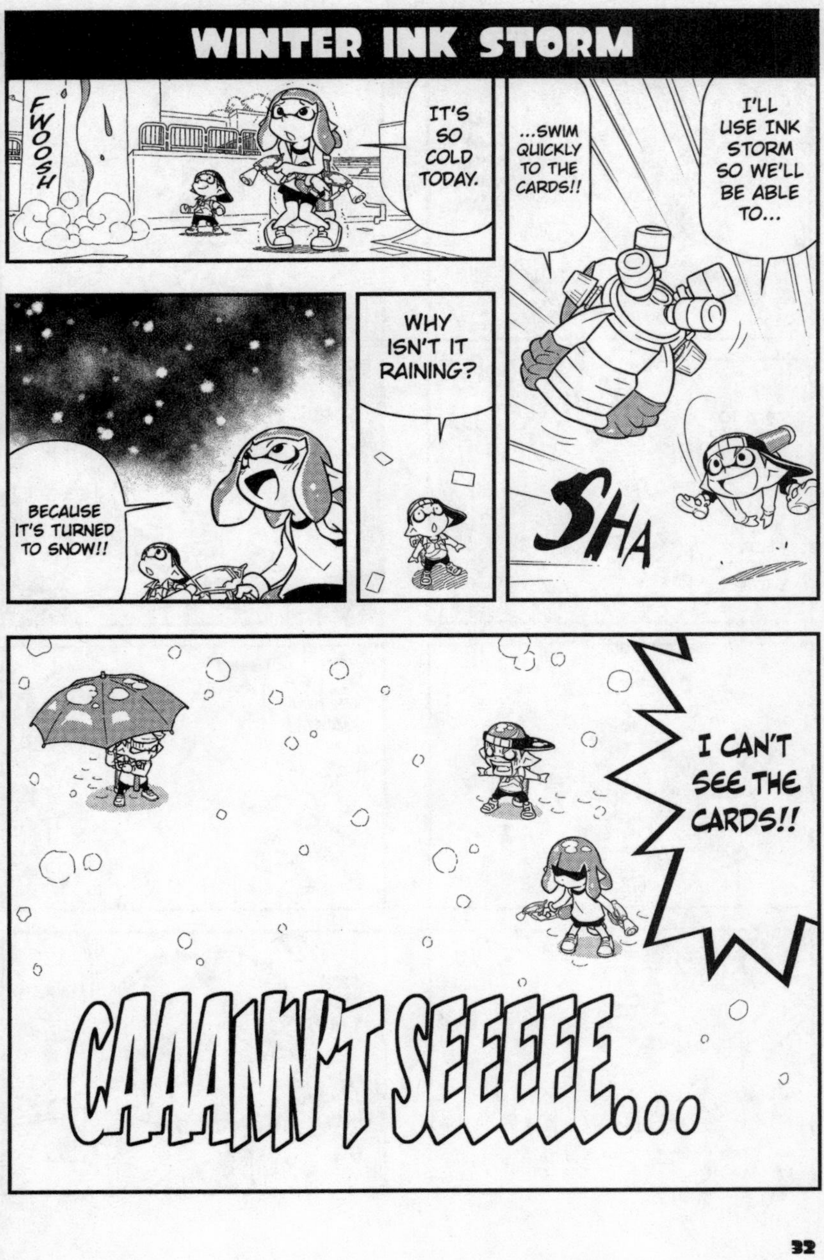
I'LL USE INK STORM SO WE'LL BE ABLE TO...
...SWIM QUICKLY TO THE CARDS!!
SHA
IT'S SO COLD TODAY.
FWOOSH
WHY ISN'T IT RAINING?
BECAUSE IT'S TURNED TO SNOW!!
I CAN'T SEE THE CARDS!!
CAAANN'T SEEEEE...

HUGE SNOW BALL

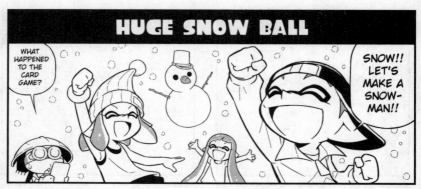

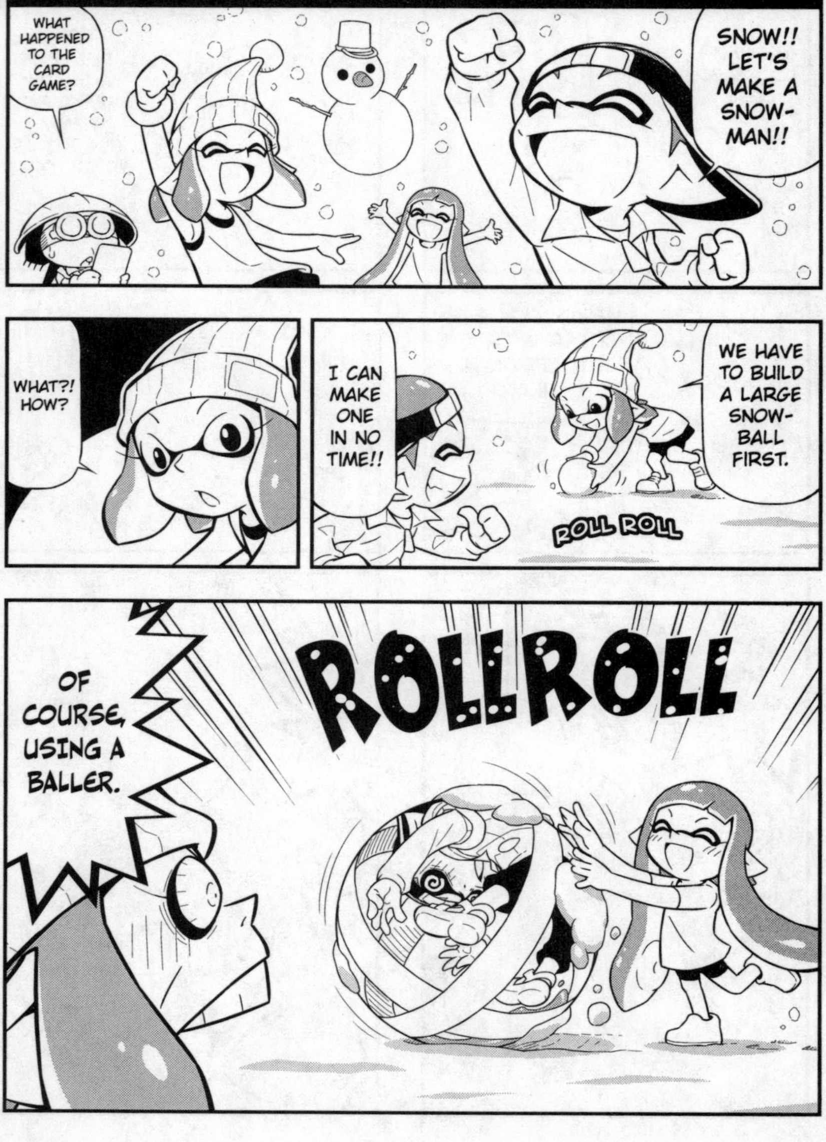
SNOW!! LET'S MAKE A SNOW-MAN!!
WHAT HAPPENED TO THE CARD GAME?
WE HAVE TO BUILD A LARGE SNOW-BALL FIRST.
ROLL ROLL
I CAN MAKE ONE IN NO TIME!!
WHAT?! HOW?
ROLLROLL
OF COURSE, USING A BALLER.

SNOW MAN

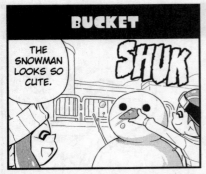

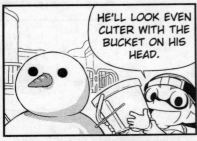

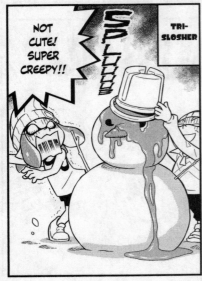

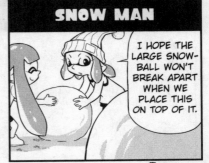

I HOPE THE LARGE SNOW-BALL WON'T BREAK APART WHEN WE PLACE THIS ON TOP OF IT.
FWUMP
LOOKS FINE.
IT'S NOT FINE...
HIT!!

BUCKET

SHUK
THE SNOWMAN LOOKS SO CUTE.
HE'LL LOOK EVEN CUTER WITH THE BUCKET ON HIS HEAD.
TRI-SLOSHER
SPLUUUU
NOT CUTE! SUPER CREEPY!!

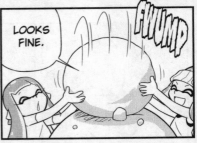

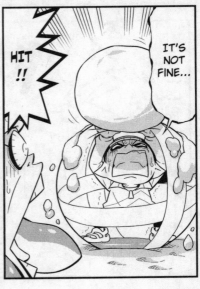

IGLOO BRELLA

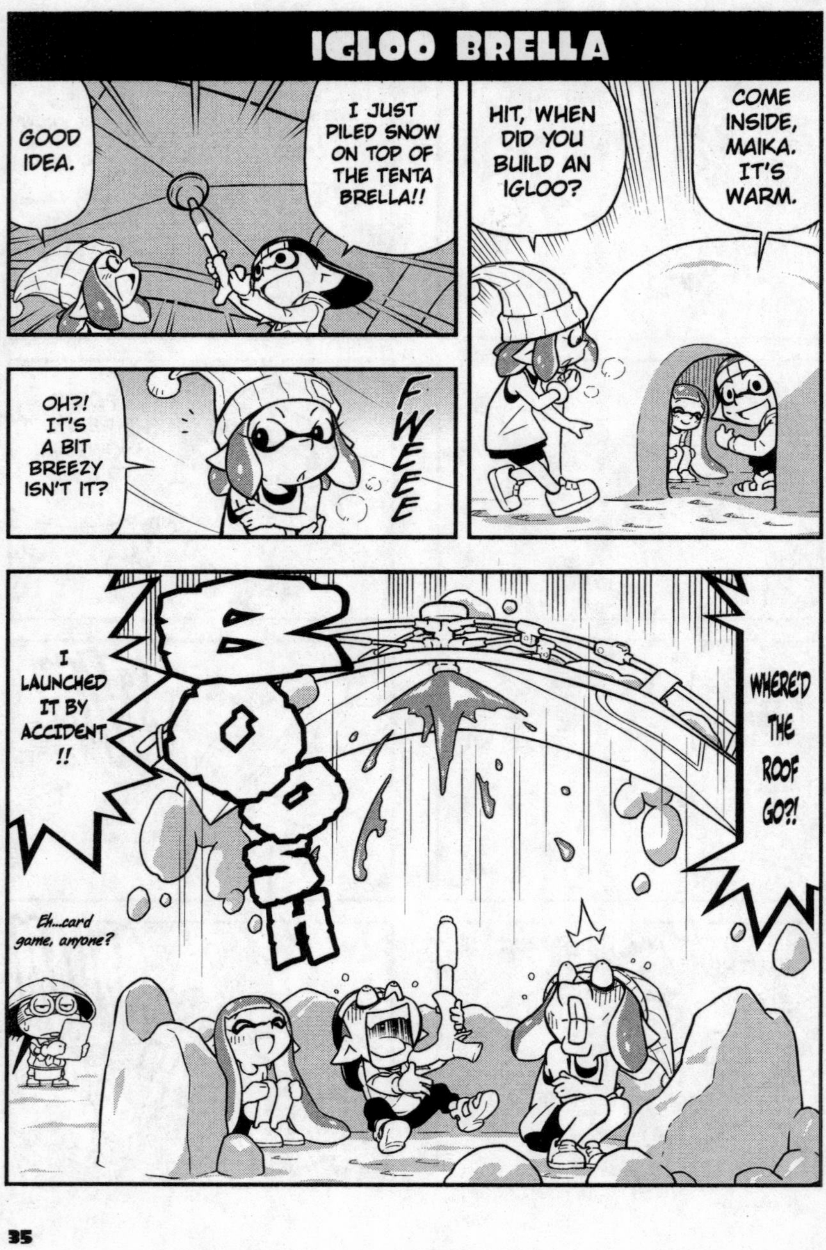
COME INSIDE, MAIKA. IT'S WARM.
HIT, WHEN DID YOU BUILD AN IGLOO?
I JUST PILED SNOW ON TOP OF THE TENTA BRELLA!!
GOOD IDEA.
FWEEE
OH?! IT'S A BIT BREEZY ISN'T IT?
WHERE'D THE ROOF GO?!
BOOSH
I LAUNCHED IT BY ACCIDENT!!
Eh...card game, anyone?

SNOW RABBIT

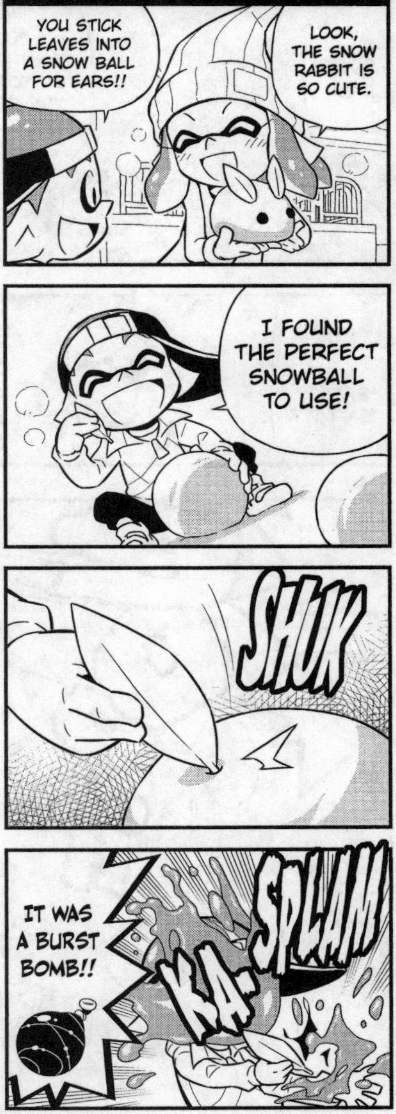
LOOK, THE SNOW RABBIT IS SO CUTE.
YOU STICK LEAVES INTO A SNOW BALL FOR EARS!!
I FOUND THE PERFECT SNOWBALL TO USE!
SHUK
KA-SPLAM
IT WAS A BURST BOMB!!

SLED

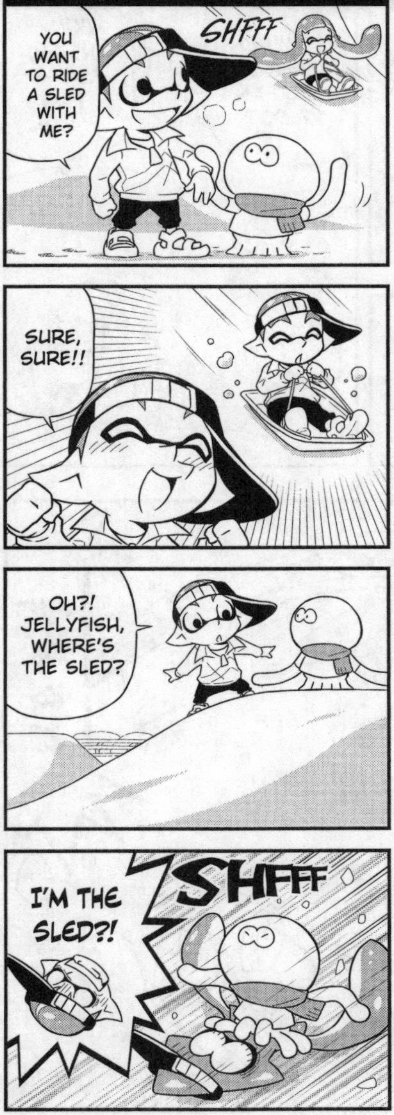
SHFFF
YOU WANT TO RIDE A SLED WITH ME?
SURE, SURE!!
OH?! JELLYFISH, WHERE'S THE SLED?
SHFFF
I'M THE SLED?!

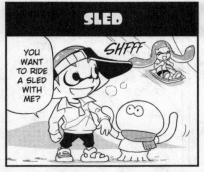

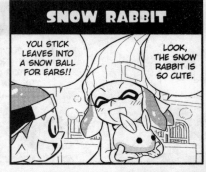

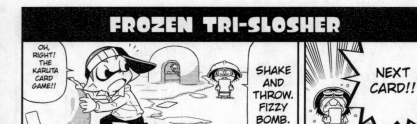

FROZEN TRI-SLOSHER

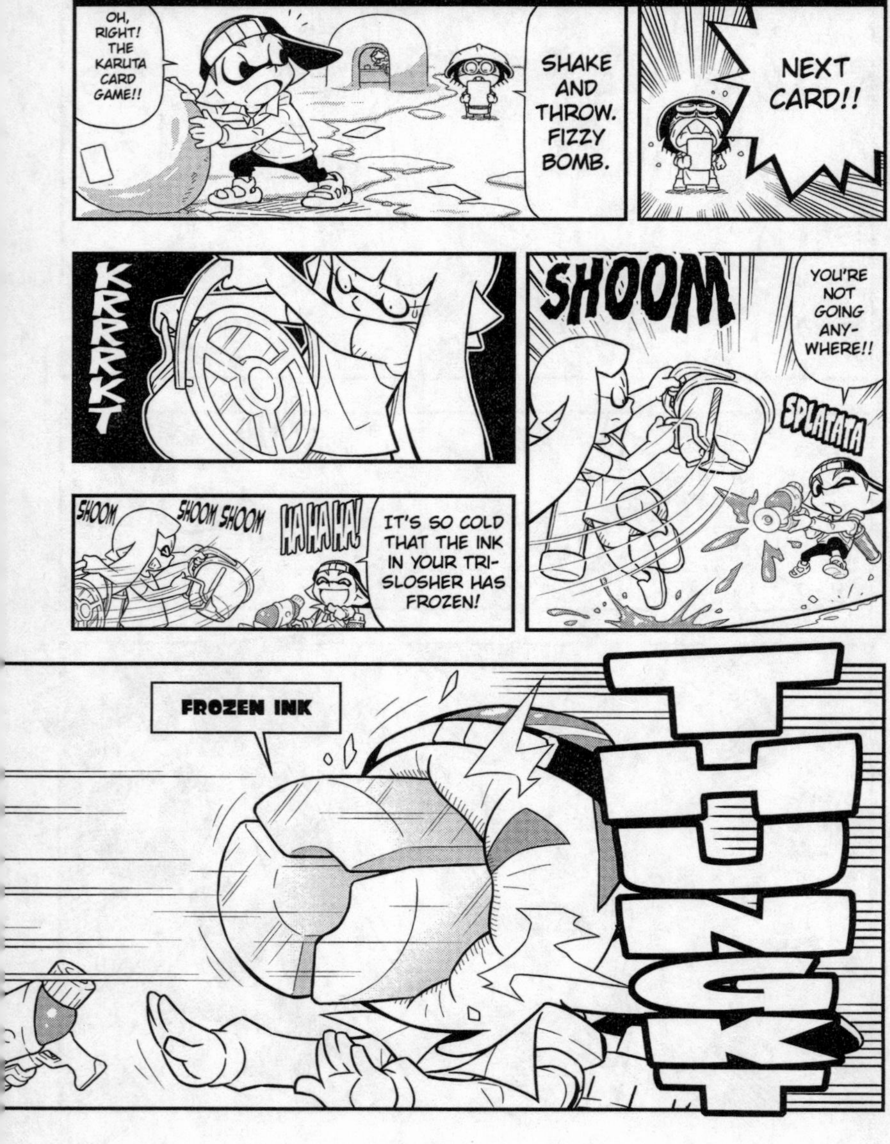
NEXT CARD!!
SHAKE AND THROW. FIZZY BOMB.
OH, RIGHT! THE KARUTA CARD GAME!!
SHOOM
YOU'RE NOT GOING ANYWHERE!!
SPLATATA
KRRRKT
IT'S SO COLD THAT THE INK IN YOUR TRI-SLOSHER HAS FROZEN!
HA HA HA!
SHOOM SHOOM
SHOOM
THUNK
FROZEN INK

HIT WITH THE STAMP

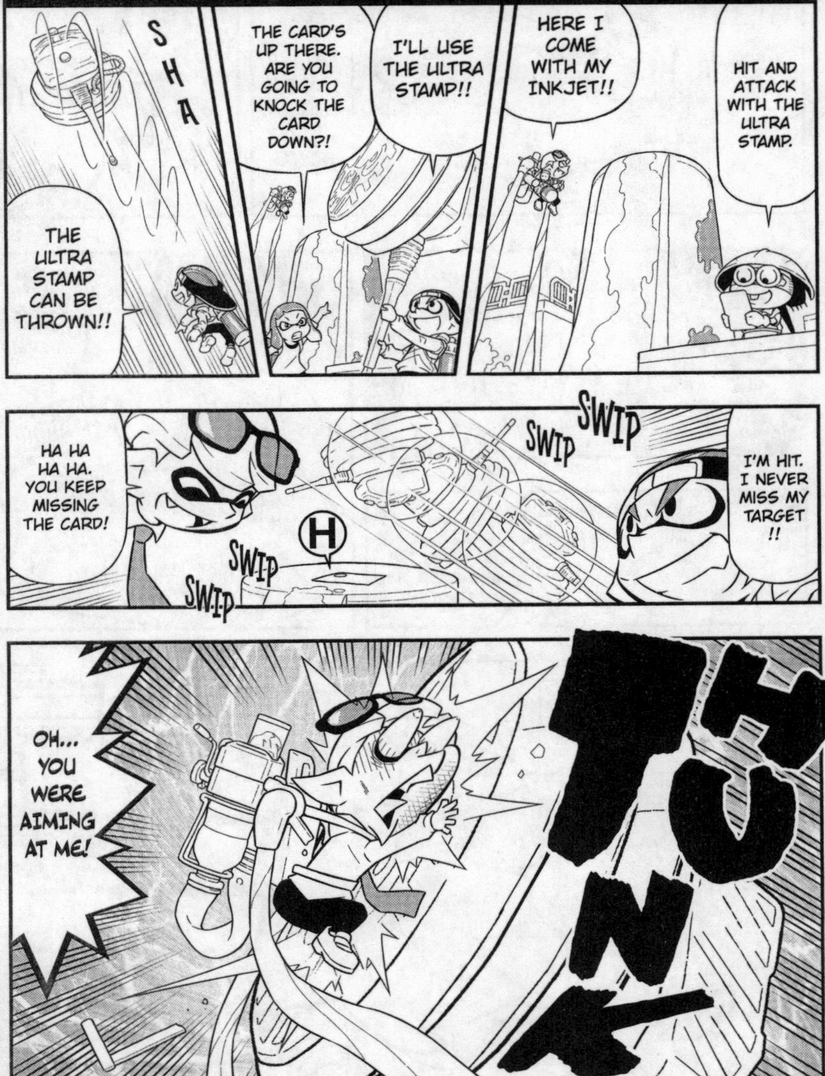
HIT AND ATTACK WITH THE ULTRA STAMP.
HERE I COME WITH MY INKJET!!
I'LL USE THE ULTRA STAMP!!
THE CARD'S UP THERE. ARE YOU GOING TO KNOCK THE CARD DOWN?!
SHA
THE ULTRA STAMP CAN BE THROWN!!
SWIP
SWIP
I'M HIT. I NEVER MISS MY TARGET!!
HA HA HA HA. YOU KEEP MISSING THE CARD!
H
SWIP
SWIP
THUNK
OH... YOU WERE AIMING AT ME!

TIME FOR
HAY FEVER!

FASHIONABLE GEAR

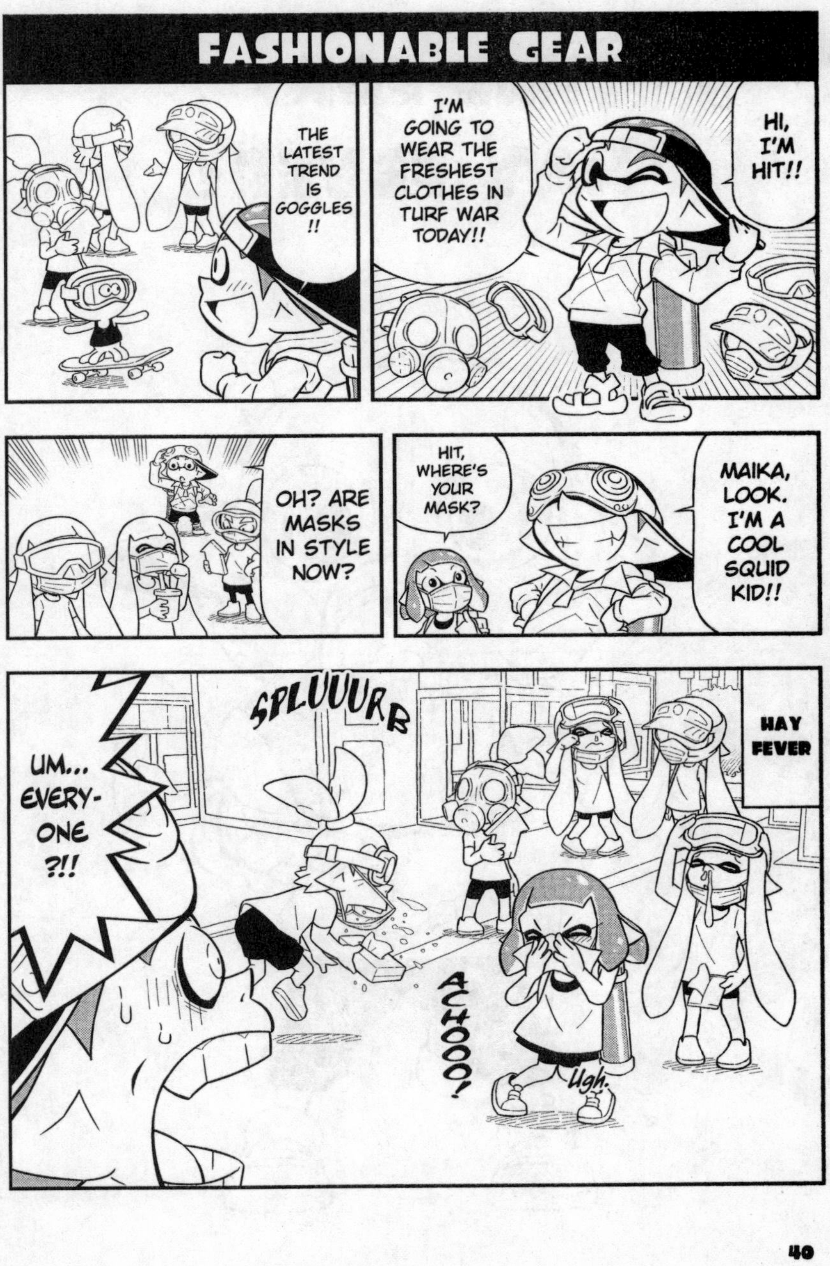
HI, I'M HIT!!
I'M GOING TO WEAR THE FRESHEST CLOTHES IN TURF WAR TODAY!!
THE LATEST TREND IS GOGGLES!!
MAIKA, LOOK. I'M A COOL SQUID KID!!
HIT, WHERE'S YOUR MASK?
OH? ARE MASKS IN STYLE NOW?
HAY FEVER
SPLUUURB
UM... EVERY-ONE?!!
ACHOOO!
Ugh.

POLLEN

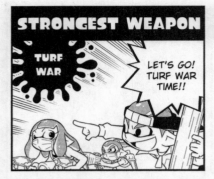

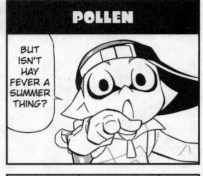

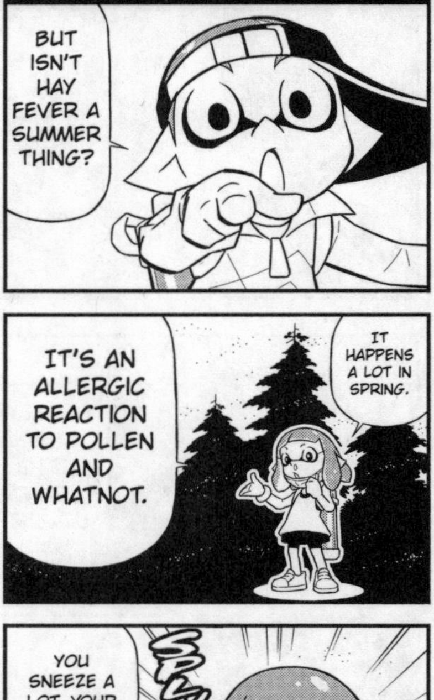
BUT ISN'T HAY FEVER A SUMMER THING?
IT HAPPENS A LOT IN SPRING.
IT'S AN ALLERGIC REACTION TO POLLEN AND WHATNOT.
YOU SNEEZE A LOT, YOUR NOSE RUNS, AND YOUR EYES GET ITCHY TOO.
SO "POLLEN" IS A FANCY WAY OF SAYING "MOSQUITO POOP," RIGHT?
PLIP
I DON'T EVEN KNOW HOW TO RESPOND TO THAT...

STRONGEST WEAPON

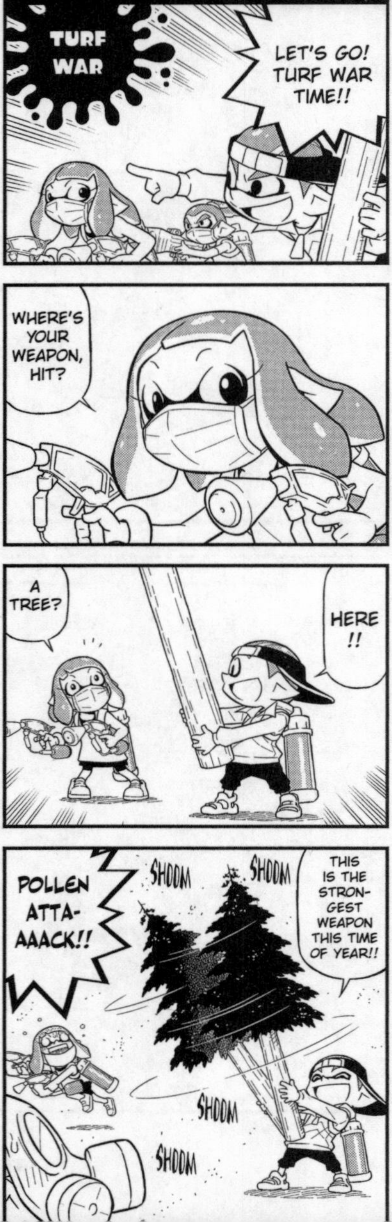
LET'S GO! TURF WAR TIME!!
TURF WAR
WHERE'S YOUR WEAPON, HIT?
HERE!!
A TREE?
THIS IS THE STRONGEST WEAPON THIS TIME OF YEAR!!
SHOOM
SHOOM
POLLEN ATTA-AAACK!!
SHOOM
SHOOM

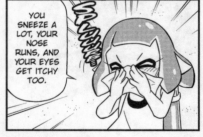

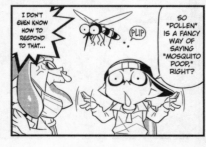

SAME-COLORED INK

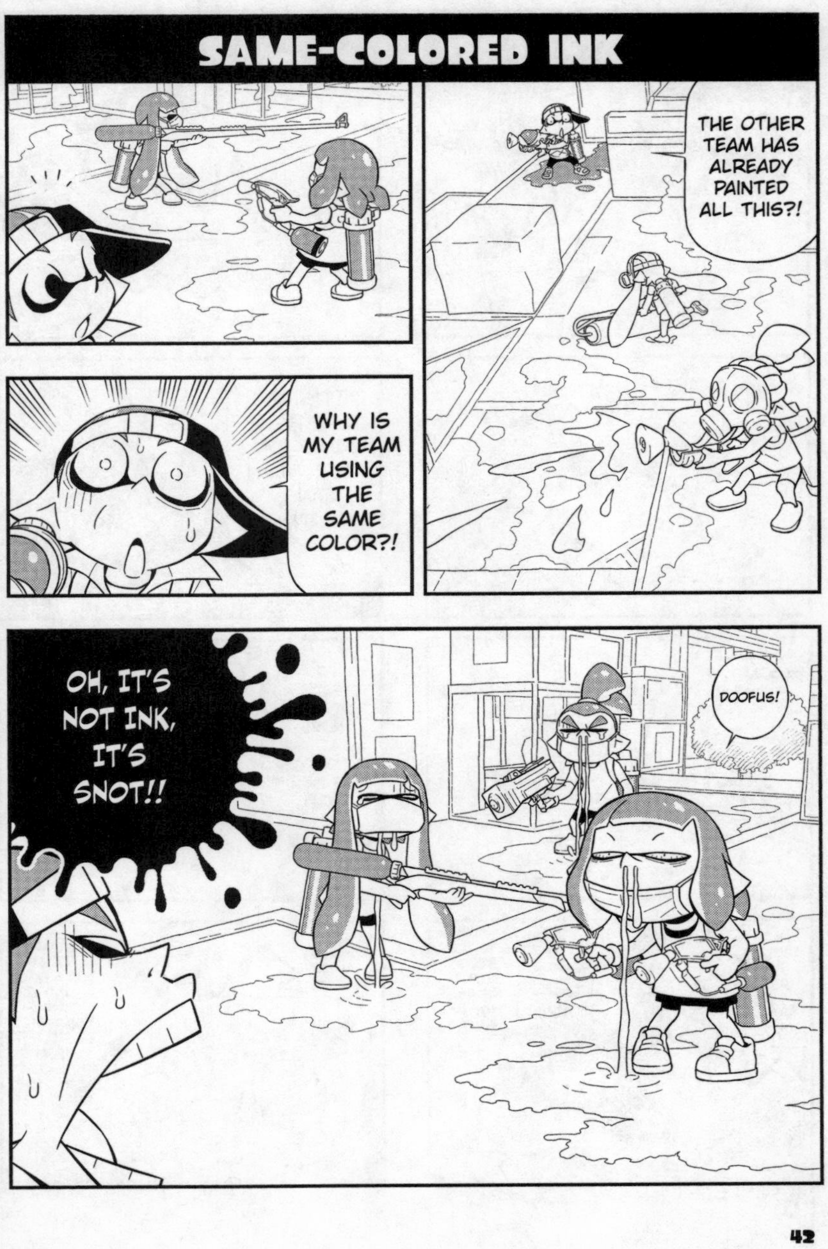
THE OTHER TEAM HAS ALREADY PAINTED ALL THIS?!
WHY IS MY TEAM USING THE SAME COLOR?!
OH, IT'S NOT INK, IT'S SNOT!!
DOOFUS!

HIDING PLACE

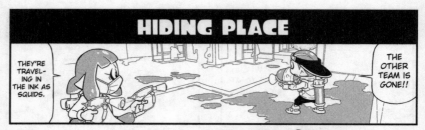

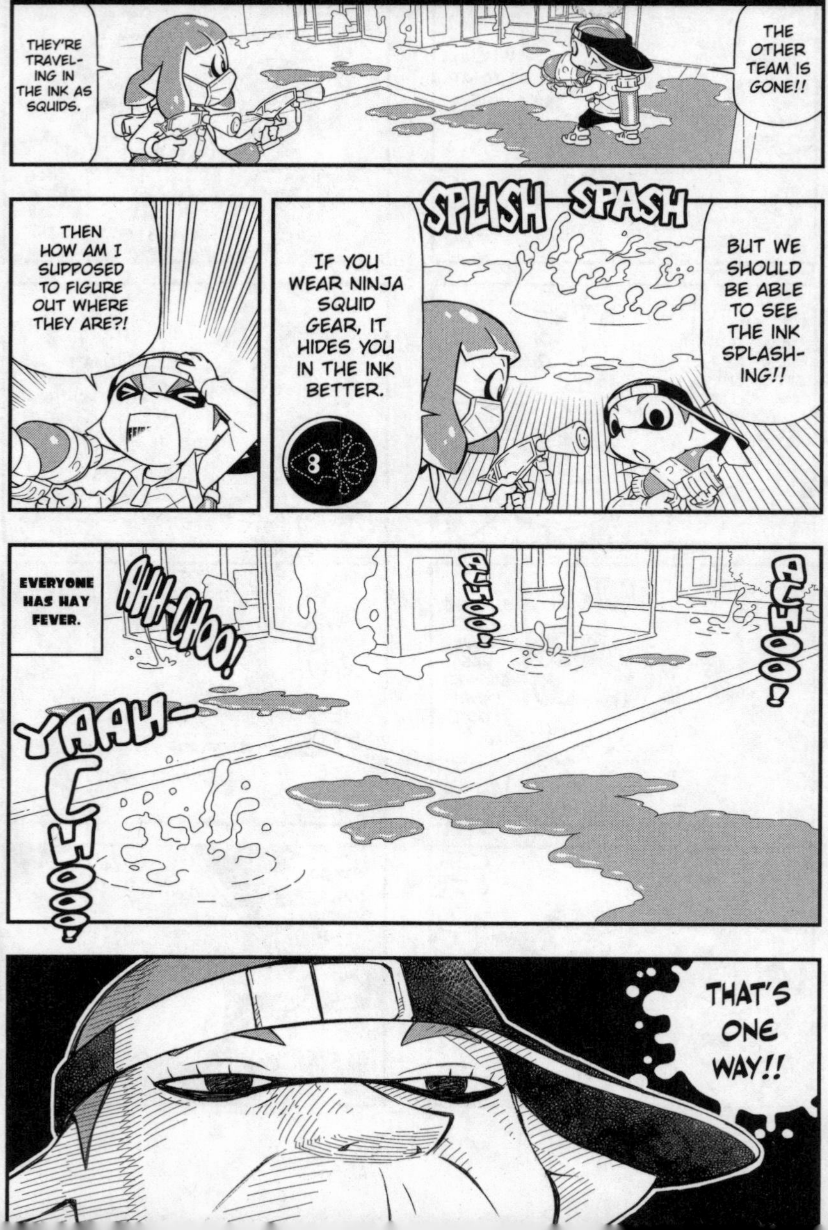
THE OTHER TEAM IS GONE!!
THEY'RE TRAVEL-ING IN THE INK AS SQUIDS.
SPLISH SPASH
BUT WE SHOULD BE ABLE TO SEE THE INK SPLASH-ING!!
IF YOU WEAR NINJA SQUID GEAR, IT HIDES YOU IN THE INK BETTER.
THEN HOW AM I SUPPOSED TO FIGURE OUT WHERE THEY ARE?!
ACHOO!
ACHOO!
AHH-CHOO!
EVERYONE HAS HAY FEVER.
YAAH-CHOOO!
THAT'S ONE WAY!!

MAP

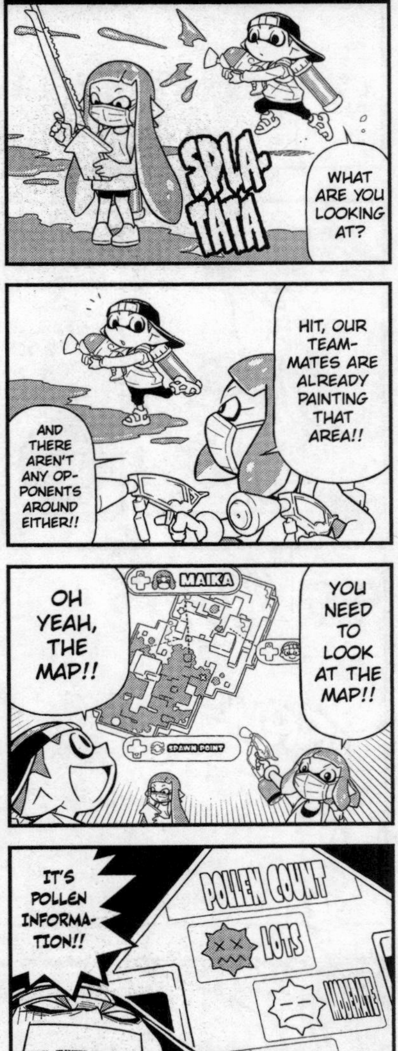
WHAT ARE YOU LOOKING AT?
SPLA-TATA
HIT, OUR TEAM-MATES ARE ALREADY PAINTING THAT AREA!!
AND THERE AREN'T ANY OP-PONENTS AROUND EITHER!!
YOU NEED TO LOOK AT THE MAP!!
MAIKA
OH YEAH, THE MAP!!
SPAWN POINT
POLLEN COUNT
LOTS
MODERATE
LOTS
IT'S POLLEN INFORMA-TION!!

SLOWING DOWN

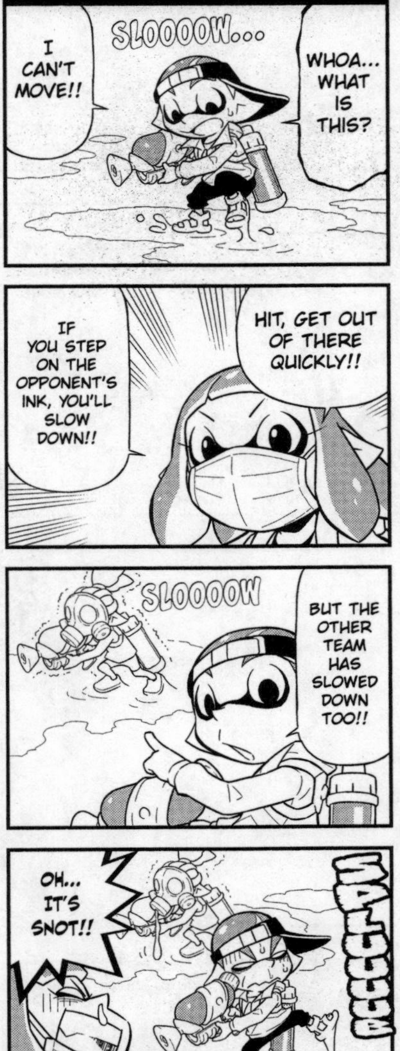
WHOA... WHAT IS THIS?
SLOOOOW...
I CAN'T MOVE!!
HIT, GET OUT OF THERE QUICKLY!!
IF YOU STEP ON THE OPPONENT'S INK, YOU'LL SLOW DOWN!!
BUT THE OTHER TEAM HAS SLOWED DOWN TOO!!
SLOOOOW
SPLUGGGG
OH... IT'S SNOT!!

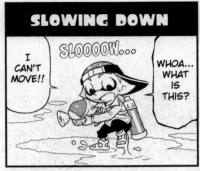

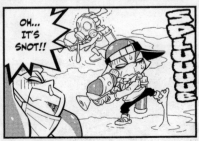

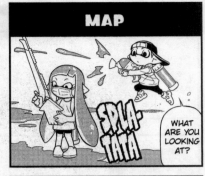

SHIELD WALL

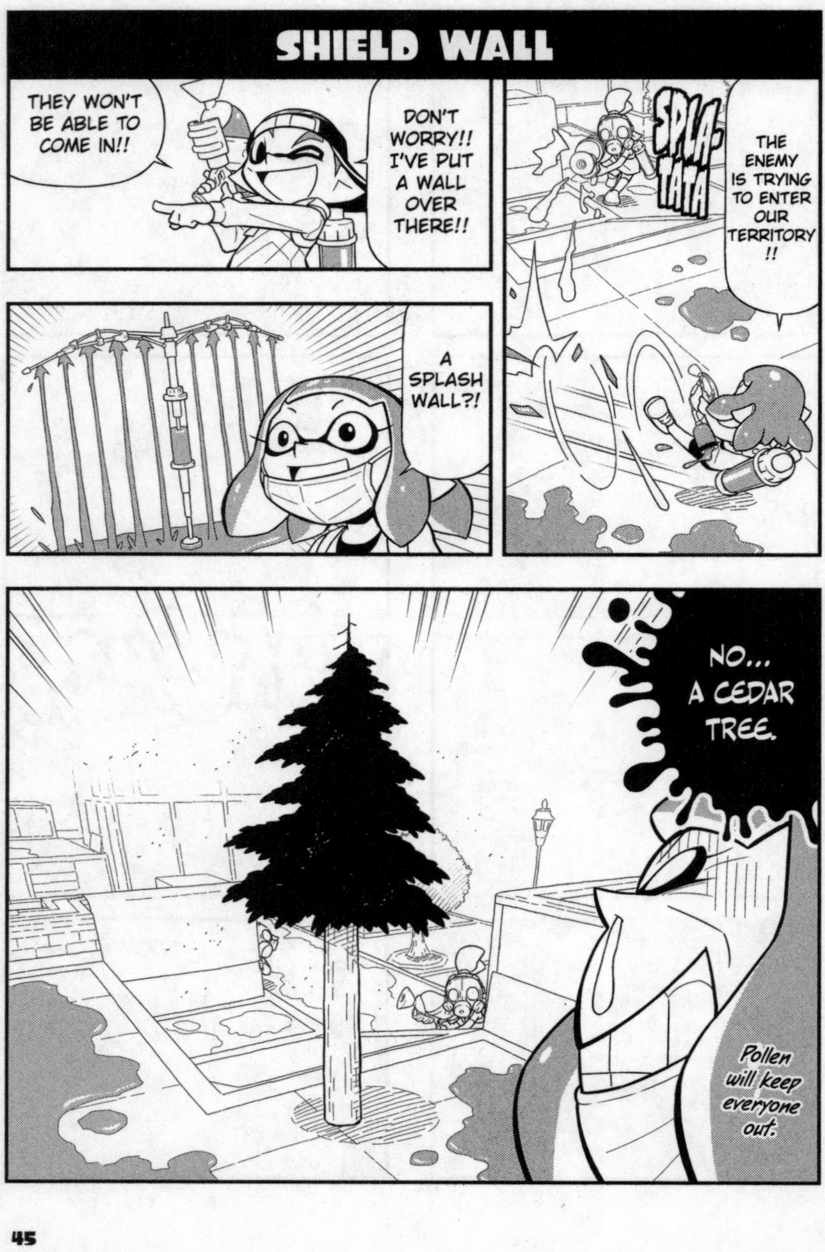
THE ENEMY IS TRYING TO ENTER OUR TERRITORY!!
SPLA-TATA
DON'T WORRY!! I'VE PUT A WALL OVER THERE!!
THEY WON'T BE ABLE TO COME IN!!
A SPLASH WALL?!
NO... A CEDAR TREE.
Pollen will keep everyone out.

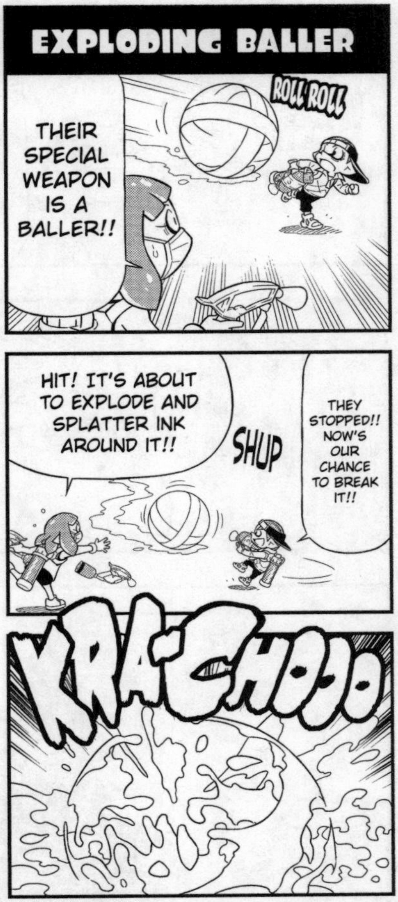
EXPLODING BALLER
ROLL ROLL
THEIR SPECIAL WEAPON IS A BALLER!!
THEY STOPPED!! NOW'S OUR CHANCE TO BREAK IT!!
HIT! IT'S ABOUT TO EXPLODE AND SPLATTER INK AROUND IT!!
SHUP
KRA-CHOOO
Ewww...
SPLUUUB...
GROSS!!
Snot again?!

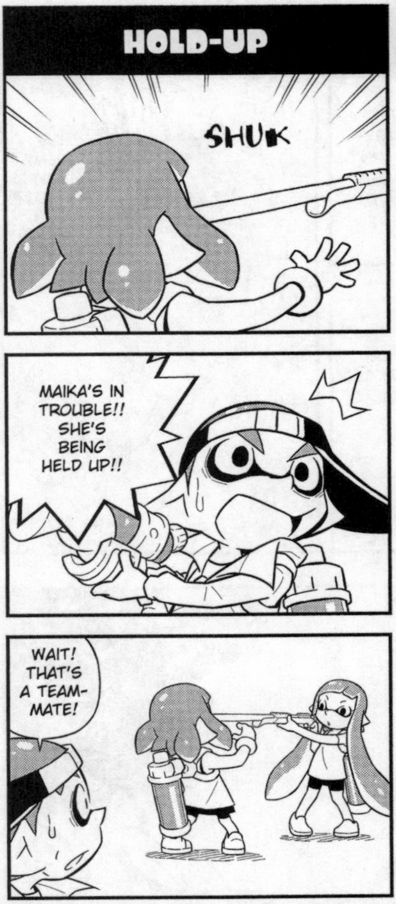
HOLD-UP
SHUK
MAIKA'S IN TROUBLE!! SHE'S BEING HELD UP!!
WAIT! THAT'S A TEAM-MATE!
NOSE RINSE?!
SHWAAA

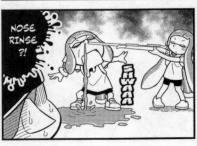

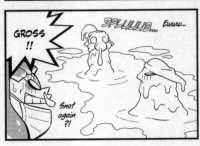

WEAPON MALFUNCTION

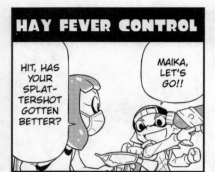

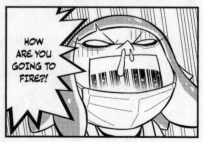

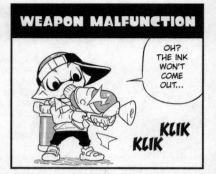

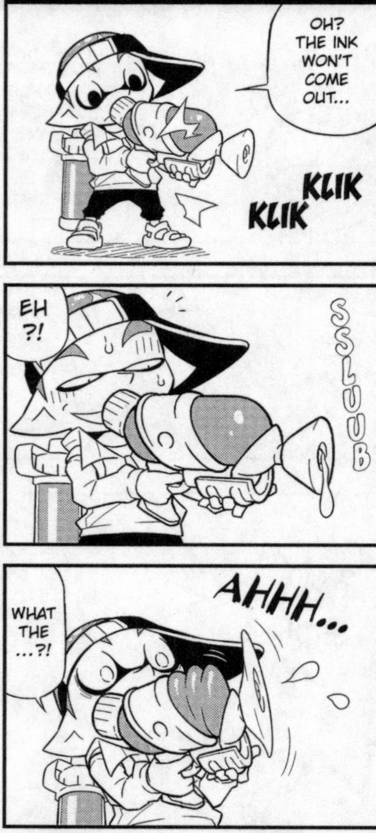
OH? THE INK WON'T COME OUT...
KLIK KLIK
SSLUUB
EH ?!
AHHH...
WHAT THE ...?!
AH-CHOO
THE WEAPON HAS HAY FEVER TOO!!

HAY FEVER CONTROL

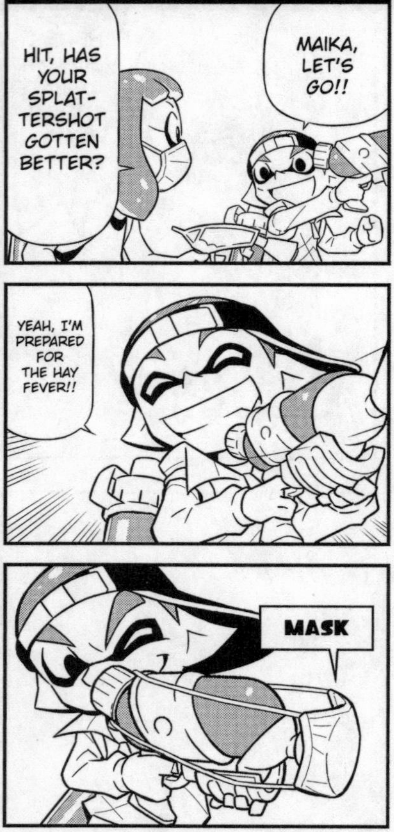
MAIKA, LET'S GO!!
HIT, HAS YOUR SPLAT-TERSHOT GOTTEN BETTER?
YEAH, I'M PREPARED FOR THE HAY FEVER!!
MASK
HOW ARE YOU GOING TO FIRE?!

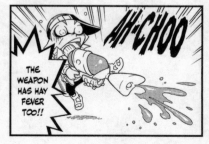

ULTIMATE SPECIAL WEAPON

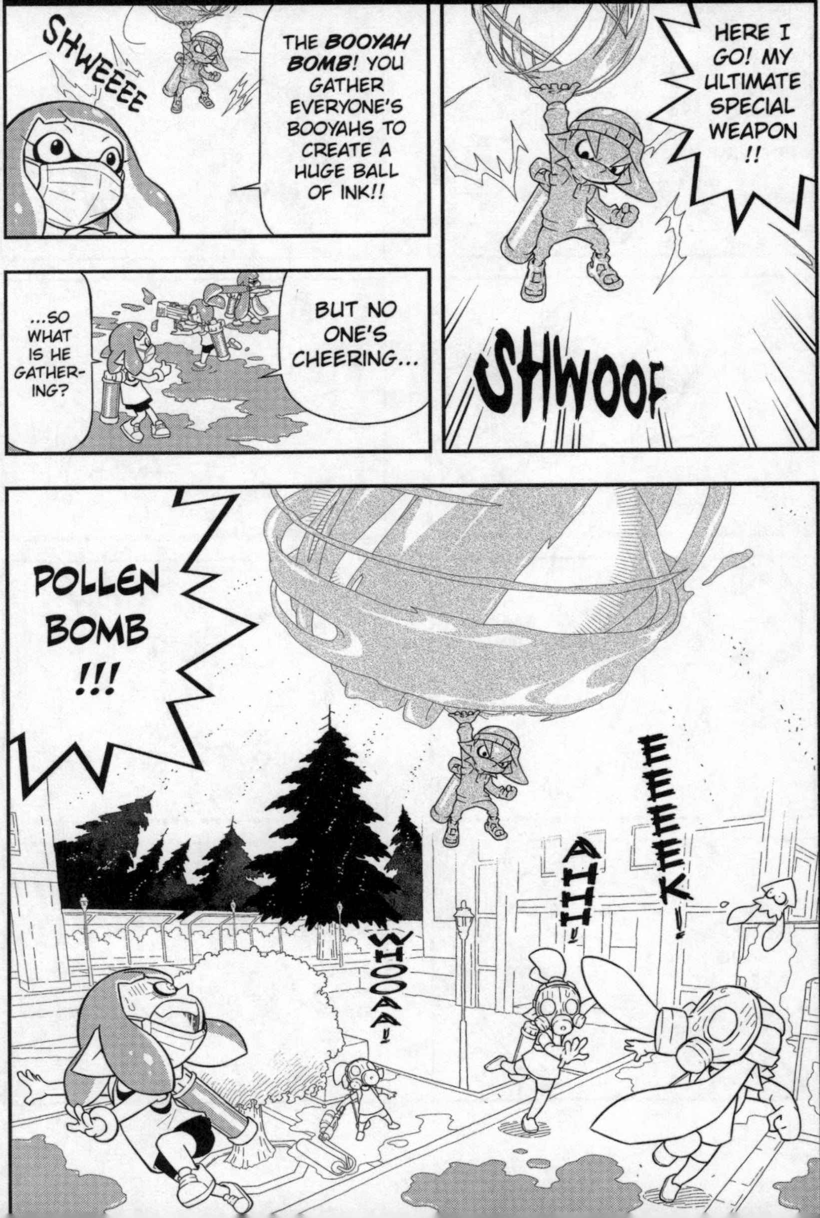
HERE I GO! MY ULTIMATE SPECIAL WEAPON !!
SHWOOF
SHWEEEEE
THE BOOYAH BOMB! YOU GATHER EVERYONE'S BOOYAHS TO CREATE A HUGE BALL OF INK!!
BUT NO ONE'S CHEERING...
...SO WHAT IS HE GATHER-ING?
POLLEN BOMB !!!
EEEEEK!
AHHH!
WHOOAA!

INK STORM OF JOY

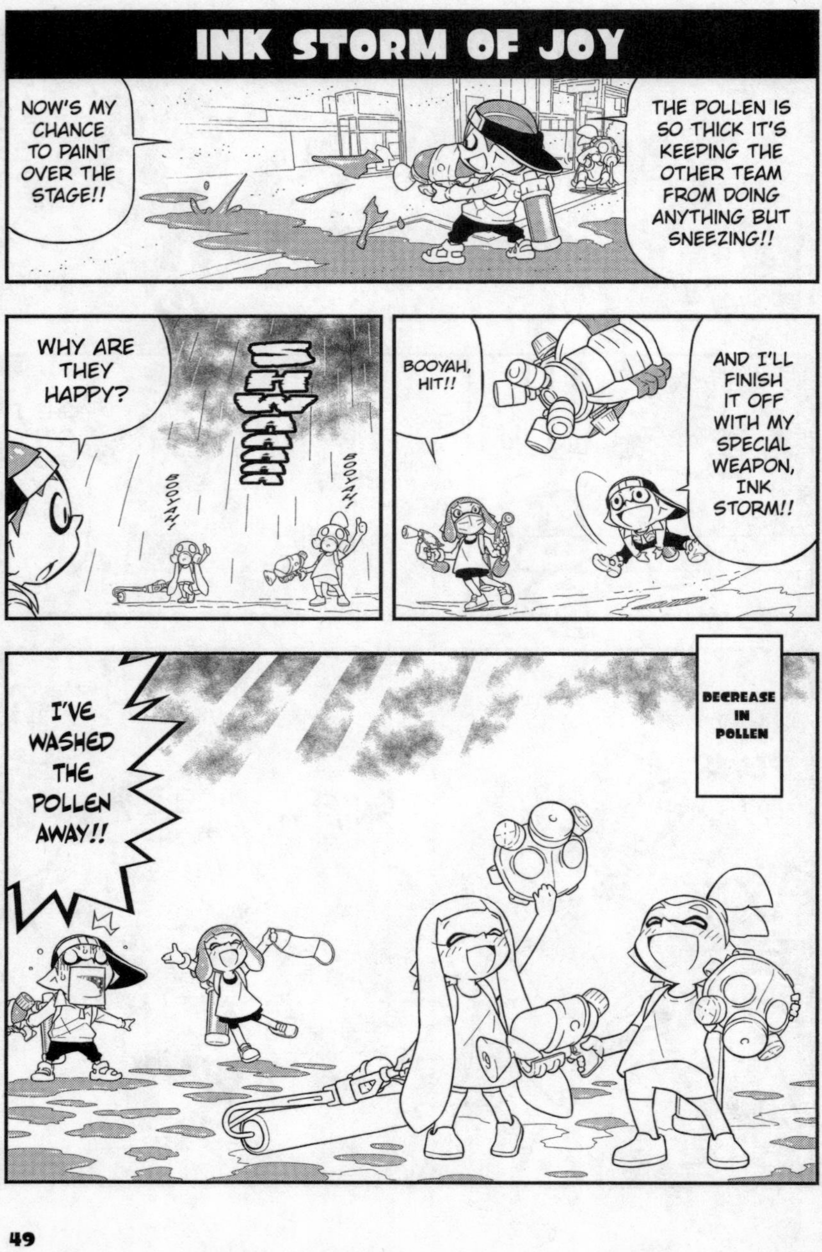
THE POLLEN IS SO THICK IT'S KEEPING THE OTHER TEAM FROM DOING ANYTHING BUT SNEEZING!!
NOW'S MY CHANCE TO PAINT OVER THE STAGE!!
AND I'LL FINISH IT OFF WITH MY SPECIAL WEAPON, INK STORM!!
BOOYAH, HIT!!
BOOYAH!
BOOYAH!
WHY ARE THEY HAPPY?
DECREASE IN POLLEN
I'VE WASHED THE POLLEN AWAY!!

TEARS OF JOY

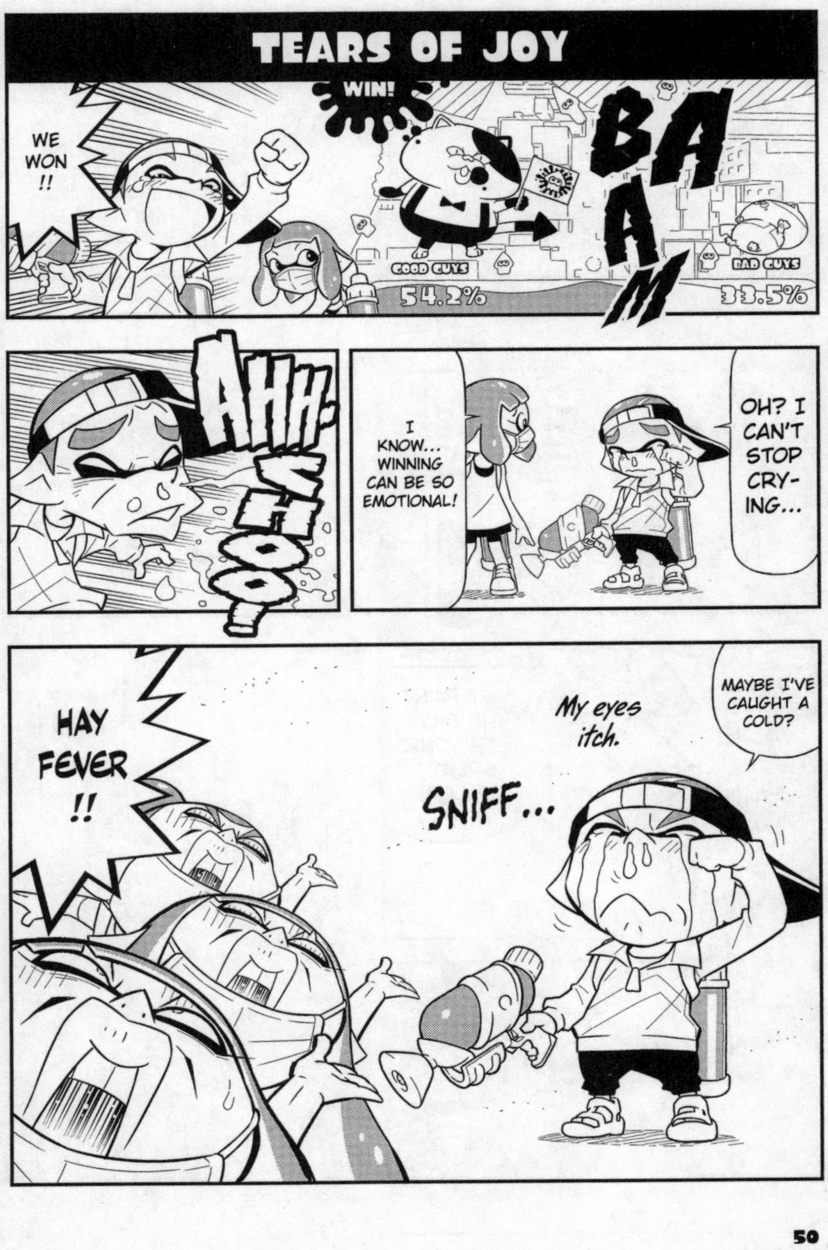
BAAM
WIN!
BAD GUYS
33.5%
GOOD GUYS
54.2%
WE WON !!
OH? I CAN'T STOP CRY-ING...
I KNOW... WINNING CAN BE SO EMOTIONAL!
AHH-CHOO
MAYBE I'VE CAUGHT A COLD?
My eyes itch.
SNIFF...
HAY FEVER !!

SPLAT ROLLER LANDSCAPE

THE BLUE PAINT MUST BE EMPTY.

GGGT...

LEAVE IT TO ME!!

JUST PAINT THE SKY WITH YOUR SPLAT ROLLER!

OR... THAT...

SQUEEE...

HERE YOU GO.

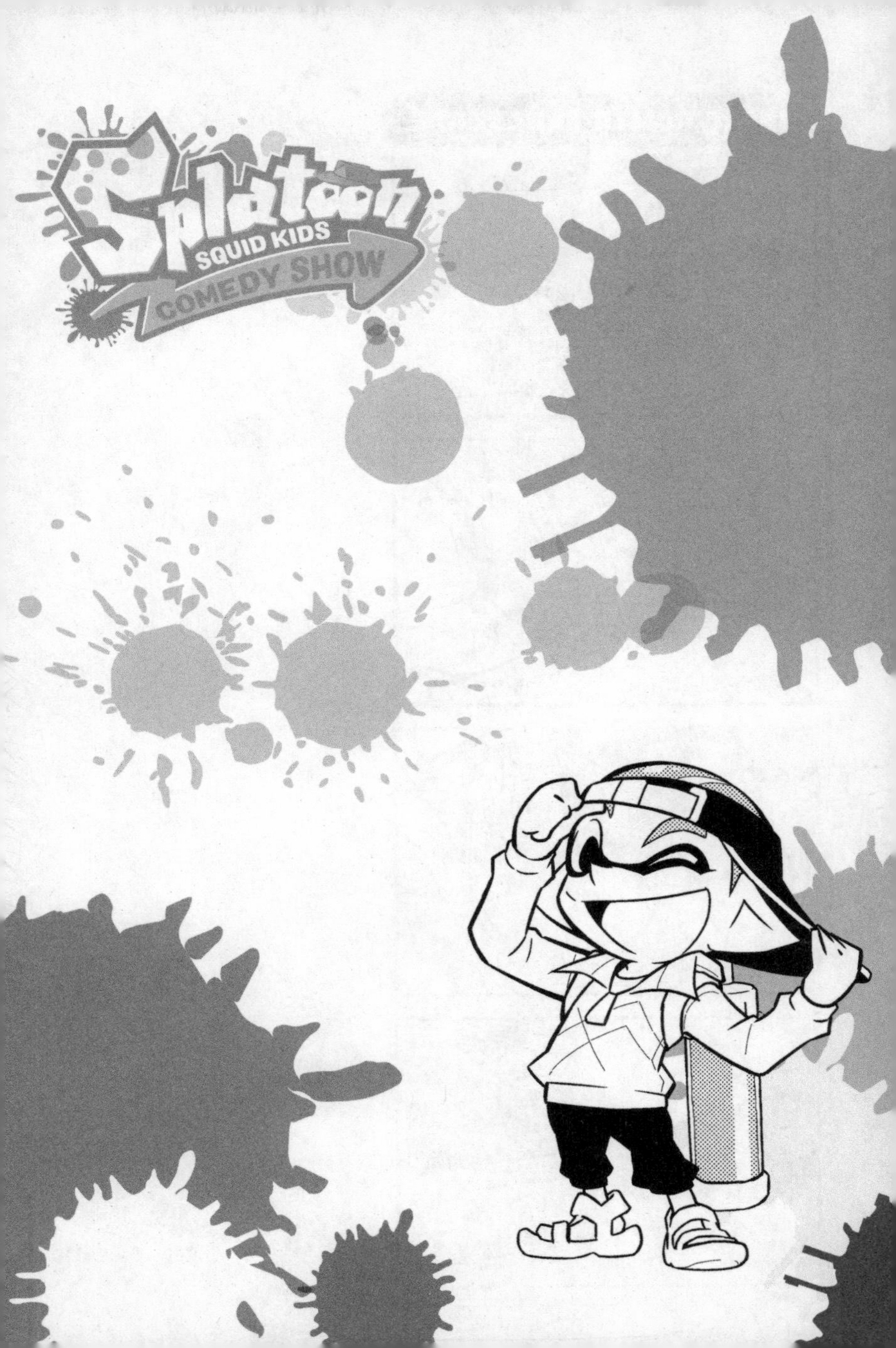
Splatoon
SQUID KIDS
COMEDY SHOW

TIME FOR A CRUISE SHIP BATTLE!

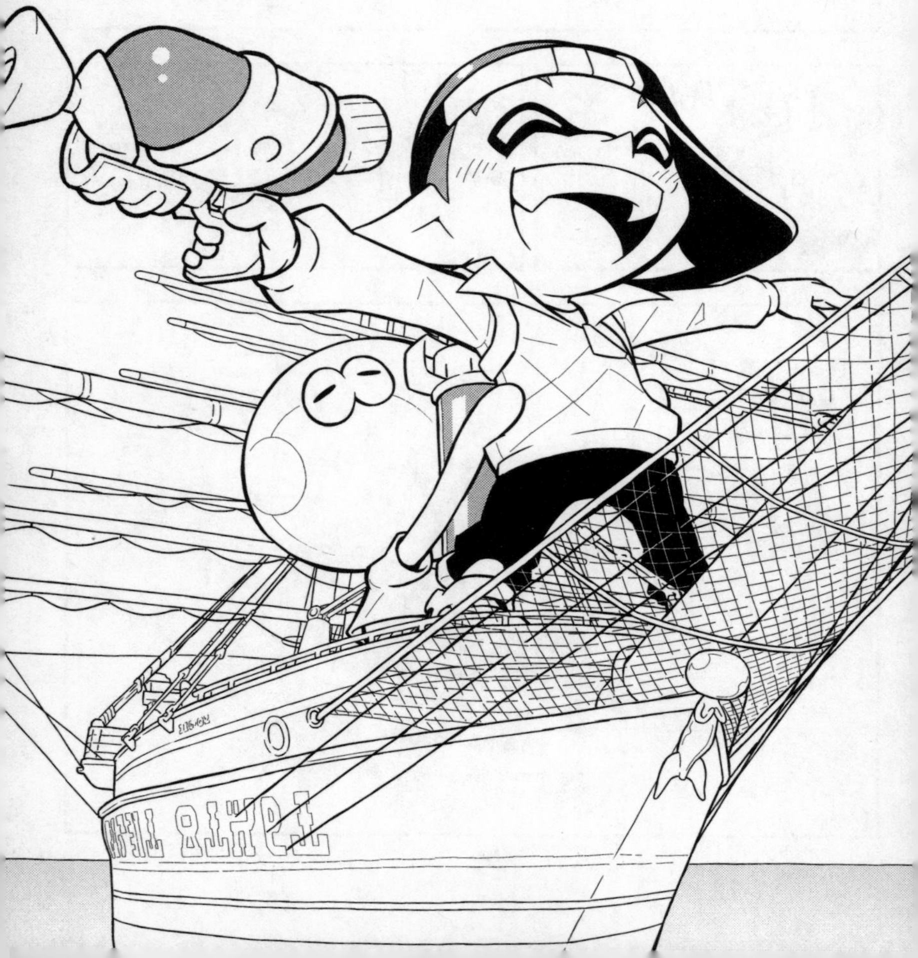

MANTA MARIA

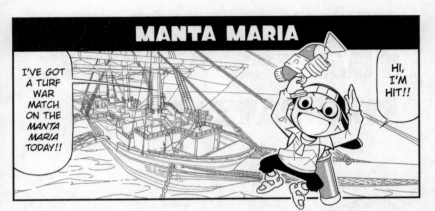

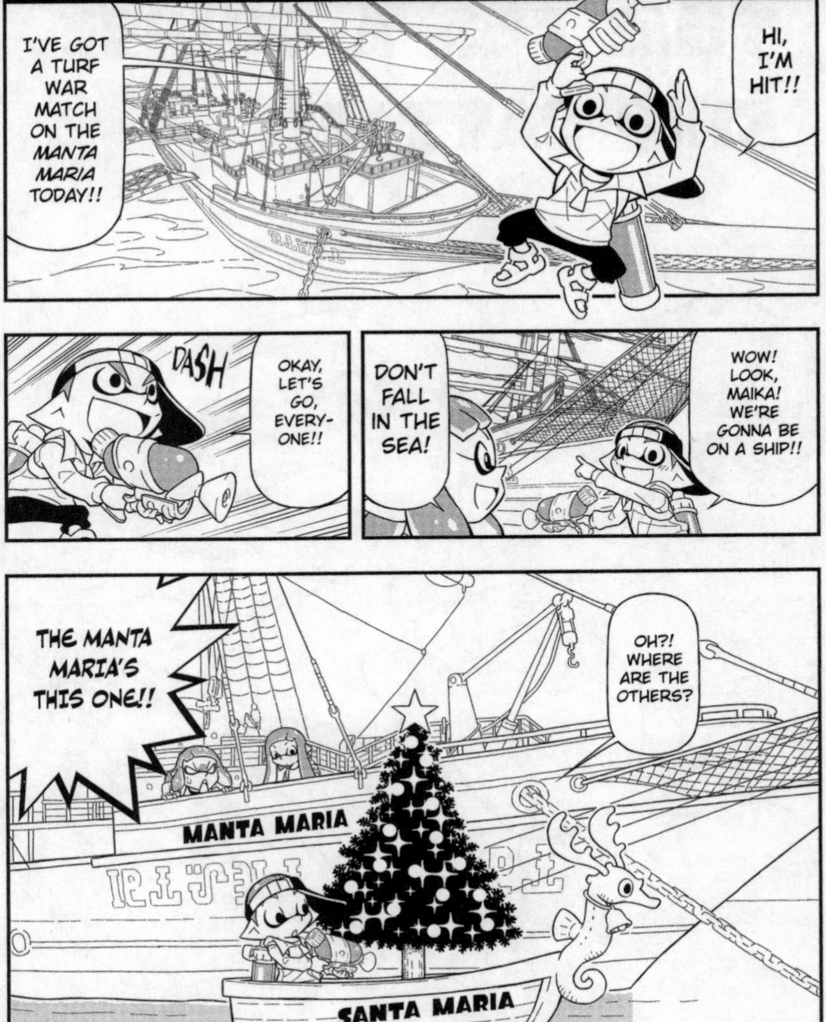
HI, I'M HIT!!
I'VE GOT A TURF WAR MATCH ON THE MANTA MARIA TODAY!!
WOW! LOOK, MAIKA! WE'RE GONNA BE ON A SHIP!!
DON'T FALL IN THE SEA!
OKAY, LET'S GO, EVERYONE!!
DASH
OH?! WHERE ARE THE OTHERS?
THE MANTA MARIA'S THIS ONE!!
MANTA MARIA
SANTA MARIA

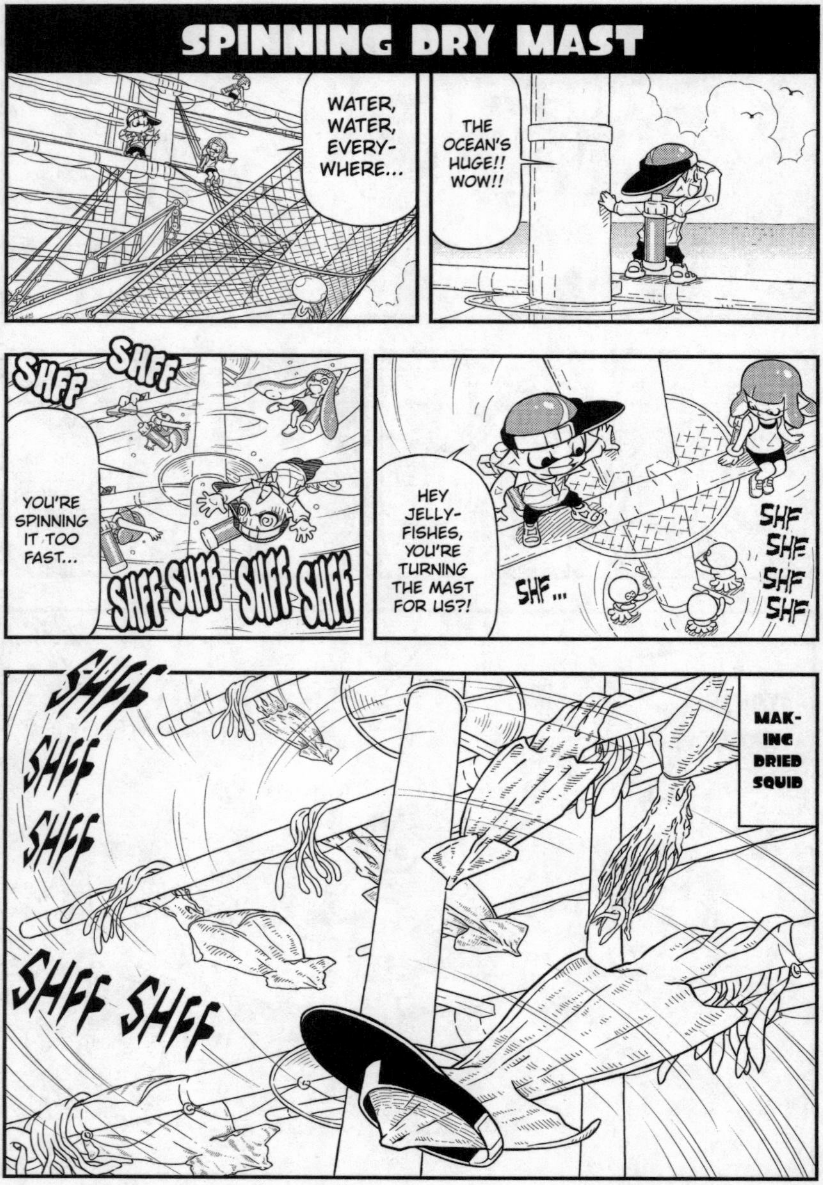
SPINNING DRY MAST
THE OCEAN'S HUGE!! WOW!!
WATER, WATER, EVERY-WHERE...
SHF SHF SHF SHF
HEY JELLY-FISHES, YOU'RE TURNING THE MAST FOR US?!
SHF...
SHFF SHFF
YOU'RE SPINNING IT TOO FAST...
SHFF SHFF SHFF SHFF
MAK-ING DRIED SQUID
SHFF SHFF SHFF
SHFF SHFF

LONG WAY TO GO

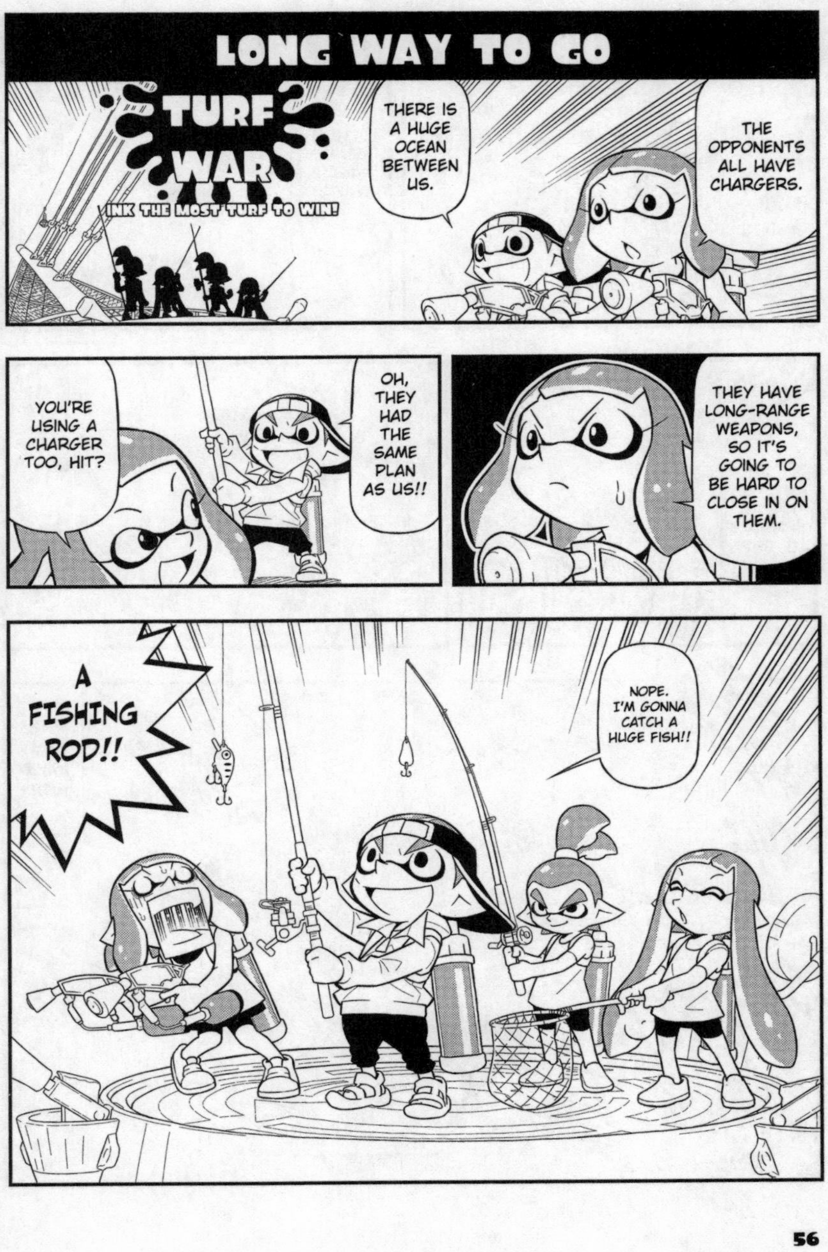
THE OPPONENTS ALL HAVE CHARGERS.
THERE IS A HUGE OCEAN BETWEEN US.
TURF WAR
INK THE MOST TURF TO WIN!
THEY HAVE LONG-RANGE WEAPONS, SO IT'S GOING TO BE HARD TO CLOSE IN ON THEM.
OH, THEY HAD THE SAME PLAN AS US!!
YOU'RE USING A CHARGER TOO, HIT?
NOPE. I'M GONNA CATCH A HUGE FISH!!
A FISHING ROD!!

RAIN COVER

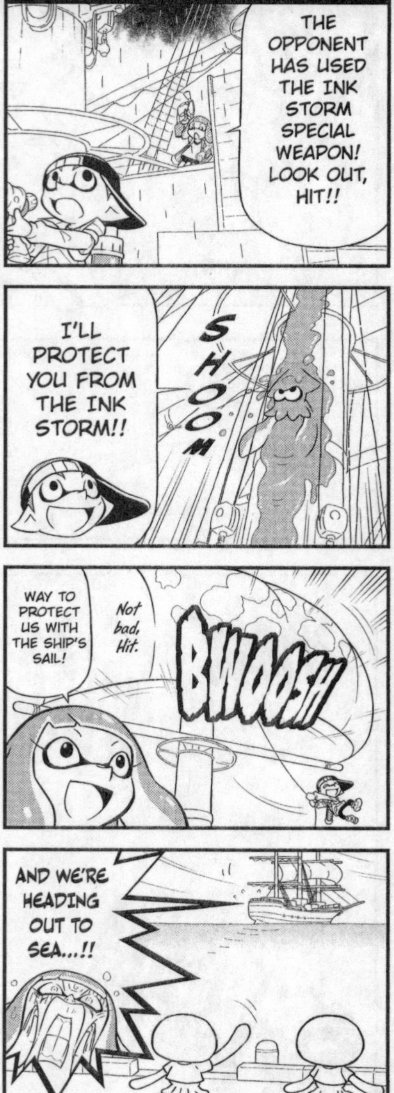
THE OPPONENT HAS USED THE INK STORM SPECIAL WEAPON! LOOK OUT, HIT!!
SHOOOM
I'LL PROTECT YOU FROM THE INK STORM!!
BWOOSH
Not bad, Hit.
WAY TO PROTECT US WITH THE SHIP'S SAIL!
AND WE'RE HEADING OUT TO SEA...!!

HELPER OF THE SEA

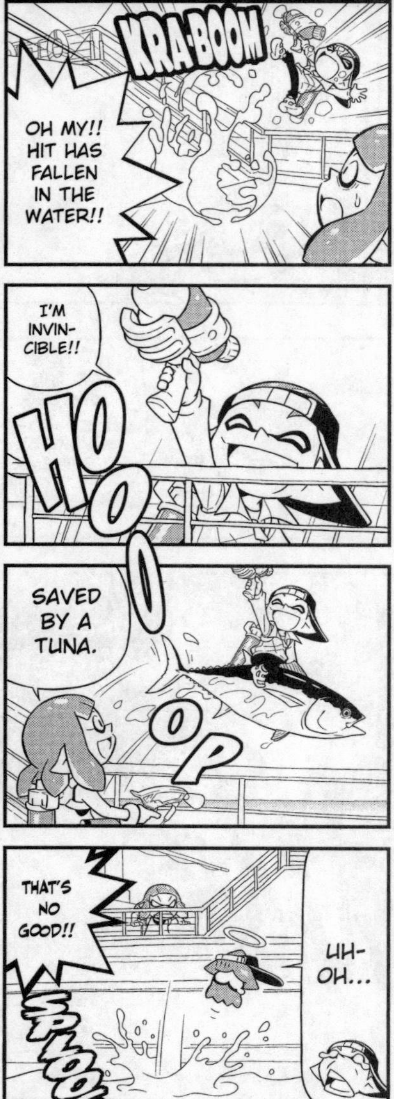
KRA-BOOM
OH MY!! HIT HAS FALLEN IN THE WATER!!
I'M INVINCIBLE!!
HOOOOP
SAVED BY A TUNA.
UH-OH...
THAT'S NO GOOD!!
SPLOOOSH

LOCK ON EVERYBODY

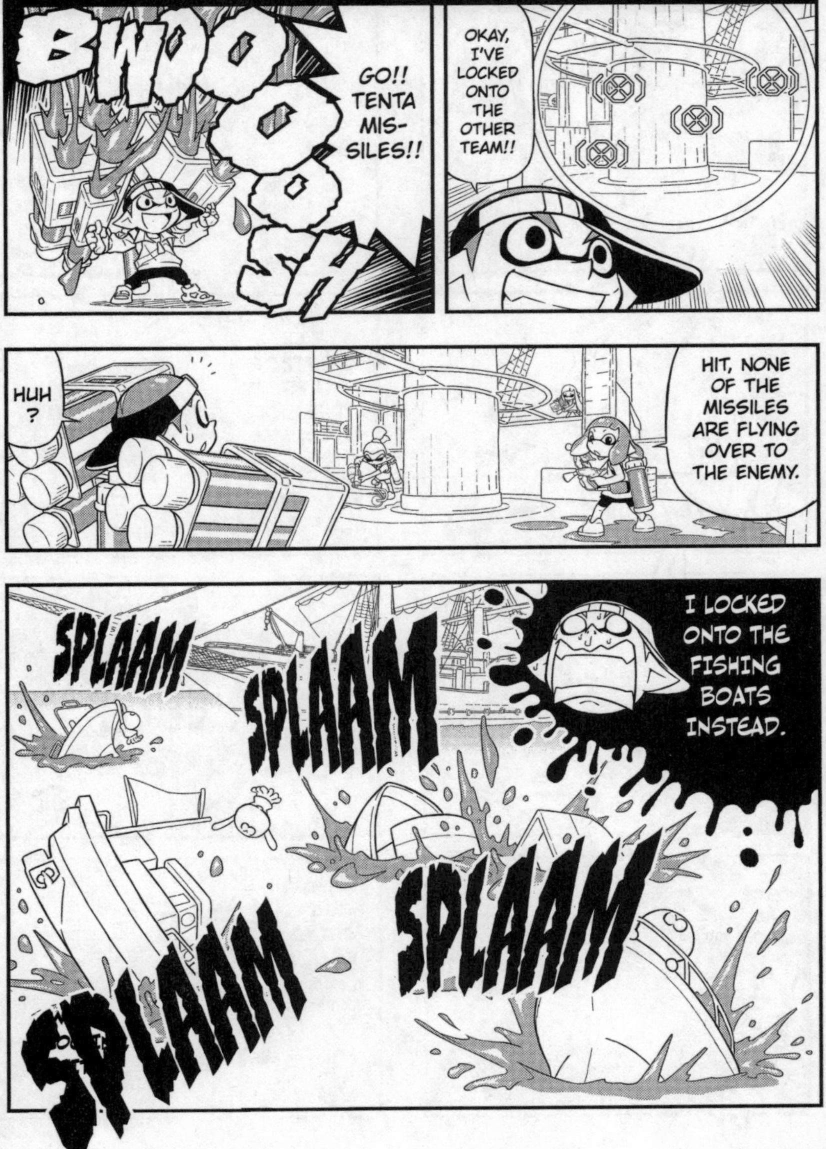
OKAY, I'VE LOCKED ONTO THE OTHER TEAM!!
BWOOOOOSH
GO!! TENTA MISSILES!!
HIT, NONE OF THE MISSILES ARE FLYING OVER TO THE ENEMY.
HUH?
I LOCKED ONTO THE FISHING BOATS INSTEAD.
SPLAAM
SPLAAM
SPLAAM
SPLAAM

THE RIGHT BAIT

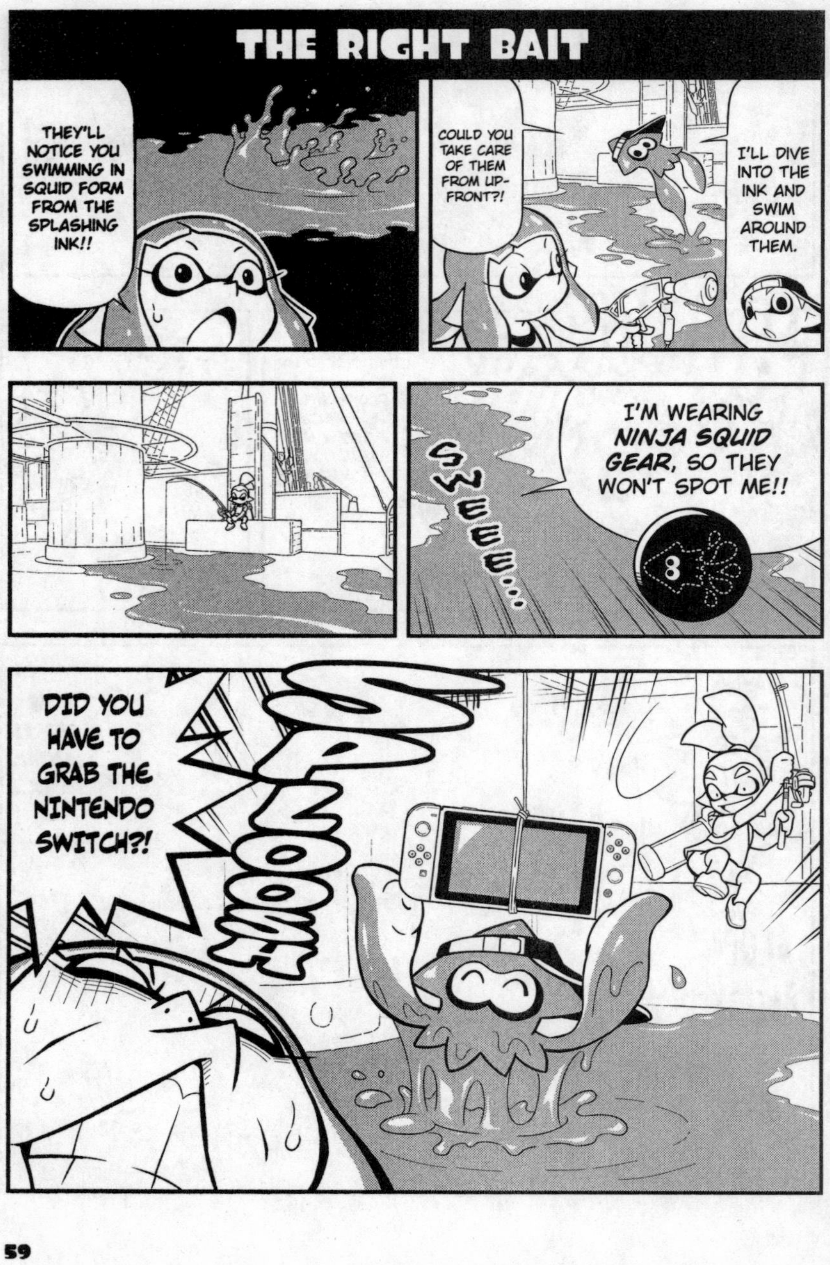

I'LL DIVE INTO THE INK AND SWIM AROUND THEM.
COULD YOU TAKE CARE OF THEM FROM UP-FRONT?!
THEY'LL NOTICE YOU SWIMMING IN SQUID FORM FROM THE SPLASHING INK!!
I'M WEARING NINJA SQUID GEAR, SO THEY WON'T SPOT ME!!
SWEEE...
SPLOOSH
DID YOU HAVE TO GRAB THE NINTENDO SWITCH?!

POWERFUL SPLASHDOWN

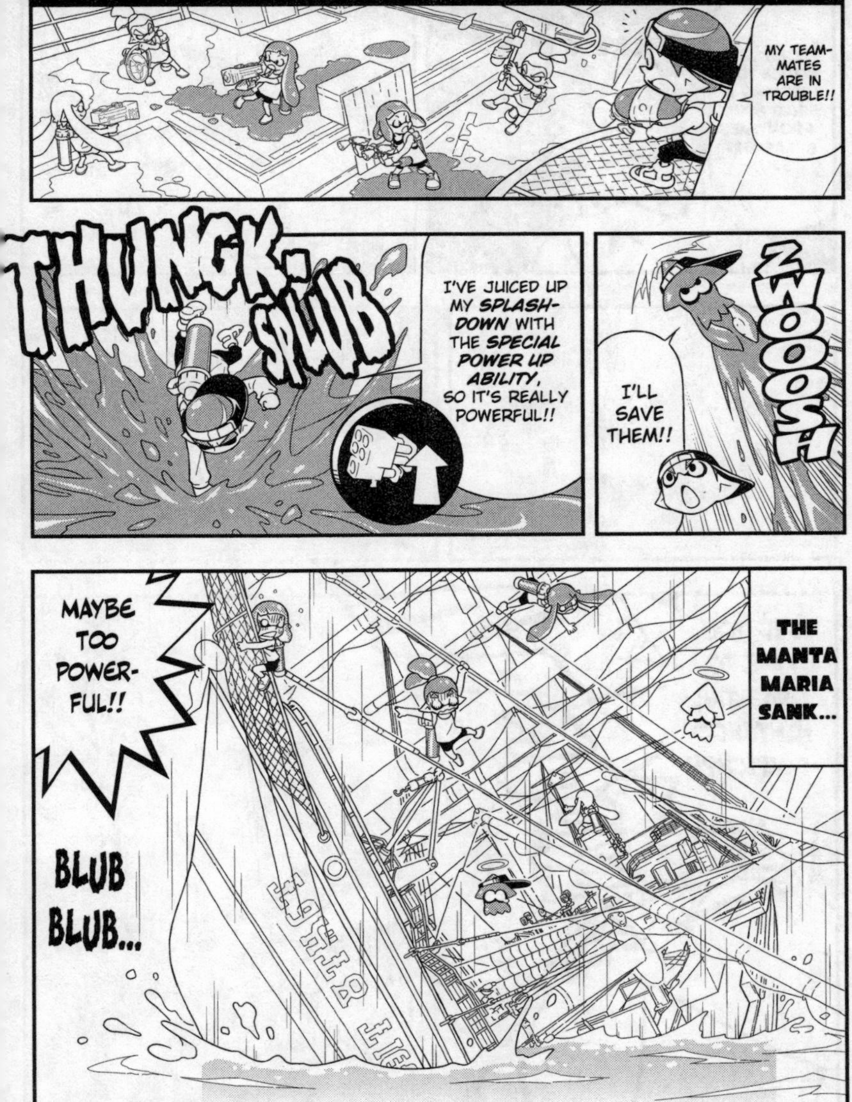
MY TEAM-MATES ARE IN TROUBLE!!
I'LL SAVE THEM!!
ZWOOOSH
THUNCK-SPLUB
I'VE JUICED UP MY *SPLASH-DOWN* WITH THE *SPECIAL POWER UP ABILITY*, SO IT'S REALLY POWERFUL!!
THE MANTA MARIA SANK...
MAYBE TOO POWER-FUL!!
BLUB BLUB...

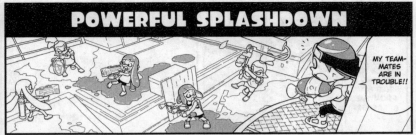

SPECIAL POWER UP INK STORM

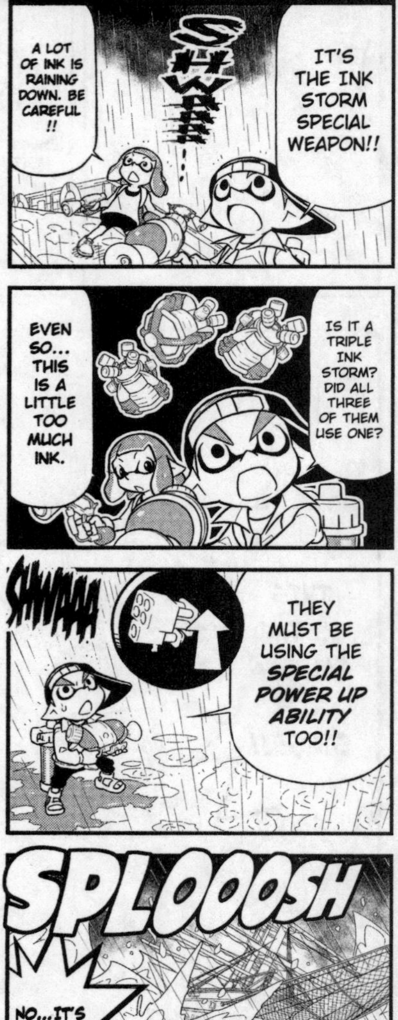
IT'S THE INK STORM SPECIAL WEAPON!!
SHWAAA
A LOT OF INK IS RAINING DOWN. BE CAREFUL !!
IS IT A TRIPLE INK STORM? DID ALL THREE OF THEM USE ONE?
EVEN SO... THIS IS A LITTLE TOO MUCH INK.
THEY MUST BE USING THE SPECIAL POWER UP ABILITY TOO!!
SHWAAA
SPLOOOSH
NO...IT'S A REAL STORM!!

HIGH-WIND WARNING

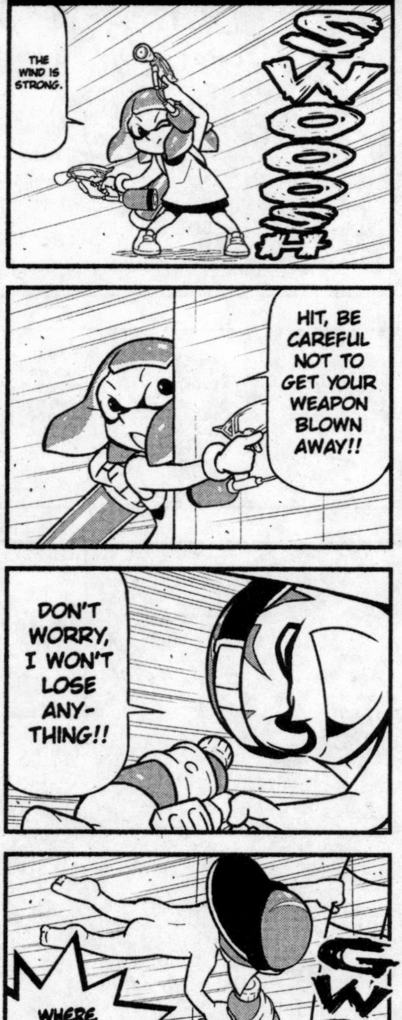
SWOOOOSH
THE WIND IS STRONG.
HIT, BE CAREFUL NOT TO GET YOUR WEAPON BLOWN AWAY!!
DON'T WORRY, I WON'T LOSE ANY-THING!!
GWOOSH
WHERE ARE YOUR CLOTHES?

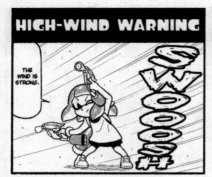

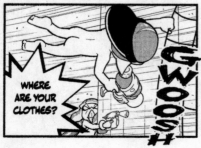

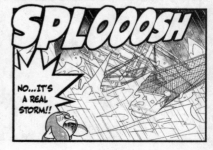

MAROONED SHIP

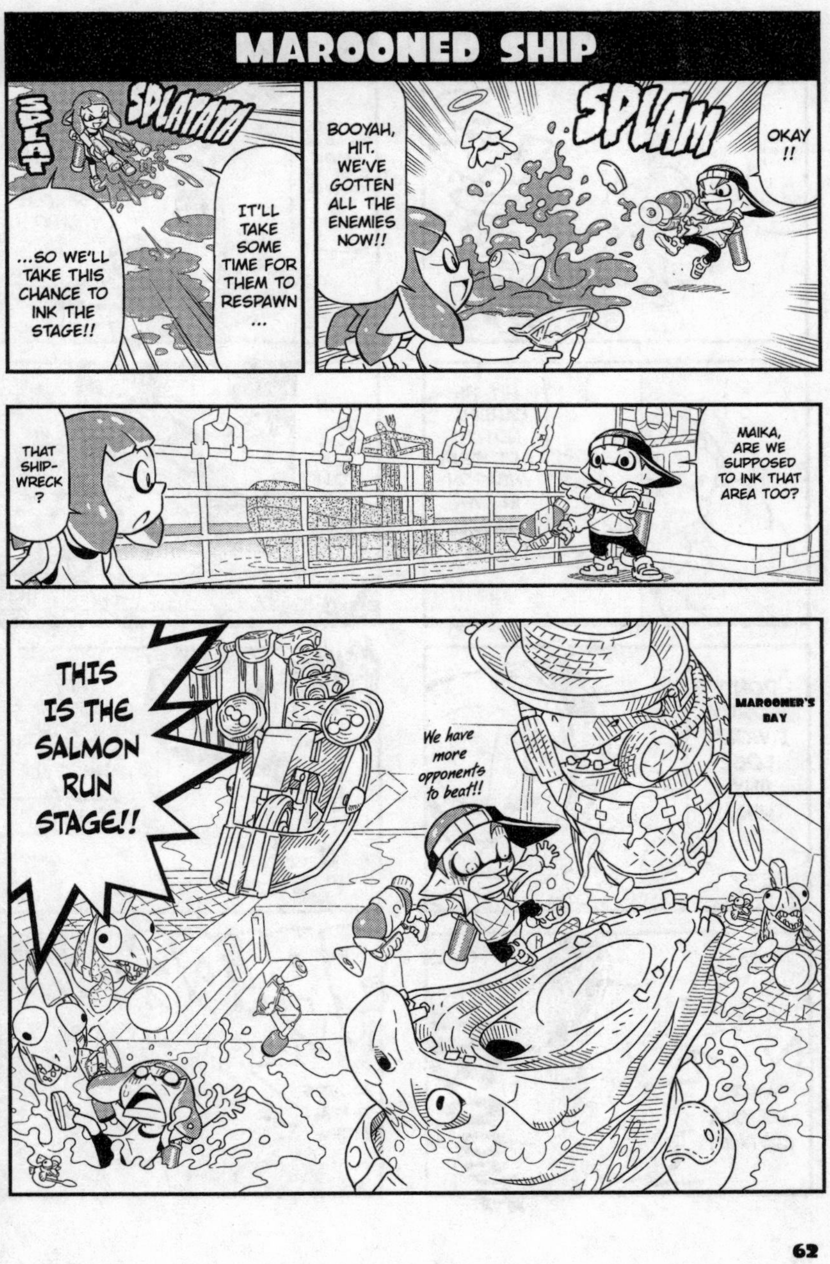
OKAY!!
SPLAM
BOOYAH, HIT. WE'VE GOTTEN ALL THE ENEMIES NOW!!
SPLATATA
SPLAT
IT'LL TAKE SOME TIME FOR THEM TO RESPAWN ...
...SO WE'LL TAKE THIS CHANCE TO INK THE STAGE!!
MAIKA, ARE WE SUPPOSED TO INK THAT AREA TOO?
THAT SHIP-WRECK?
MAROONER'S BAY
We have more opponents to beat!!
THIS IS THE SALMON RUN STAGE!!

GREAT VOYAGE

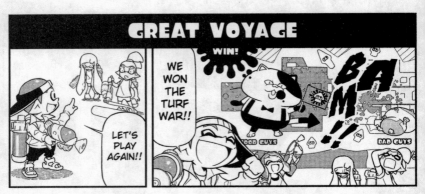

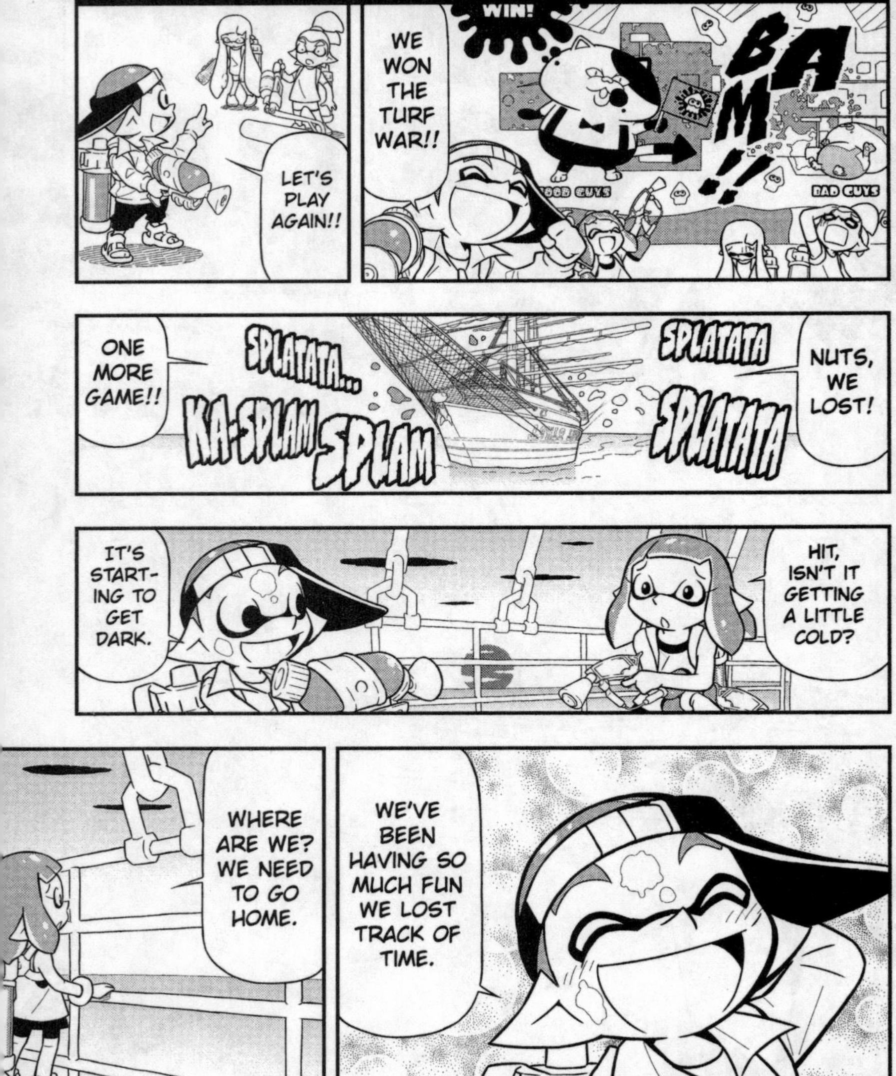
WIN!
WE WON THE TURF WAR!!
BAM!!
GOOD GUYS
BAD GUYS
LET'S PLAY AGAIN!!
NUTS, WE LOST!
SPLATATA
SPLATATA
SPLATATA...
KA-SPLAM
SPLAM
ONE MORE GAME!!
HIT, ISN'T IT GETTING A LITTLE COLD?
IT'S START-ING TO GET DARK.
WE'VE BEEN HAVING SO MUCH FUN WE LOST TRACK OF TIME.
WHERE ARE WE? WE NEED TO GO HOME.

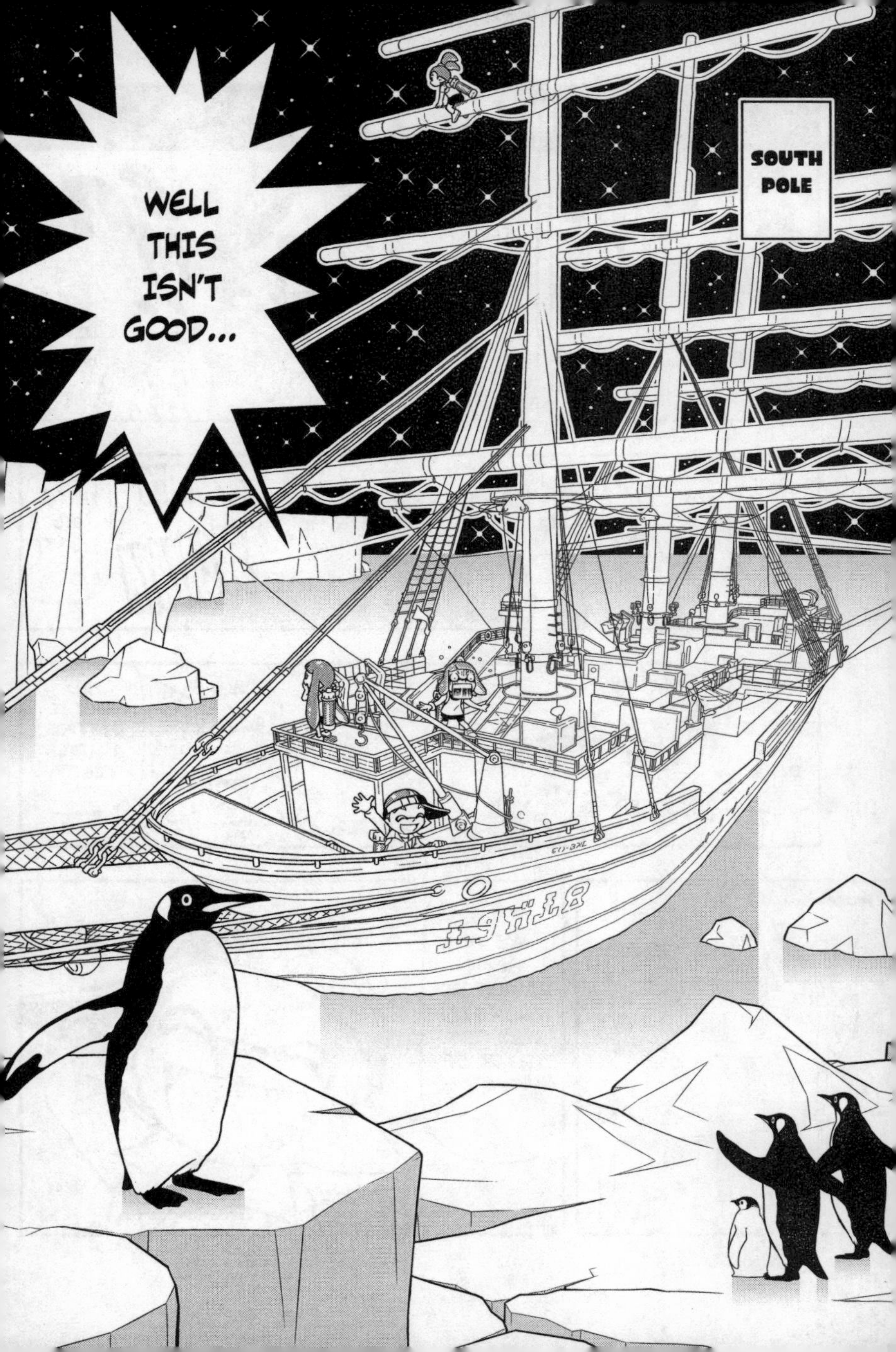
SOUTH POLE
WELL THIS ISN'T GOOD...

FIREFIGHTING

SOMEONE, BRING ME WATER!! THE FIRE'S SPREADING!!

KRRSHAA...

SHOOM

SLOSHING MACHINE!!

IT'S STILL BURNING!!

KRRSHAA...

THAT WAS YOUR LAUNDRY!!

FWIP FWIP

HUH?

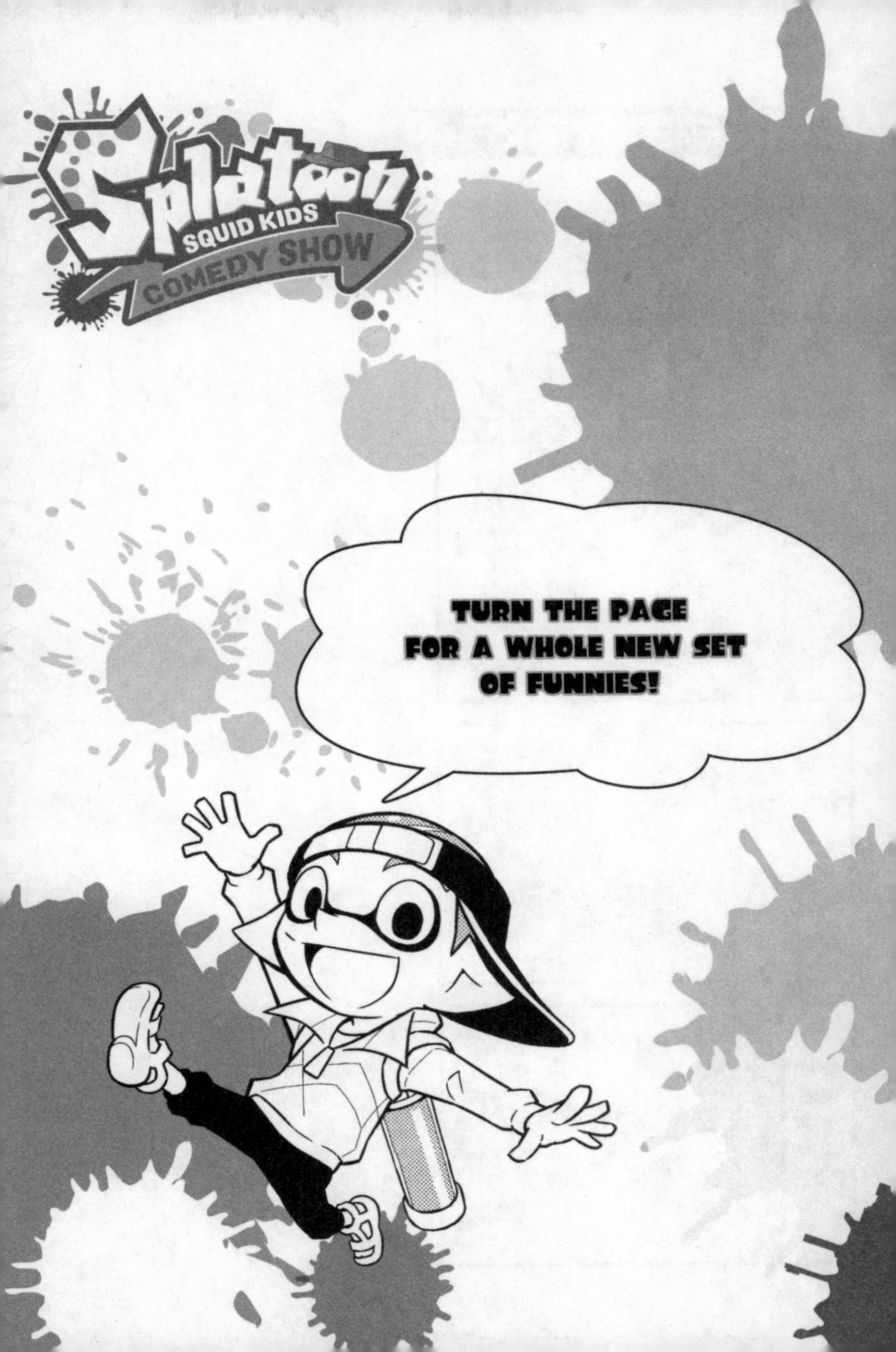
Splatoon
SQUID KIDS
COMEDY SHOW
TURN THE PAGE FOR A WHOLE NEW SET OF FUNNIES!

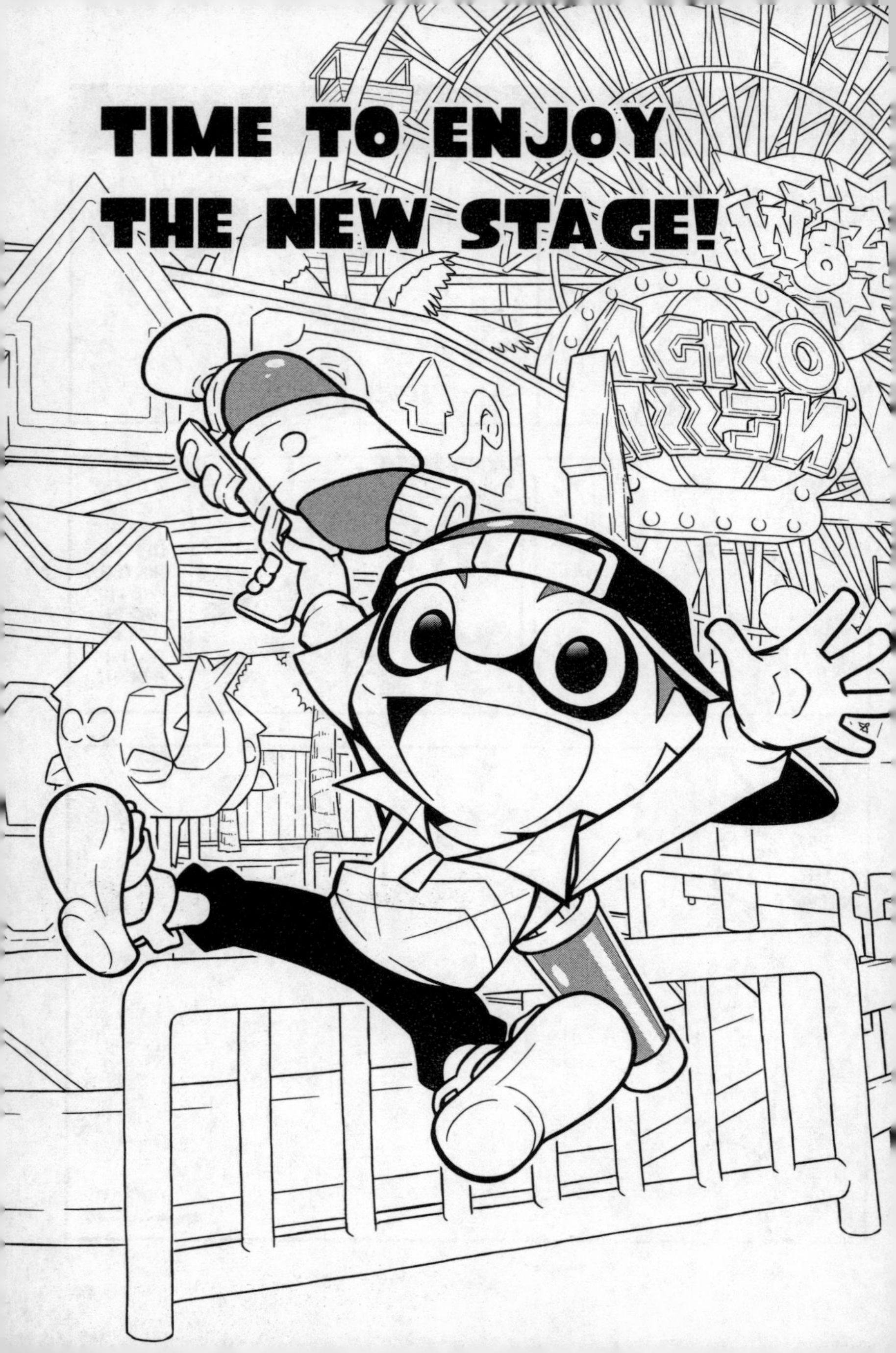
TIME TO ENJOY
THE NEW STAGE!

WAHOO WORLD

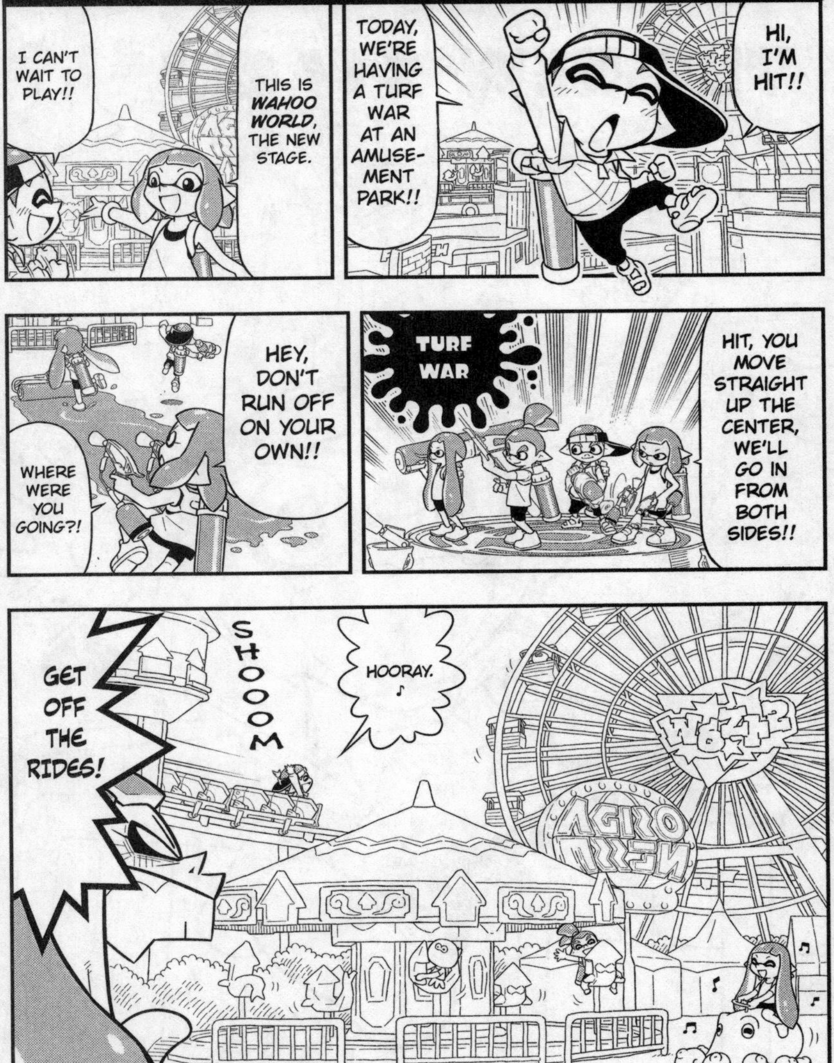

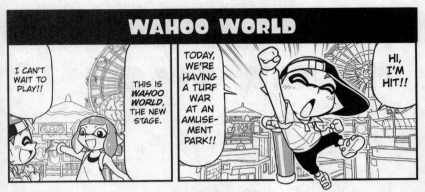

HI, I'M HIT!!
TODAY, WE'RE HAVING A TURF WAR AT AN AMUSEMENT PARK!!
THIS IS *WAHOO WORLD*, THE NEW STAGE.
I CAN'T WAIT TO PLAY!!
HIT, YOU MOVE STRAIGHT UP THE CENTER, WE'LL GO IN FROM BOTH SIDES!!
TURF WAR
HEY, DON'T RUN OFF ON YOUR OWN!!
WHERE WERE YOU GOING?!
HOORAY. ♪
SHOOOOM
GET OFF THE RIDES!

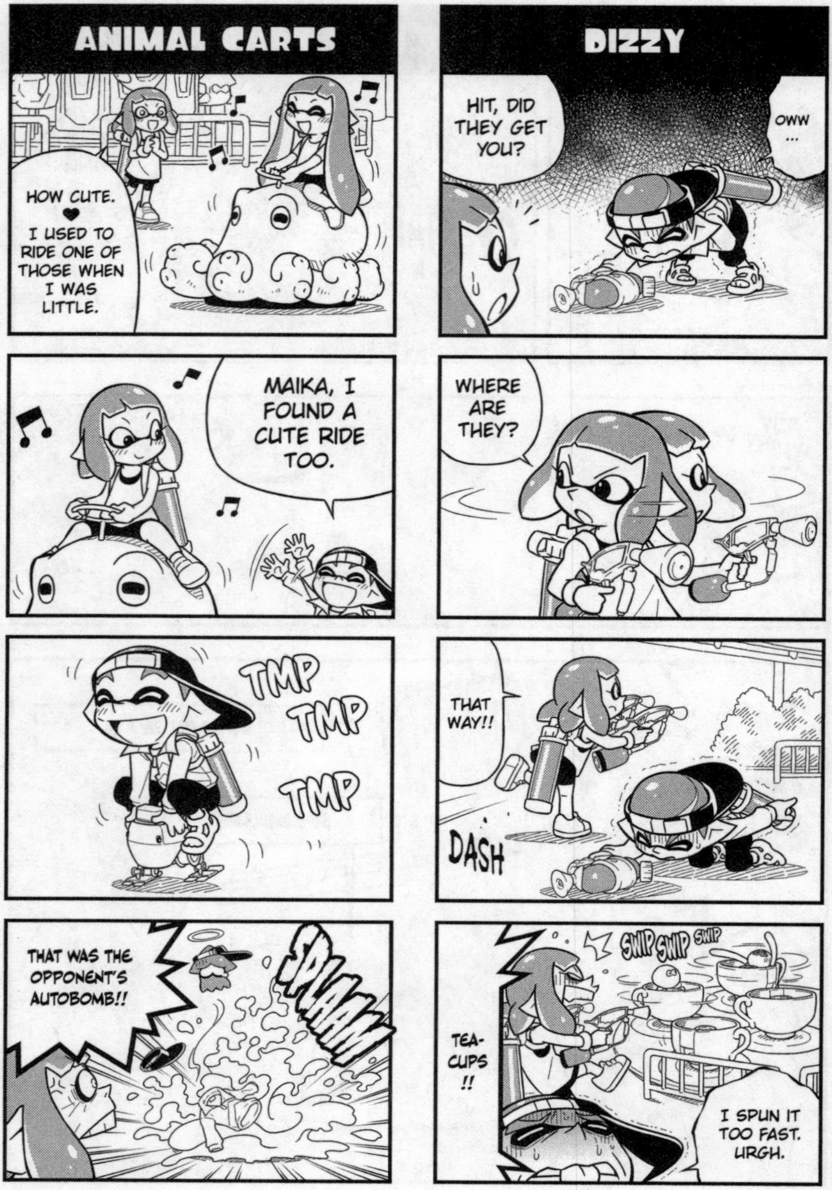
DIZZY
HIT, DID THEY GET YOU?
OWW ...
WHERE ARE THEY?
THAT WAY!!
DASH
TEA-CUPS !!
SWIP SWIP SWIP
I SPUN IT TOO FAST. URGH.
ANIMAL CARTS
HOW CUTE. ❤ I USED TO RIDE ONE OF THOSE WHEN I WAS LITTLE.
MAIKA, I FOUND A CUTE RIDE TOO.
TMP TMP TMP
THAT WAS THE OPPONENT'S AUTOBOMB!!
SPLAAAW

AUTOMATIC INKING MACHINES

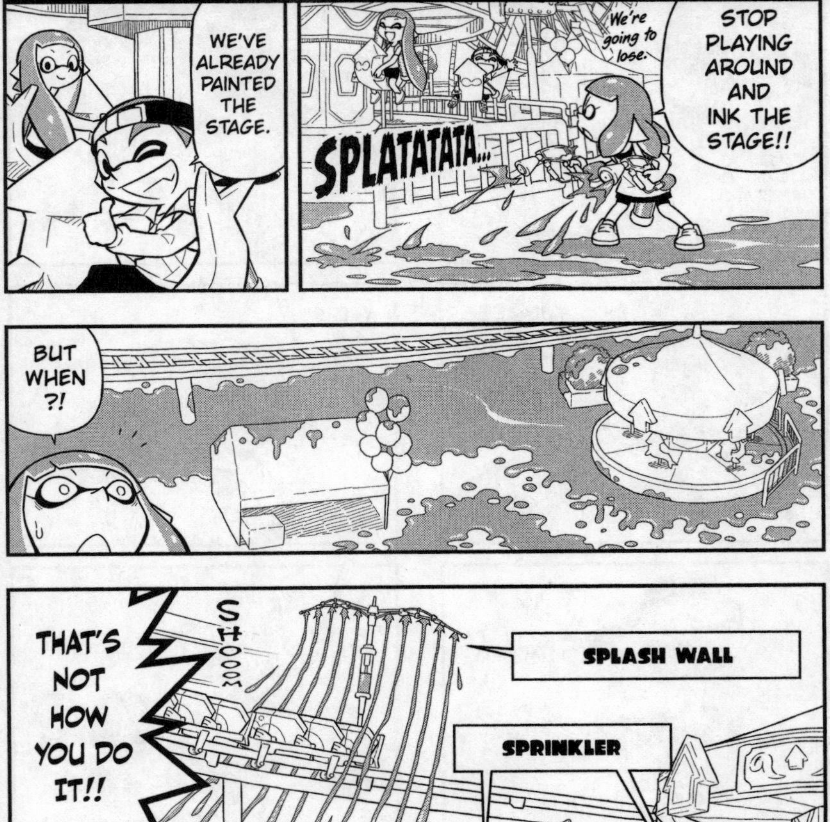

STOP PLAYING AROUND AND INK THE STAGE!!
We're going to lose.
SPLATATATA...
WE'VE ALREADY PAINTED THE STAGE.
BUT WHEN ?!
SPLASH WALL
SHOOOM
THAT'S NOT HOW YOU DO IT!!
SPRINKLER

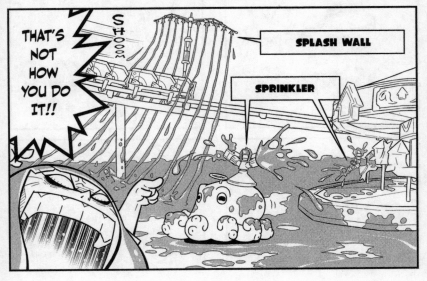

SUPER JUMP

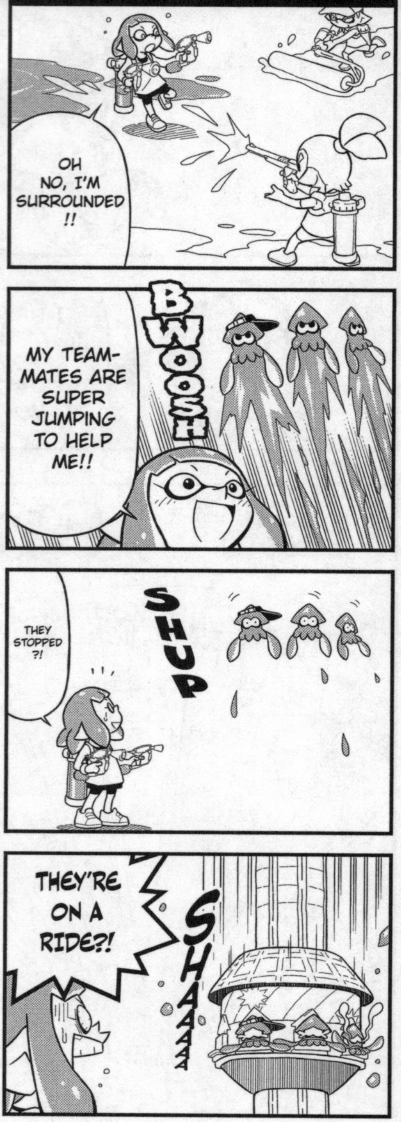
OH NO, I'M SURROUNDED !!
BWOOSH
MY TEAM-MATES ARE SUPER JUMPING TO HELP ME!!
SHUP
THEY STOPPED ?!
SHAAAAA
THEY'RE ON A RIDE?!

BOMB LAUNCHER

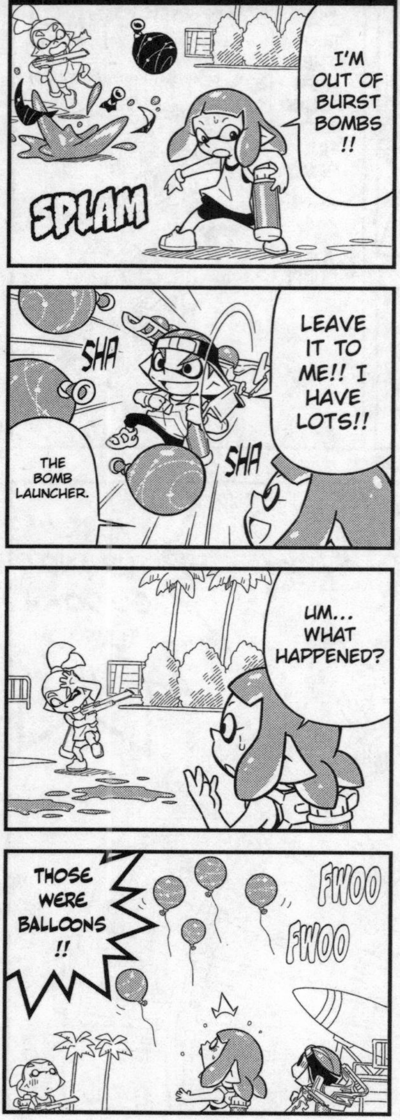
I'M OUT OF BURST BOMBS !!
SPLAM
LEAVE IT TO ME!! I HAVE LOTS!!
SHA
SHA
THE BOMB LAUNCHER.
UM... WHAT HAPPENED?
FWOO
FWOO
THOSE WERE BALLOONS !!

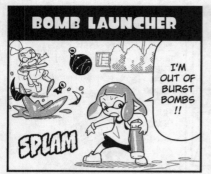

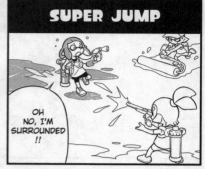

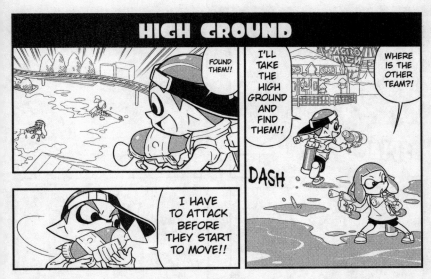

HIGH GROUND

WHERE IS THE OTHER TEAM?!
I'LL TAKE THE HIGH GROUND AND FIND THEM!!
DASH
FOUND THEM!!
I HAVE TO ATTACK BEFORE THEY START TO MOVE!!
HURRY UP AND GO DOWN ALREADY!!
SWOOO...
FERRIS WHEEL

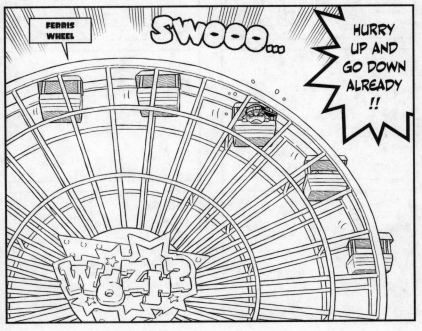

PIRATE SHIP

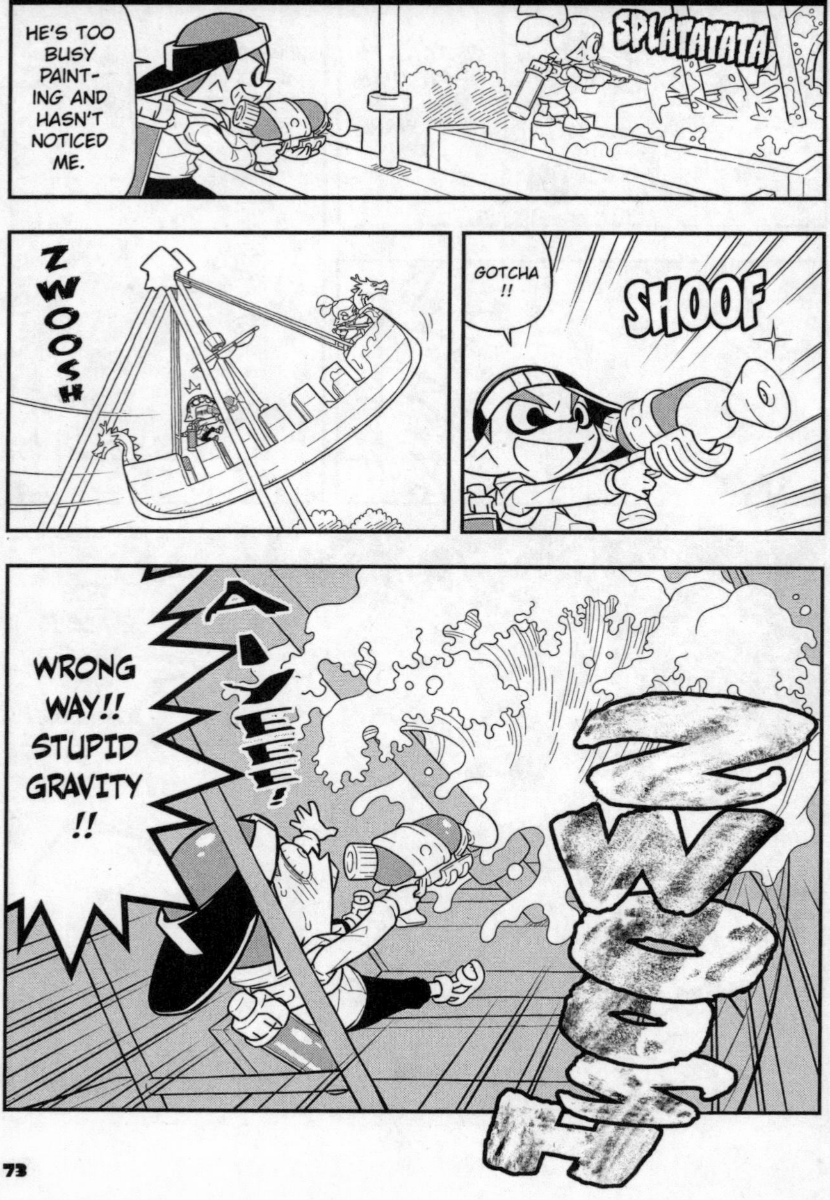
SPLATATATA
HE'S TOO BUSY PAINT-ING AND HASN'T NOTICED ME.
GOTCHA!!
SHOOF
ZWOOSH
AIYEEE!
WRONG WAY!! STUPID GRAVITY!!
ZWOOSH

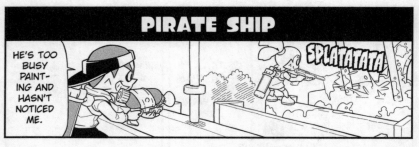

MIDWAY MONSTERS

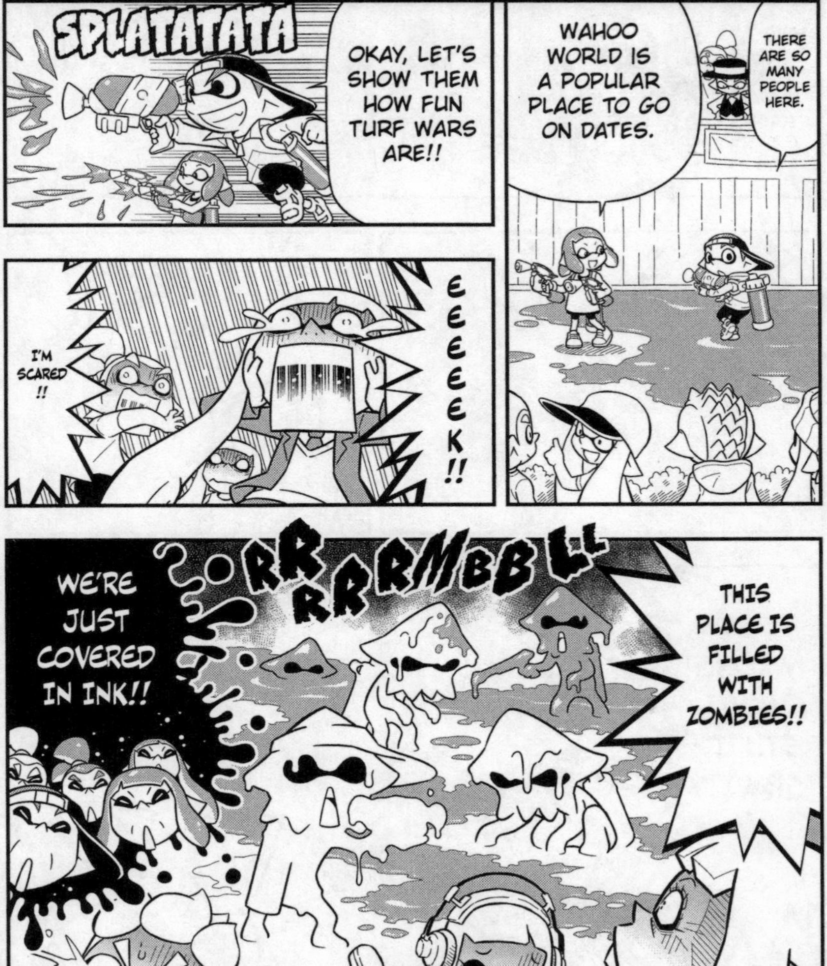
THERE ARE SO MANY PEOPLE HERE.
WAHOO WORLD IS A POPULAR PLACE TO GO ON DATES.
OKAY, LET'S SHOW THEM HOW FUN TURF WARS ARE!!
SPLATATATA
EEEEEEK!!
I'M SCARED!!
RRRRRMBBLL
THIS PLACE IS FILLED WITH ZOMBIES!!
WE'RE JUST COVERED IN INK!!

TIME FOR AN EXCITING CLAM BLITZ AT A MINE!

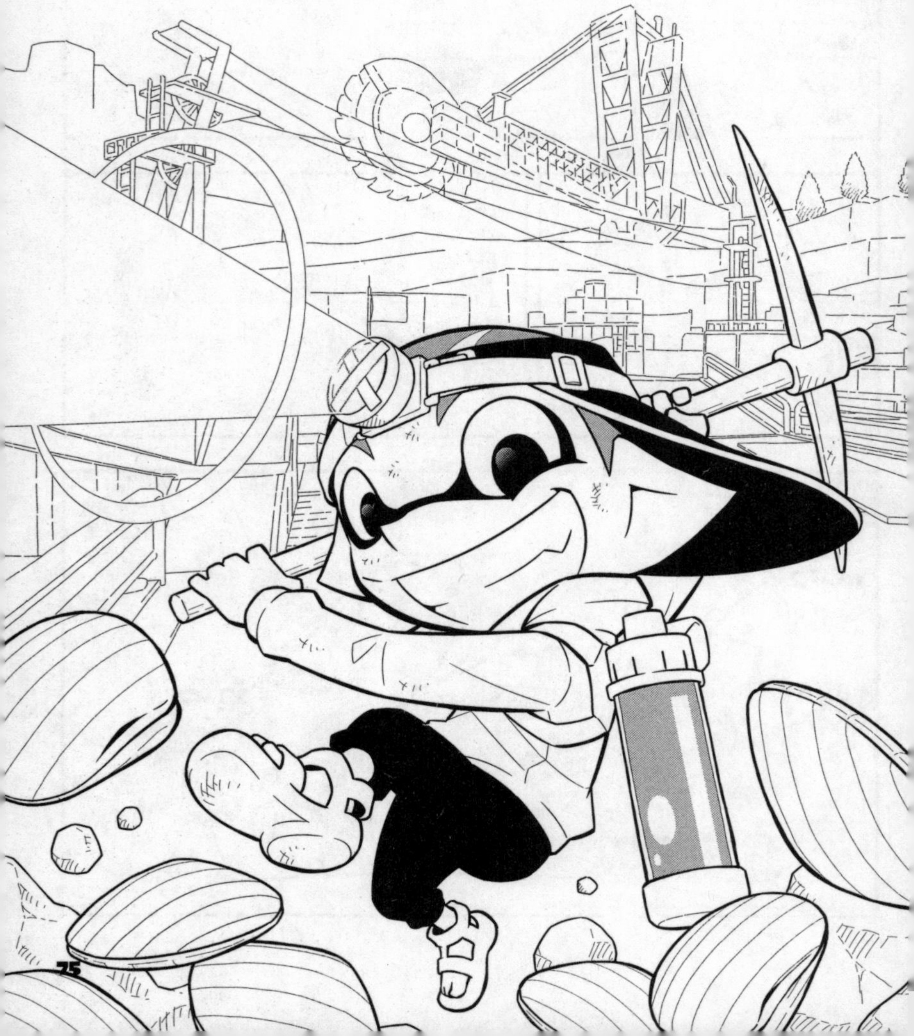

PIRANHA PIT

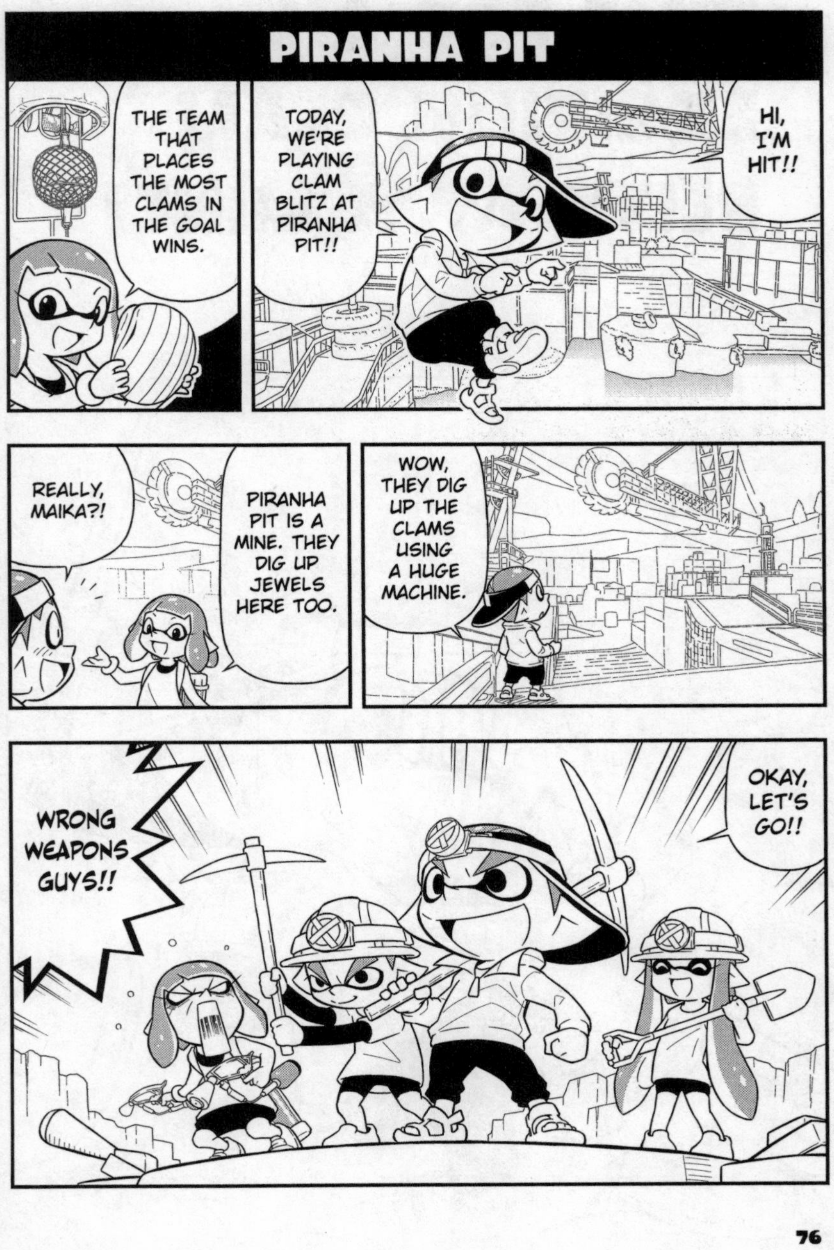
HI, I'M HIT!!
TODAY, WE'RE PLAYING CLAM BLITZ AT PIRANHA PIT!!
THE TEAM THAT PLACES THE MOST CLAMS IN THE GOAL WINS.
WOW, THEY DIG UP THE CLAMS USING A HUGE MACHINE.
PIRANHA PIT IS A MINE. THEY DIG UP JEWELS HERE TOO.
REALLY, MAIKA?!
OKAY, LET'S GO!!
WRONG WEAPONS GUYS!!

KOU BATTLE

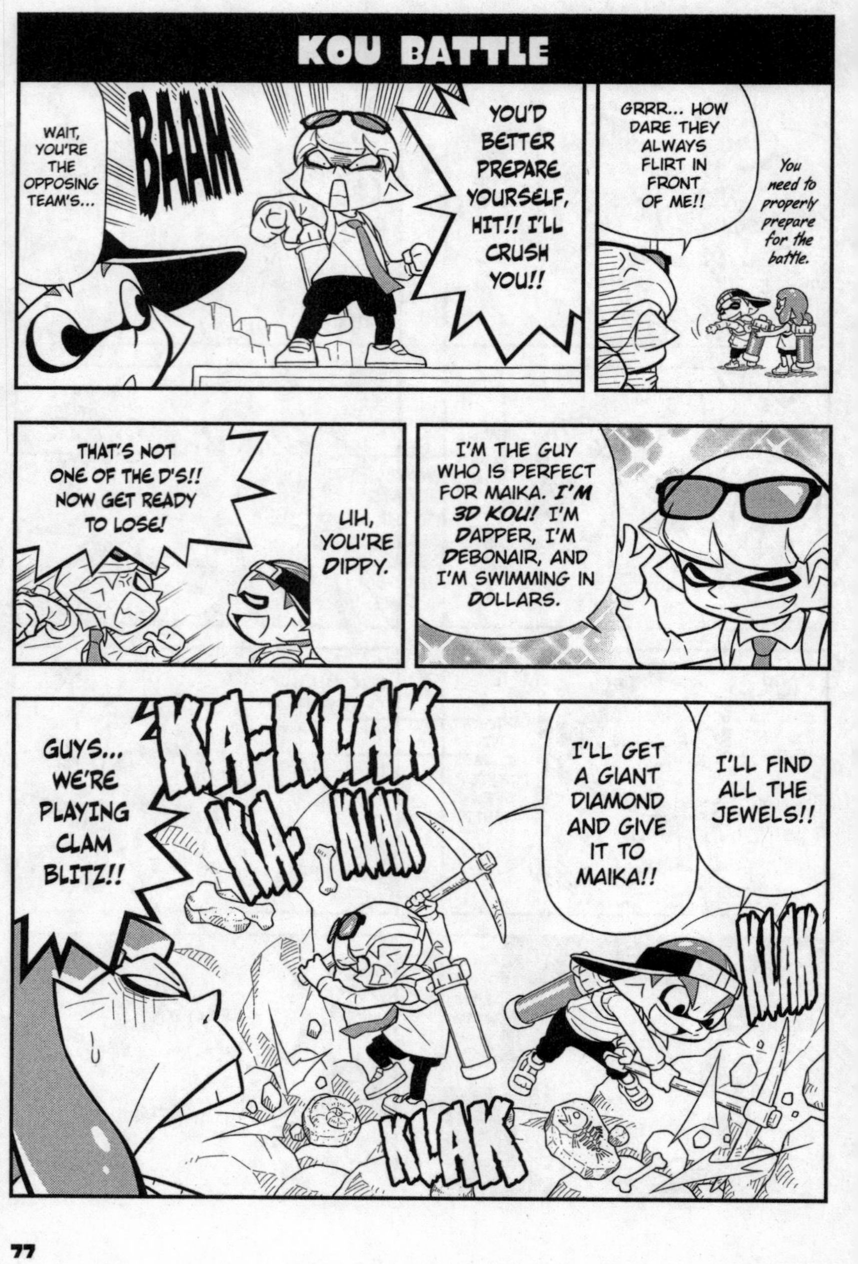
GRRR... HOW DARE THEY ALWAYS FLIRT IN FRONT OF ME!!
You need to properly prepare for the battle.
YOU'D BETTER PREPARE YOURSELF, HIT!! I'LL CRUSH YOU!!
BAAM
WAIT, YOU'RE THE OPPOSING TEAM'S...
I'M THE GUY WHO IS PERFECT FOR MAIKA. *I'M 3D KOU!* I'M *D*APPER, I'M *D*EBONAIR, AND I'M SWIMMING IN *D*OLLARS.
UH, YOU'RE *D*IPPY.
THAT'S NOT ONE OF THE D'S!! NOW GET READY TO LOSE!
I'LL FIND ALL THE JEWELS!!
I'LL GET A GIANT DIAMOND AND GIVE IT TO MAIKA!!
KA-KLAK
KA-KLAK
GUYS... WE'RE PLAYING CLAM BLITZ!!
KLAK
KLAK

COMPLETE

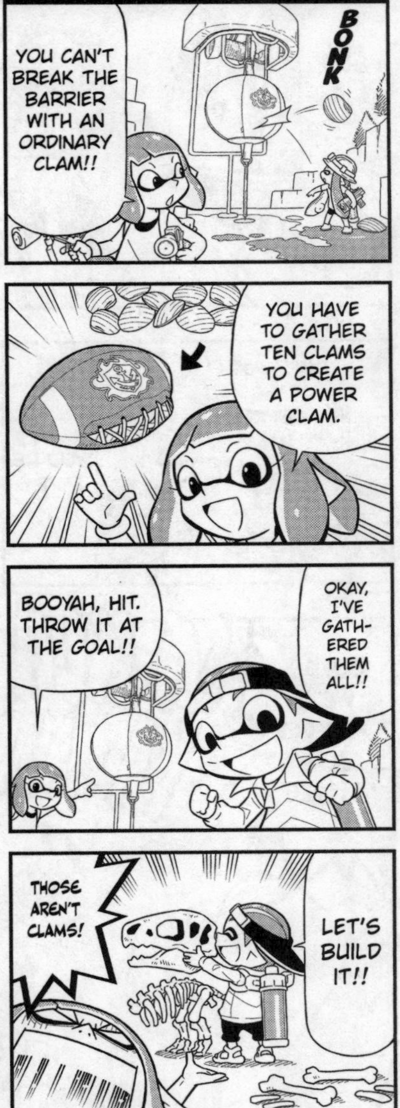

BONK
YOU CAN'T BREAK THE BARRIER WITH AN ORDINARY CLAM!!
YOU HAVE TO GATHER TEN CLAMS TO CREATE A POWER CLAM.
OKAY, I'VE GATH-ERED THEM ALL!!
BOOYAH, HIT. THROW IT AT THE GOAL!!
LET'S BUILD IT!!
THOSE AREN'T CLAMS!

FOR YOU

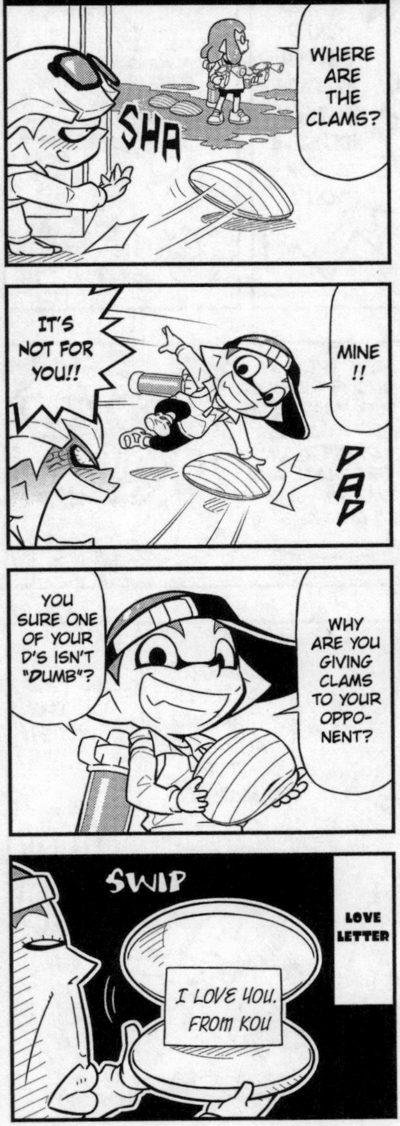

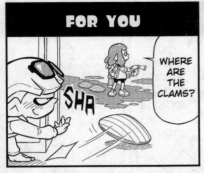

WHERE ARE THE CLAMS?
SHA
MINE!!
PAP
IT'S NOT FOR YOU!!
WHY ARE YOU GIVING CLAMS TO YOUR OPPO-NENT?
YOU SURE ONE OF YOUR D'S ISN'T "DUMB"?
LOVE LETTER
SWIP
I LOVE YOU. FROM KOU

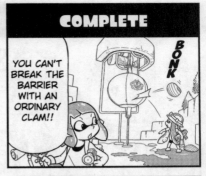

CONVEYOR BELT

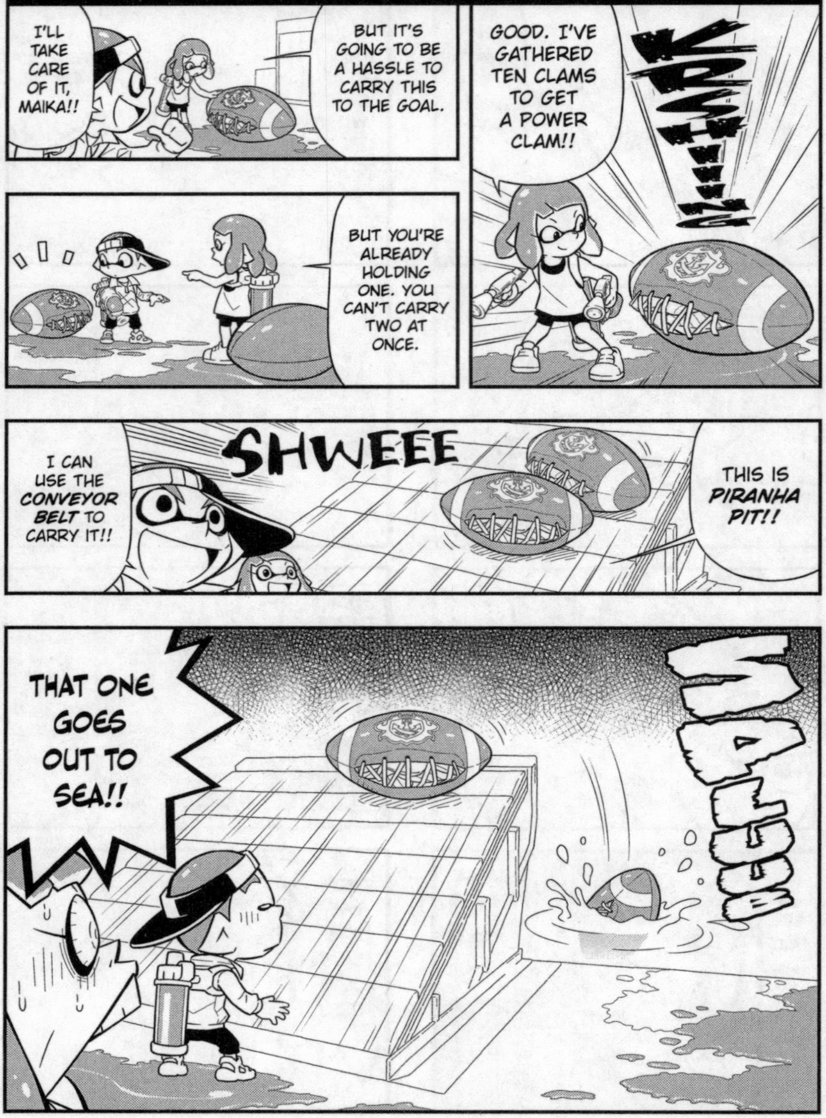
GOOD. I'VE GATHERED TEN CLAMS TO GET A POWER CLAM!!
VRSHIIING
BUT IT'S GOING TO BE A HASSLE TO CARRY THIS TO THE GOAL.
I'LL TAKE CARE OF IT, MAIKA!!
BUT YOU'RE ALREADY HOLDING ONE. YOU CAN'T CARRY TWO AT ONCE.
THIS IS *PIRANHA PIT!!*
SHWEEE
I CAN USE THE *CONVEYOR BELT* TO CARRY IT!!
THAT ONE GOES OUT TO SEA!!

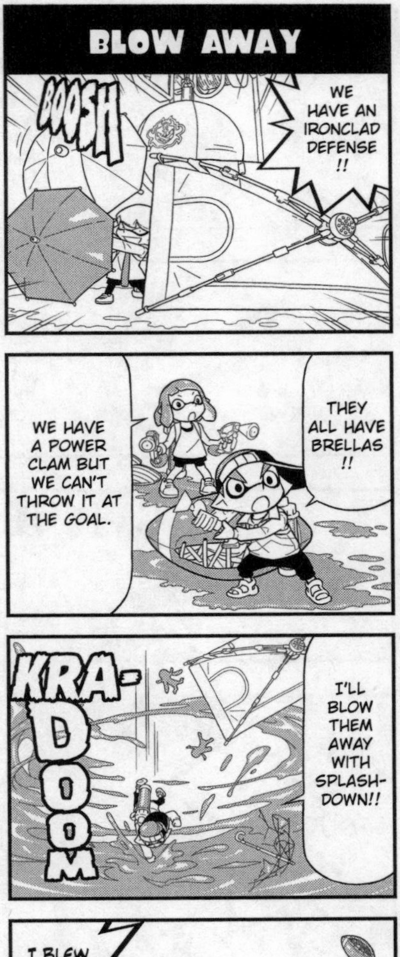
BLOW AWAY
WE HAVE AN IRONCLAD DEFENSE !!
BOOSH
THEY ALL HAVE BRELLAS !!
WE HAVE A POWER CLAM BUT WE CAN'T THROW IT AT THE GOAL.
I'LL BLOW THEM AWAY WITH SPLASH-DOWN!!
KRA-DOOM
I BLEW AWAY THE POWER CLAM TOO!!

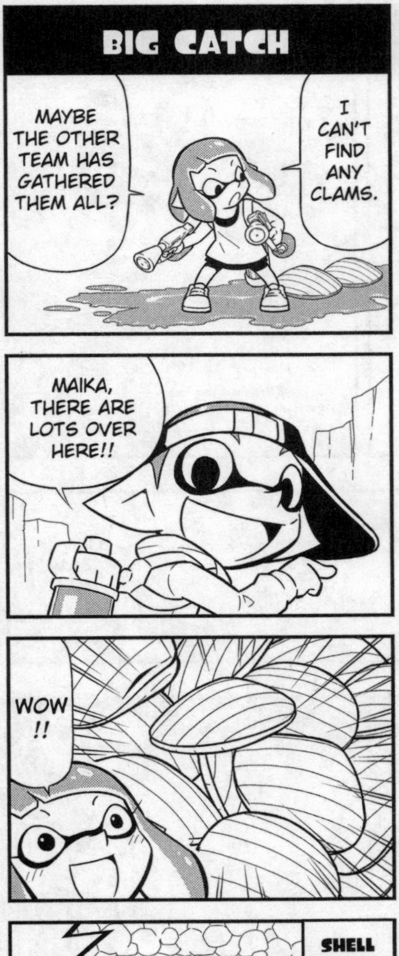
BIG CATCH
I CAN'T FIND ANY CLAMS.
MAYBE THE OTHER TEAM HAS GATHERED THEM ALL?
MAIKA, THERE ARE LOTS OVER HERE!!
WOW !!
SHELL MOUND
BUT THESE SHELLS ARE ALL FOSSILS !!

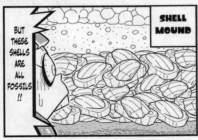

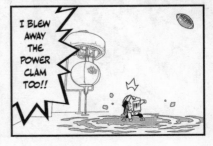

ANCIENT CLAM BLITZ

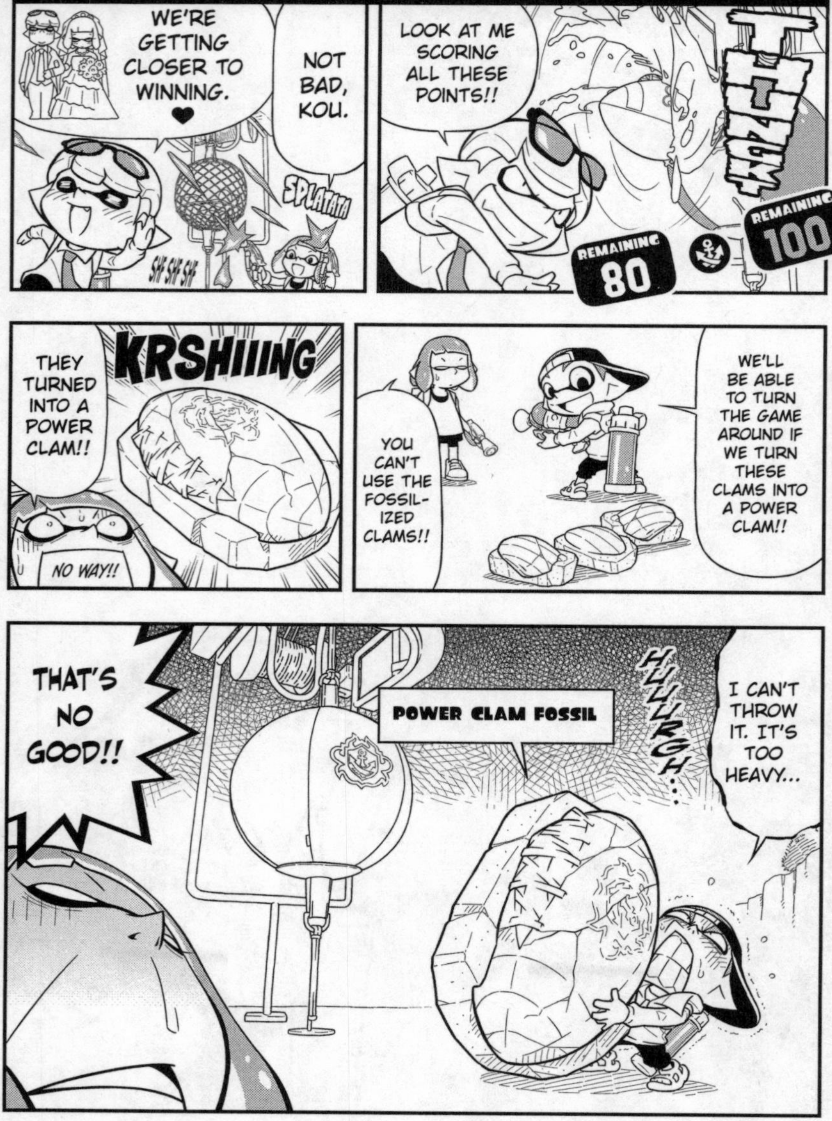
LOOK AT ME SCORING ALL THESE POINTS!!
REMAINING 100
REMAINING 80
NOT BAD, KOU.
WE'RE GETTING CLOSER TO WINNING. ❤
SPLATATA
SHF SHF SHF
WE'LL BE ABLE TO TURN THE GAME AROUND IF WE TURN THESE CLAMS INTO A POWER CLAM!!
YOU CAN'T USE THE FOSSIL-IZED CLAMS!!
KRSHIIING
THEY TURNED INTO A POWER CLAM!!
NO WAY!!
I CAN'T THROW IT. IT'S TOO HEAVY...
HUURGH...
POWER CLAM FOSSIL
THAT'S NO GOOD!!

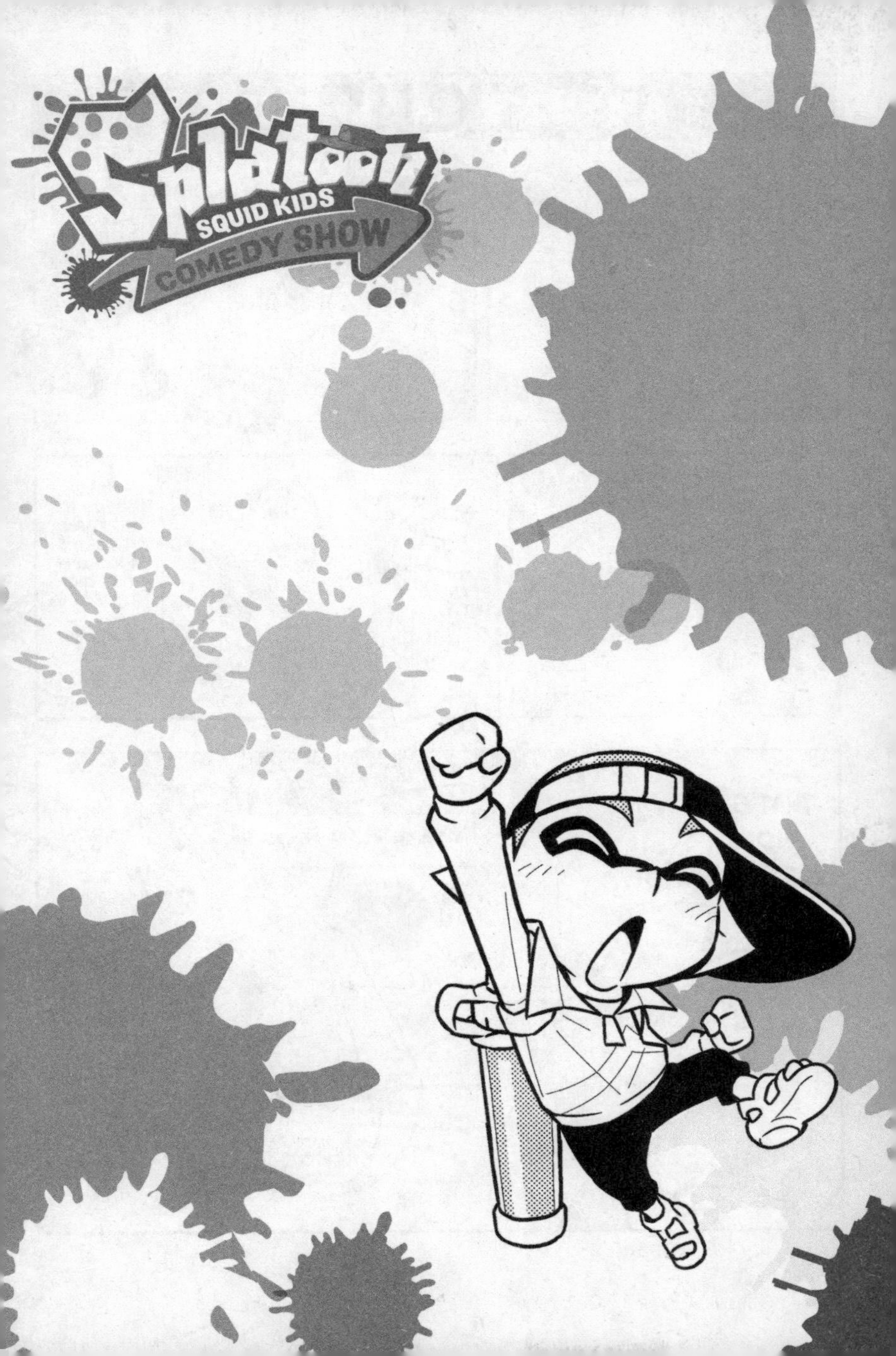
Splatoon
SQUID KIDS
COMEDY SHOW

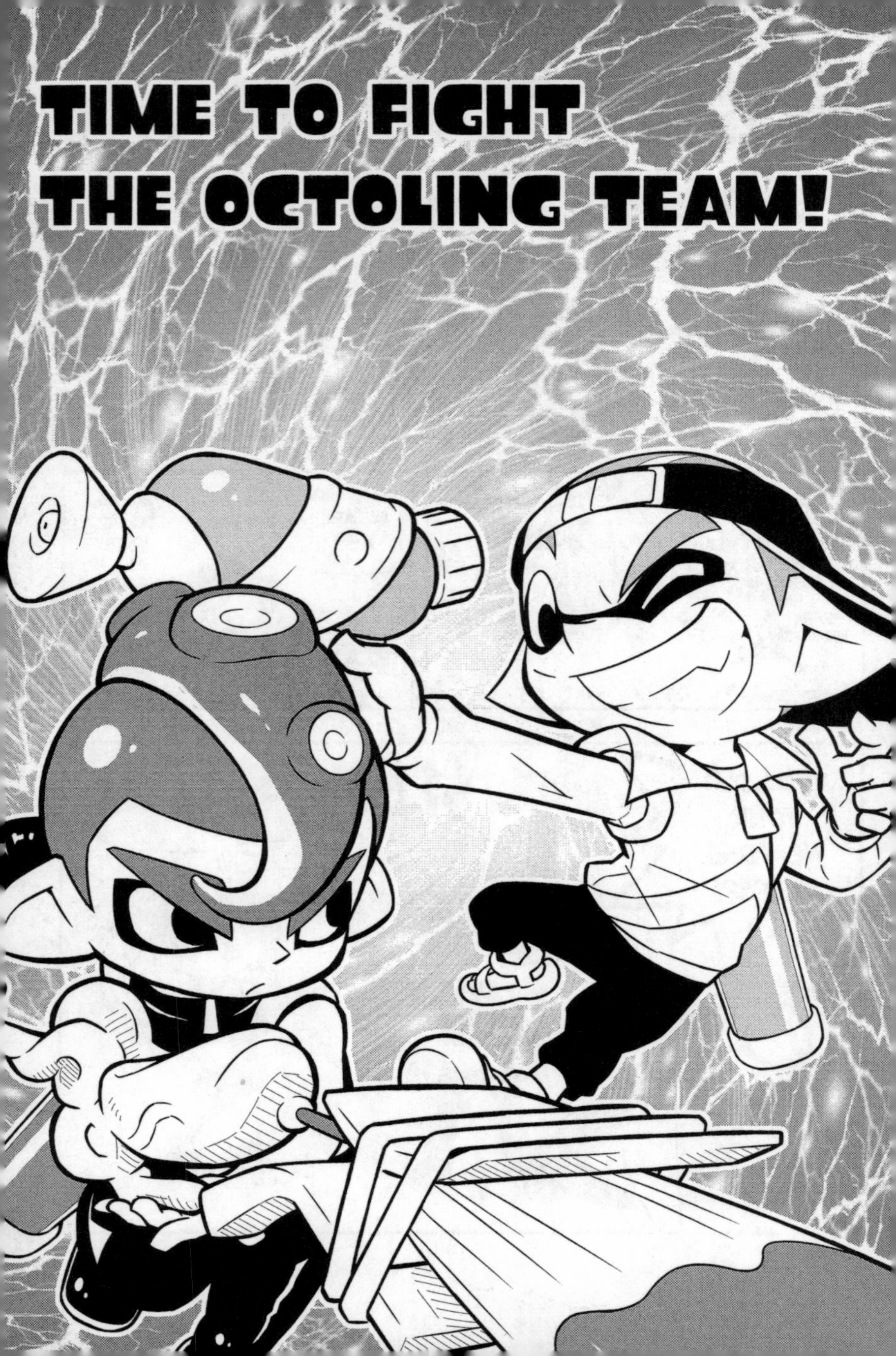
TIME TO FIGHT
THE OCTOLING TEAM!

OCTOLING TEAM

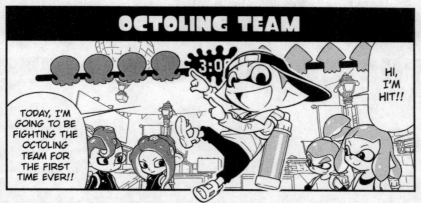

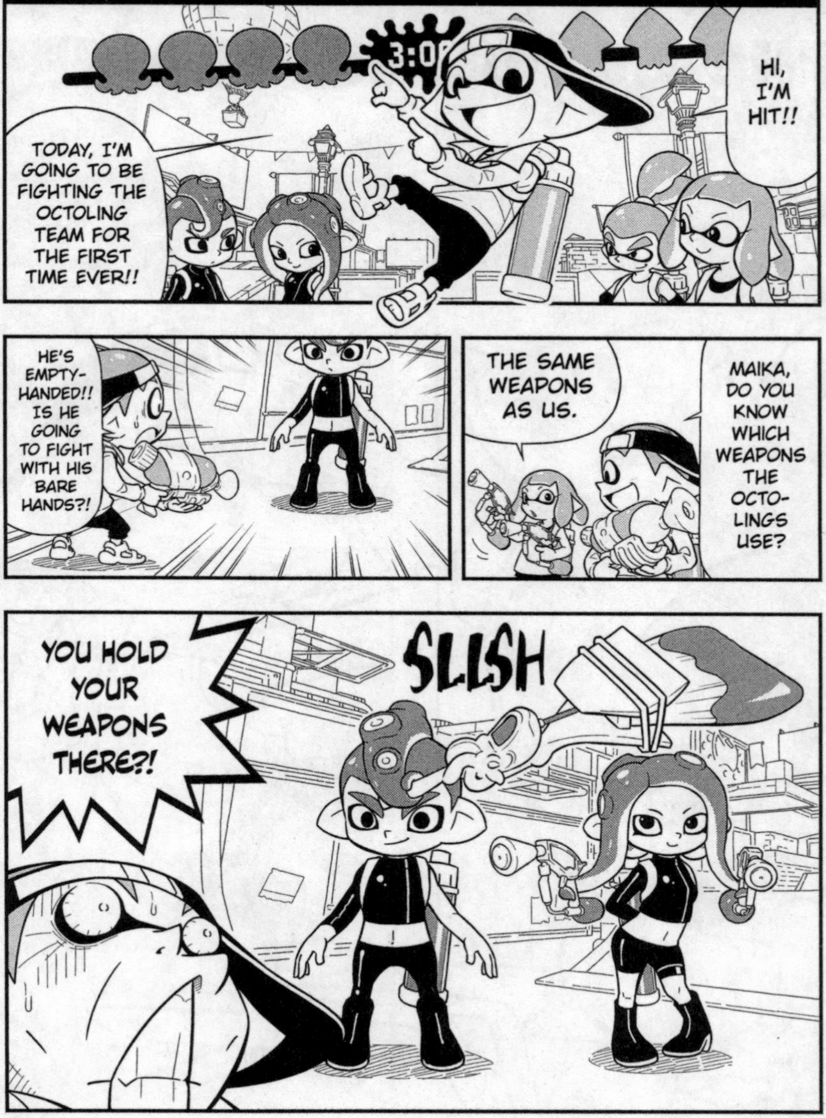
HI, I'M HIT!!
TODAY, I'M GOING TO BE FIGHTING THE OCTOLING TEAM FOR THE FIRST TIME EVER!!
MAIKA, DO YOU KNOW WHICH WEAPONS THE OCTO-LINGS USE?
THE SAME WEAPONS AS US.
HE'S EMPTY-HANDED!! IS HE GOING TO FIGHT WITH HIS BARE HANDS?!
SLISH
YOU HOLD YOUR WEAPONS THERE?!

HIDING OCTOPUS

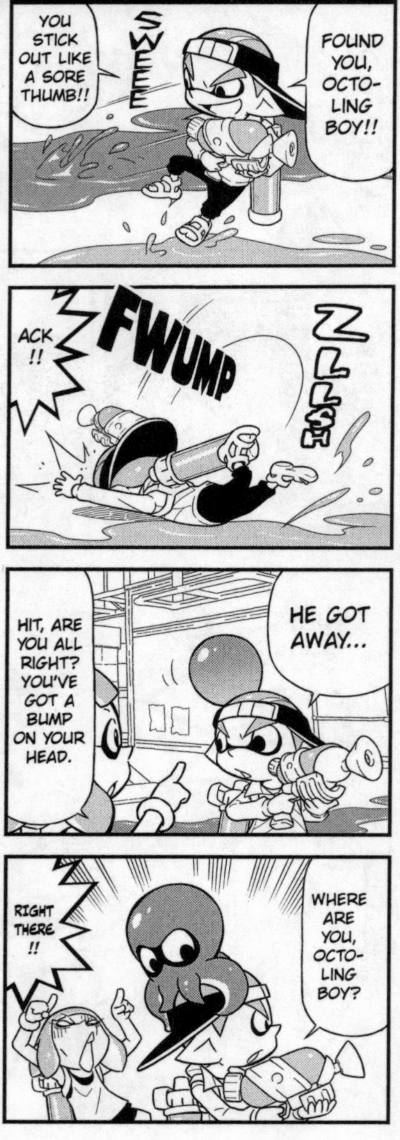
FOUND YOU, OCTO-LING BOY!!
SWEEE
YOU STICK OUT LIKE A SORE THUMB!!
ZLLSH
FWUMP
ACK!!
HE GOT AWAY...
HIT, ARE YOU ALL RIGHT? YOU'VE GOT A BUMP ON YOUR HEAD.
WHERE ARE YOU, OCTO-LING BOY?
RIGHT THERE!!

FINE OCTOPUS

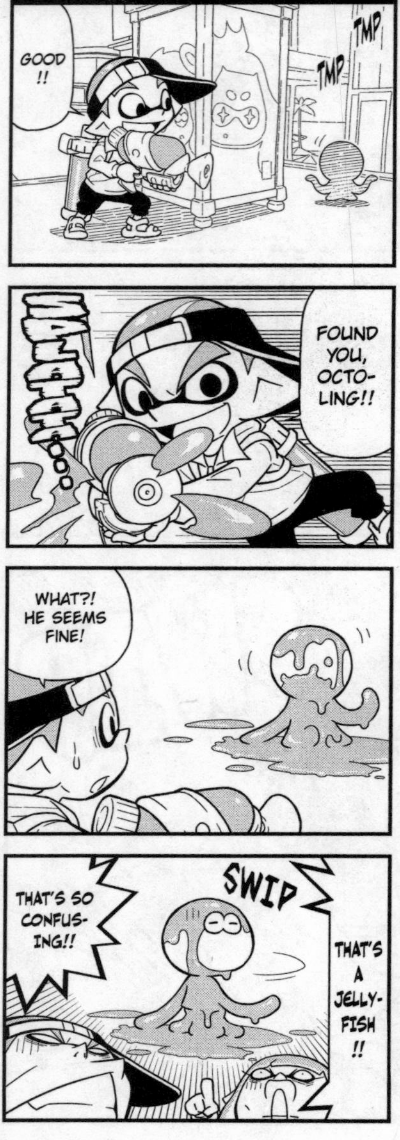
TMP
TMP
GOOD!!
FOUND YOU, OCTO-LING!!
WHAT?! HE SEEMS FINE!
SWIP
THAT'S A JELLY-FISH!!
THAT'S SO CONFUS-ING!!

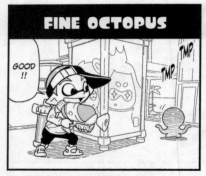

OCTOLING CATCH

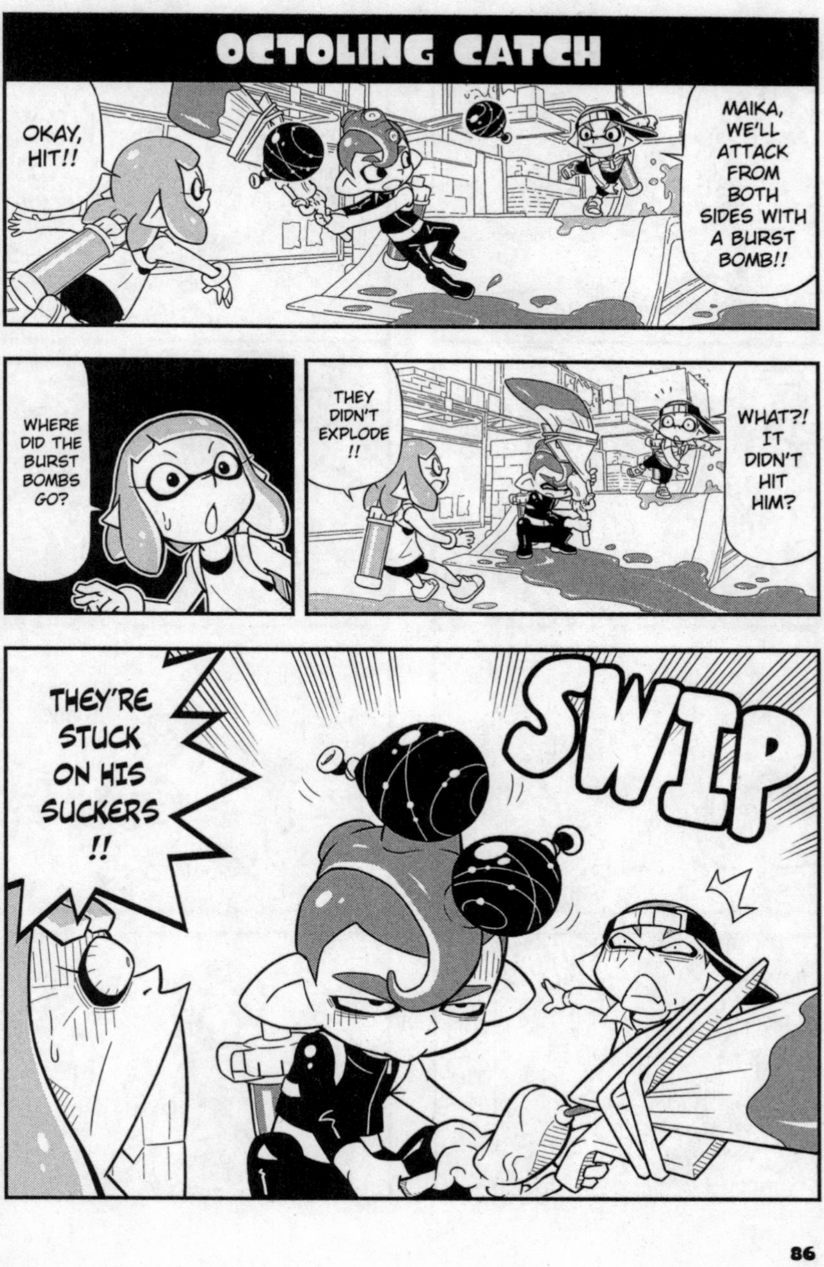
MAIKA, WE'LL ATTACK FROM BOTH SIDES WITH A BURST BOMB!!
OKAY, HIT!!
WHAT?! IT DIDN'T HIT HIM?
THEY DIDN'T EXPLODE!!
WHERE DID THE BURST BOMBS GO?
SWIP
THEY'RE STUCK ON HIS SUCKERS!!

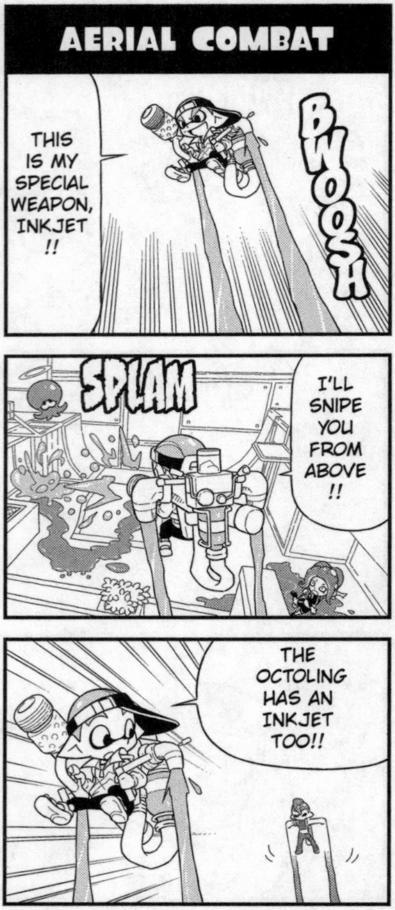
AERIAL COMBAT
BWOOSH
THIS IS MY SPECIAL WEAPON, INKJET!!
I'LL SNIPE YOU FROM ABOVE!!
SPLAM
THE OCTOLING HAS AN INKJET TOO!!
A KITE?

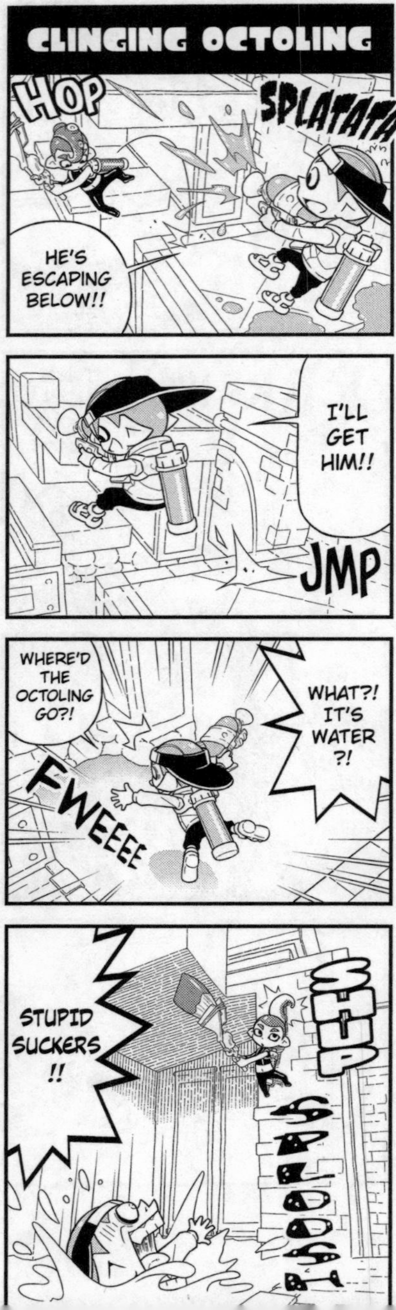
CLINGING OCTOLING
SPLATATA
HOP
HE'S ESCAPING BELOW!!
I'LL GET HIM!!
JMP
WHAT?! IT'S WATER?!
WHERE'D THE OCTOLING GO?!
FWEEEE
SHUP
STUPID SUCKERS!!
SPLOOSH

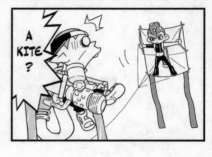

IRON PAN

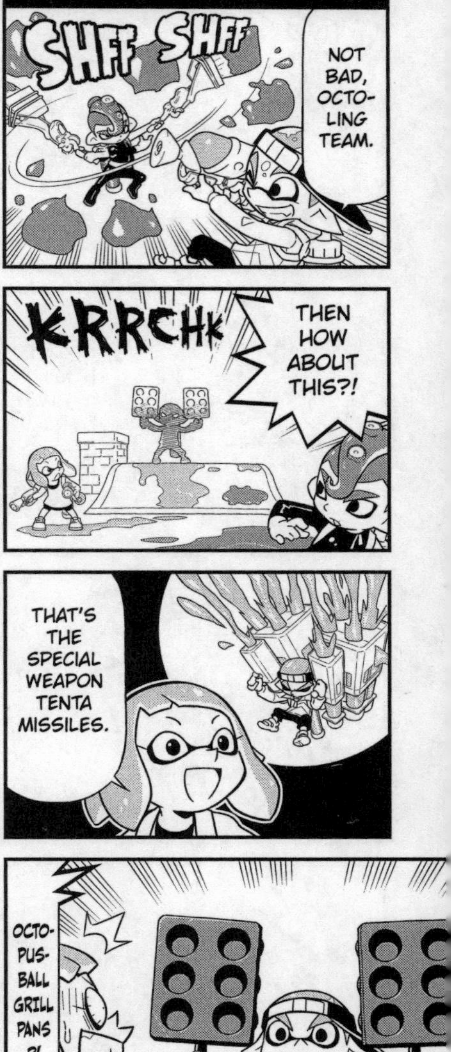

NOT BAD, OCTO-LING TEAM.
SHFF SHFF
THEN HOW ABOUT THIS?!
KRRCHK
THAT'S THE SPECIAL WEAPON TENTA MISSILES.
OCTO-PUS-BALL GRILL PANS ?!

FINISHING TOUCHES

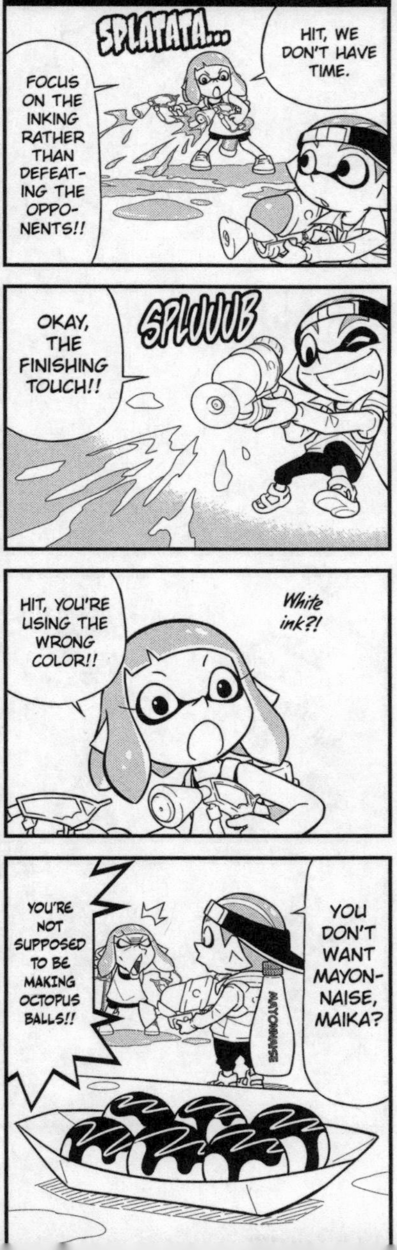

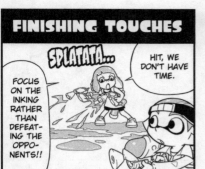

HIT, WE DON'T HAVE TIME.
SPLATATA...
FOCUS ON THE INKING RATHER THAN DEFEAT-ING THE OPPO-NENTS!!
SPLUUUB
OKAY, THE FINISHING TOUCH!!
White ink?!
HIT, YOU'RE USING THE WRONG COLOR!!
YOU DON'T WANT MAYON-NAISE, MAIKA?
MAYONNAISE
YOU'RE NOT SUPPOSED TO BE MAKING OCTOPUS BALLS!!

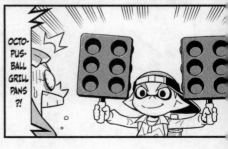

GOOD!!

THEY'RE THROWING BURST BOMBS AT EACH OTHER AT THE END OF THE GAME!!

SHA SHA

EAT THIS !!

HOW ABOUT THIS?!

I GUESS YOU'RE THE REAL DEAL.

GOOD !!

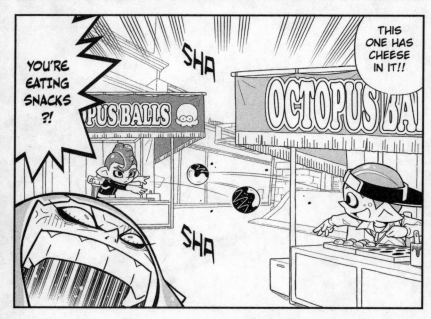

YOU'RE EATING SNACKS ?!

SHA

SHA

THIS ONE HAS CHEESE IN IT!!

PUS BALLS

OCTOPUS BA

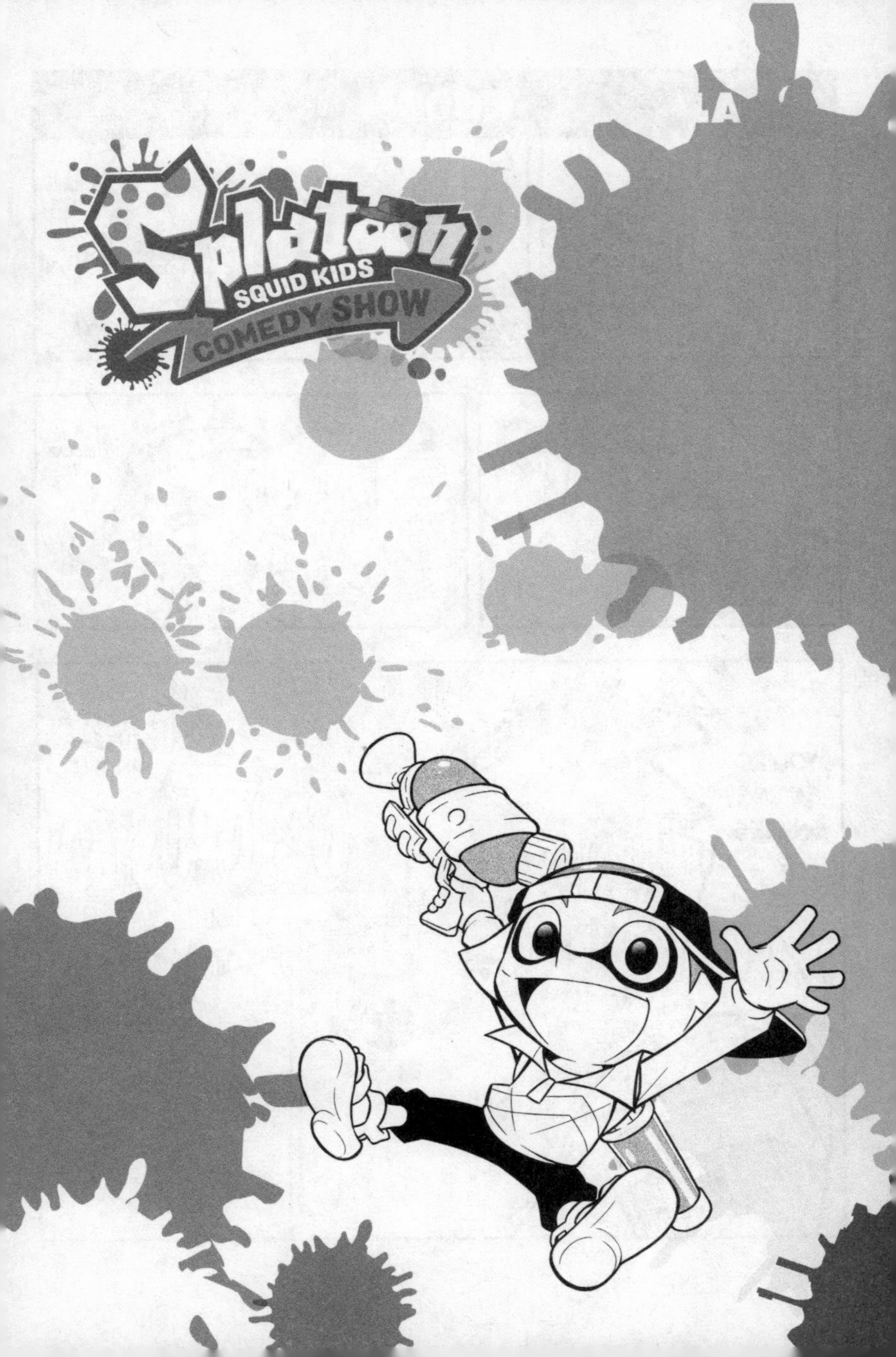
Splatoon
SQUID KIDS
COMEDY SHOW

TIME FOR A DANGEROUS POOL BATTLE!

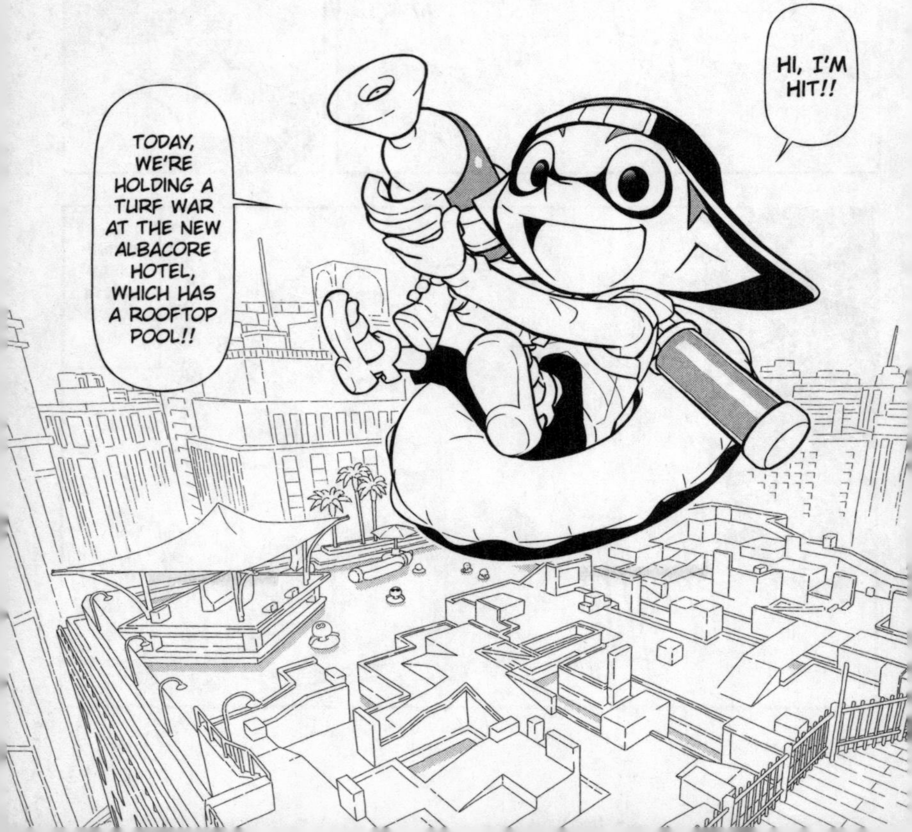
HI, I'M HIT!!
TODAY, WE'RE HOLDING A TURF WAR AT THE NEW ALBACORE HOTEL, WHICH HAS A ROOFTOP POOL!!

POOL ENTRANCE

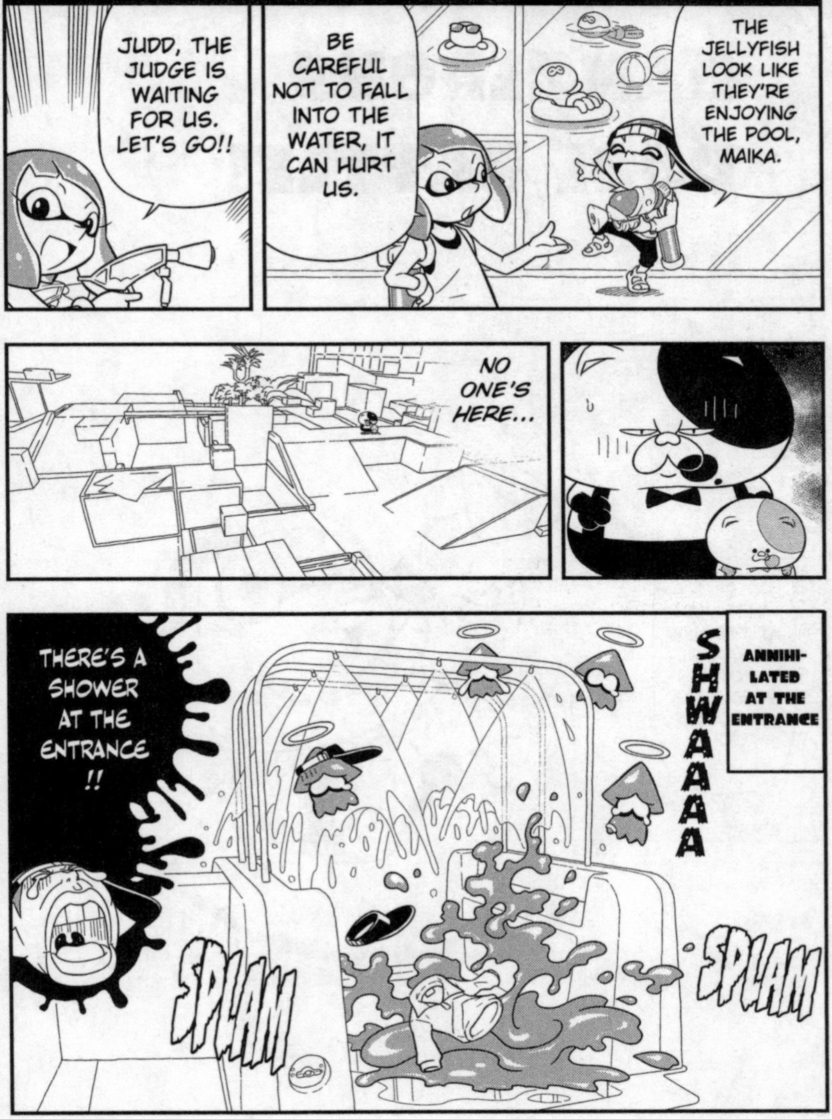

THE JELLYFISH LOOK LIKE THEY'RE ENJOYING THE POOL, MAIKA.
BE CAREFUL NOT TO FALL INTO THE WATER, IT CAN HURT US.
JUDD, THE JUDGE IS WAITING FOR US. LET'S GO!!
NO ONE'S HERE...
ANNIHILATED AT THE ENTRANCE
SHWAAAAA
SPLAM
THERE'S A SHOWER AT THE ENTRANCE !!
SPLAM

NEW ALBACORE HOTEL

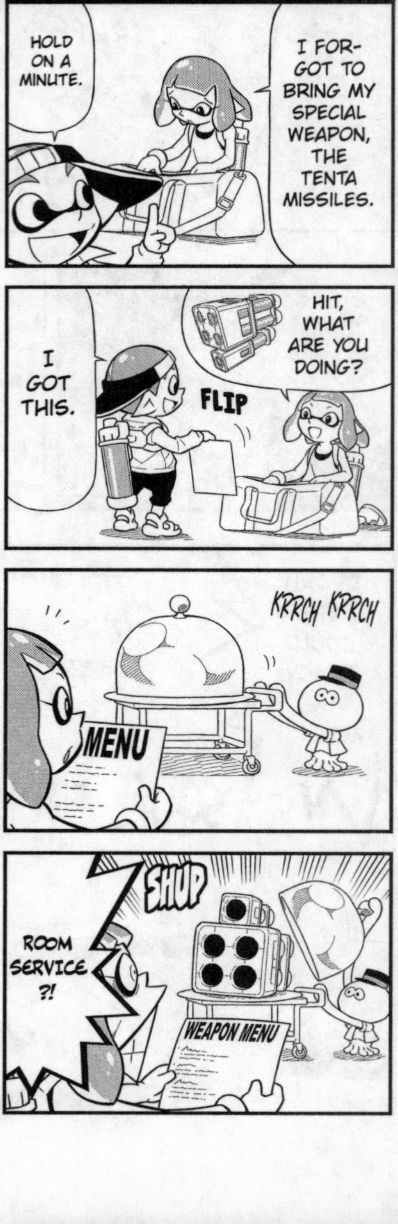
I FORGOT TO BRING MY SPECIAL WEAPON, THE TENTA MISSILES.
HOLD ON A MINUTE.
HIT, WHAT ARE YOU DOING?
FLIP
I GOT THIS.
KRRCH KRRCH
MENU
SHUP
ROOM SERVICE?!
WEAPON MENU

SNORKEL MASK

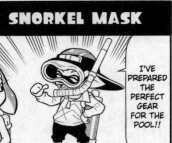

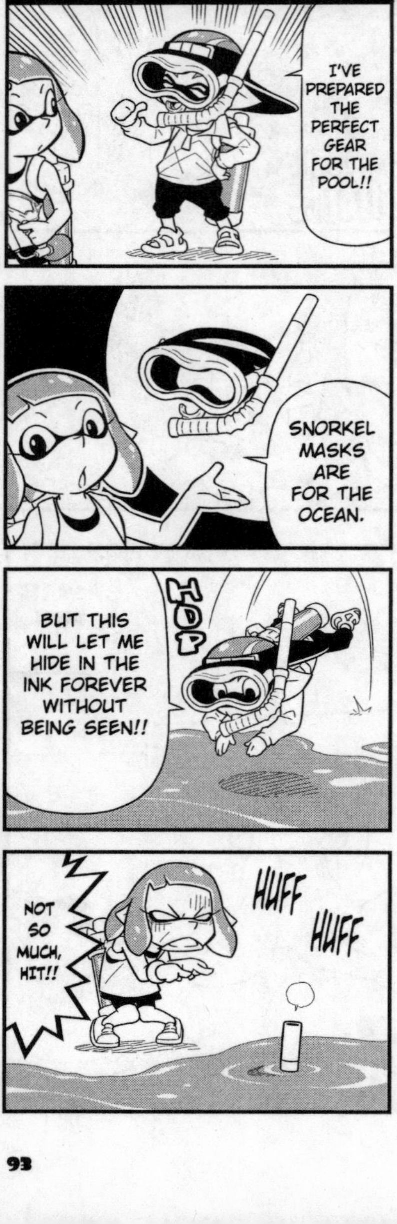
I'VE PREPARED THE PERFECT GEAR FOR THE POOL!!
SNORKEL MASKS ARE FOR THE OCEAN.
HOP
BUT THIS WILL LET ME HIDE IN THE INK FOREVER WITHOUT BEING SEEN!!
HUFF
HUFF
NOT SO MUCH, HIT!!

POPULAR POOL

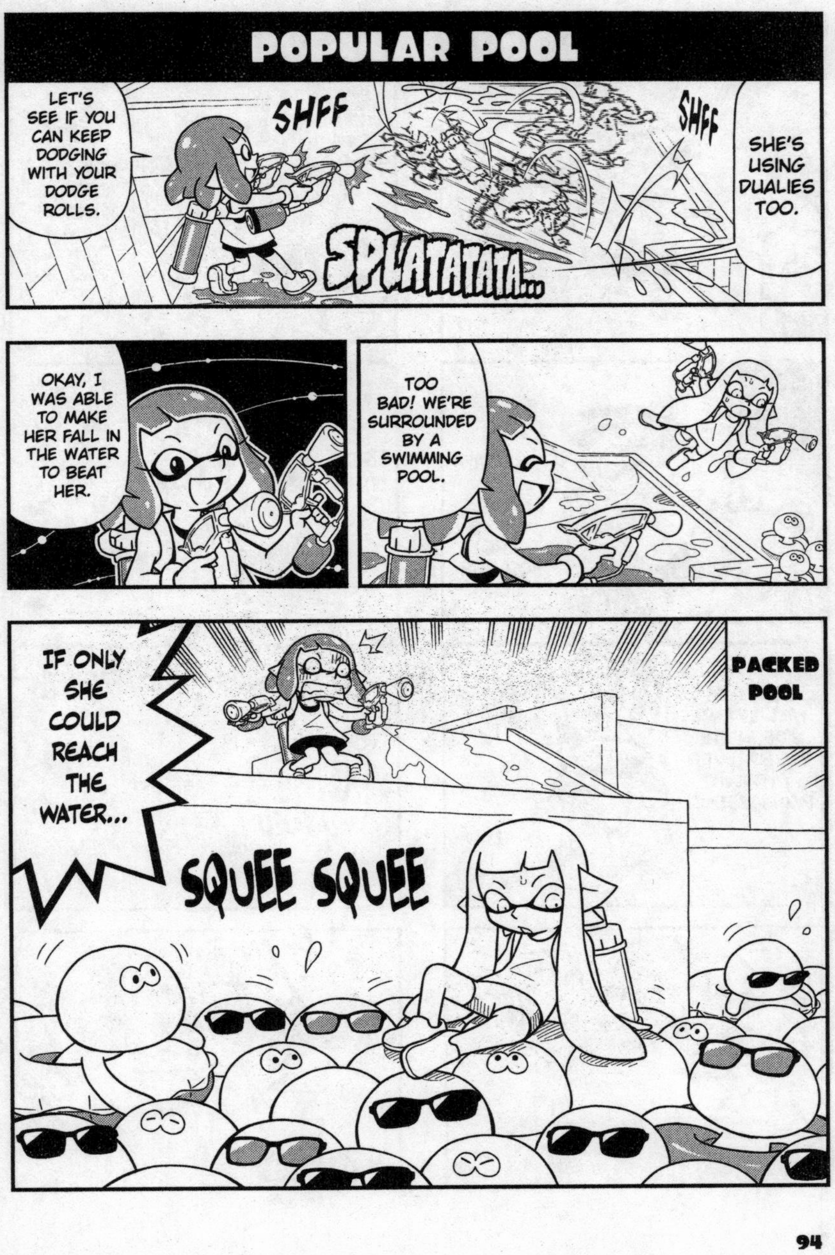

SHE'S USING DUALIES TOO.
SHFF
SHFF
LET'S SEE IF YOU CAN KEEP DODGING WITH YOUR DODGE ROLLS.
SPLATATATA...
TOO BAD! WE'RE SURROUNDED BY A SWIMMING POOL.
OKAY, I WAS ABLE TO MAKE HER FALL IN THE WATER TO BEAT HER.
PACKED POOL
IF ONLY SHE COULD REACH THE WATER...
SQUEE SQUEE

FALLING INTO THE POOL

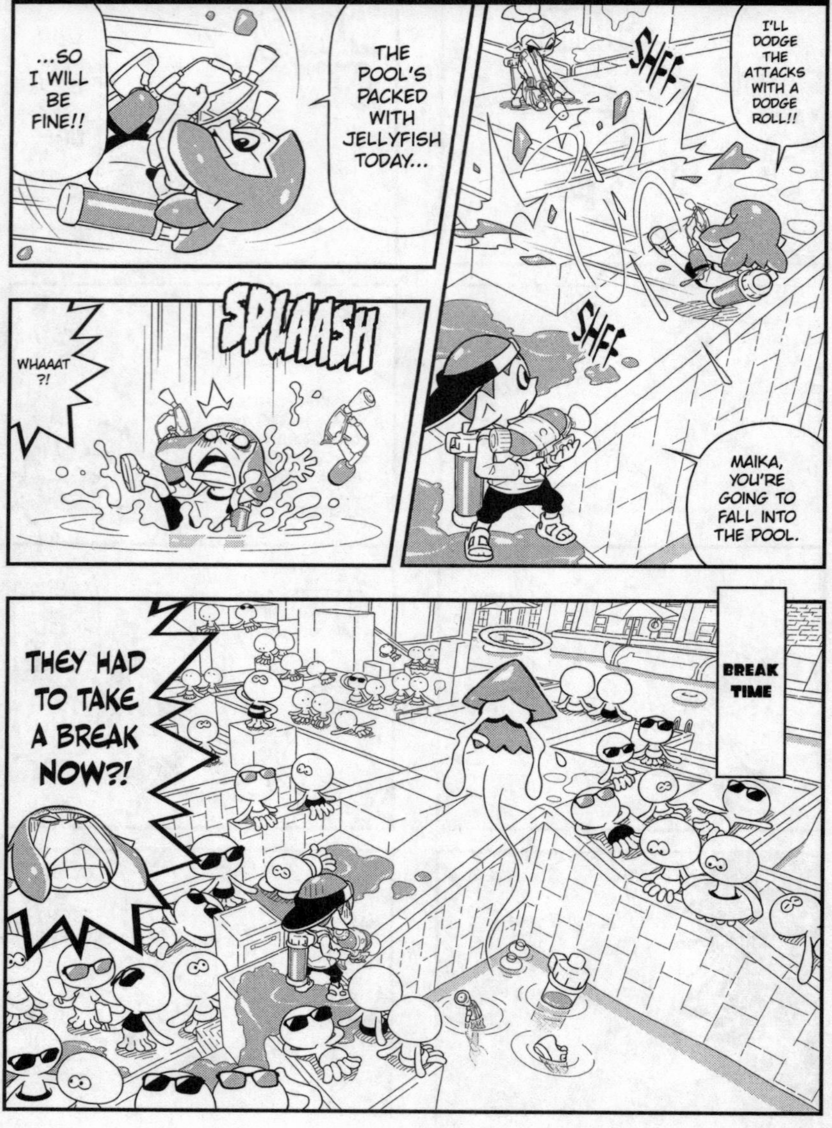
I'LL DODGE THE ATTACKS WITH A DODGE ROLL!!
SHFF
SHFF
MAIKA, YOU'RE GOING TO FALL INTO THE POOL.
THE POOL'S PACKED WITH JELLYFISH TODAY...
...SO I WILL BE FINE!!
SPLAASH
WHAAAT?!
BREAK TIME
THEY HAD TO TAKE A BREAK NOW?!

ROOM SERVICE

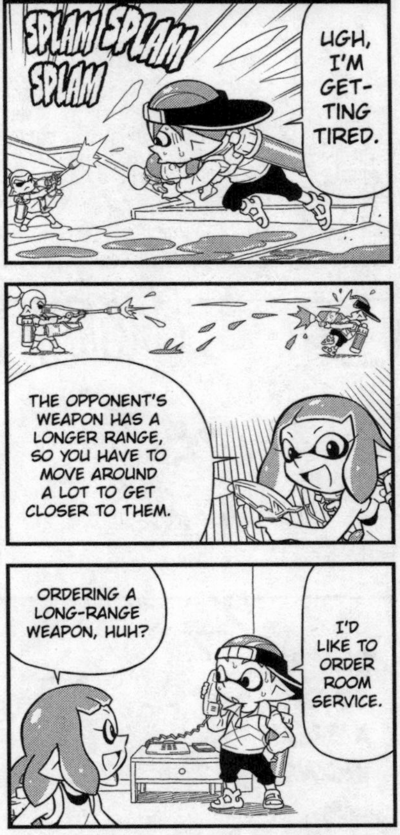
UGH, I'M GET-TING TIRED.
SPLAM SPLAM SPLAM
THE OPPONENT'S WEAPON HAS A LONGER RANGE, SO YOU HAVE TO MOVE AROUND A LOT TO GET CLOSER TO THEM.
I'D LIKE TO ORDER ROOM SERVICE.
ORDERING A LONG-RANGE WEAPON, HUH?
OOOH. ♥ RIGHT THERE.
SHUP
SHUP
A MASSAGE ?!

FALLER BALLER

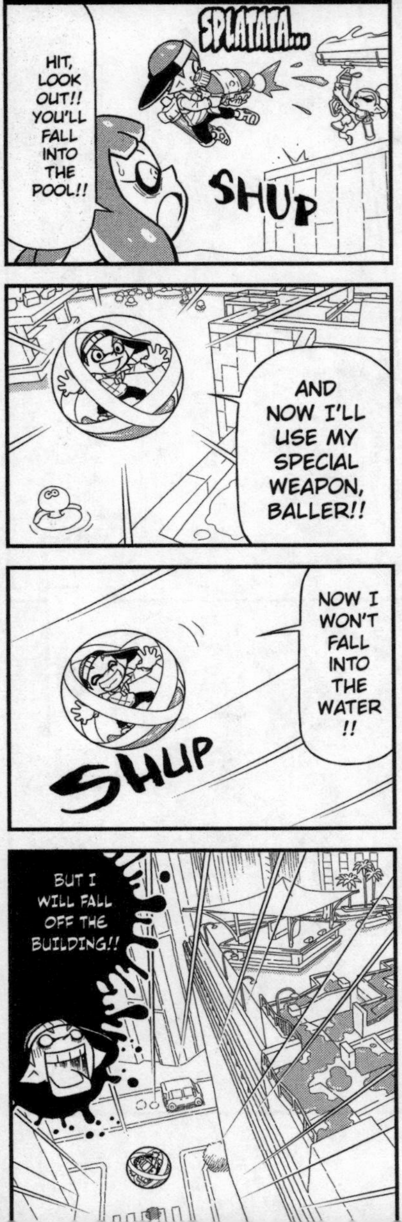
SPLATATA...
HIT, LOOK OUT!! YOU'LL FALL INTO THE POOL!!
SHUP
AND NOW I'LL USE MY SPECIAL WEAPON, BALLER!!
NOW I WON'T FALL INTO THE WATER!!
SHUP
BUT I WILL FALL OFF THE BUILDING!!

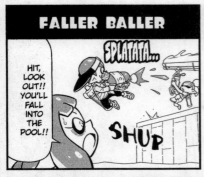

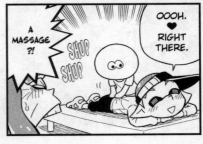

WET BODY

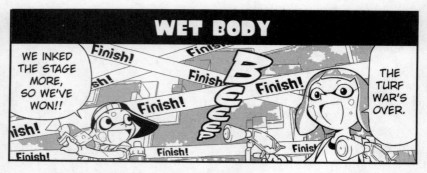

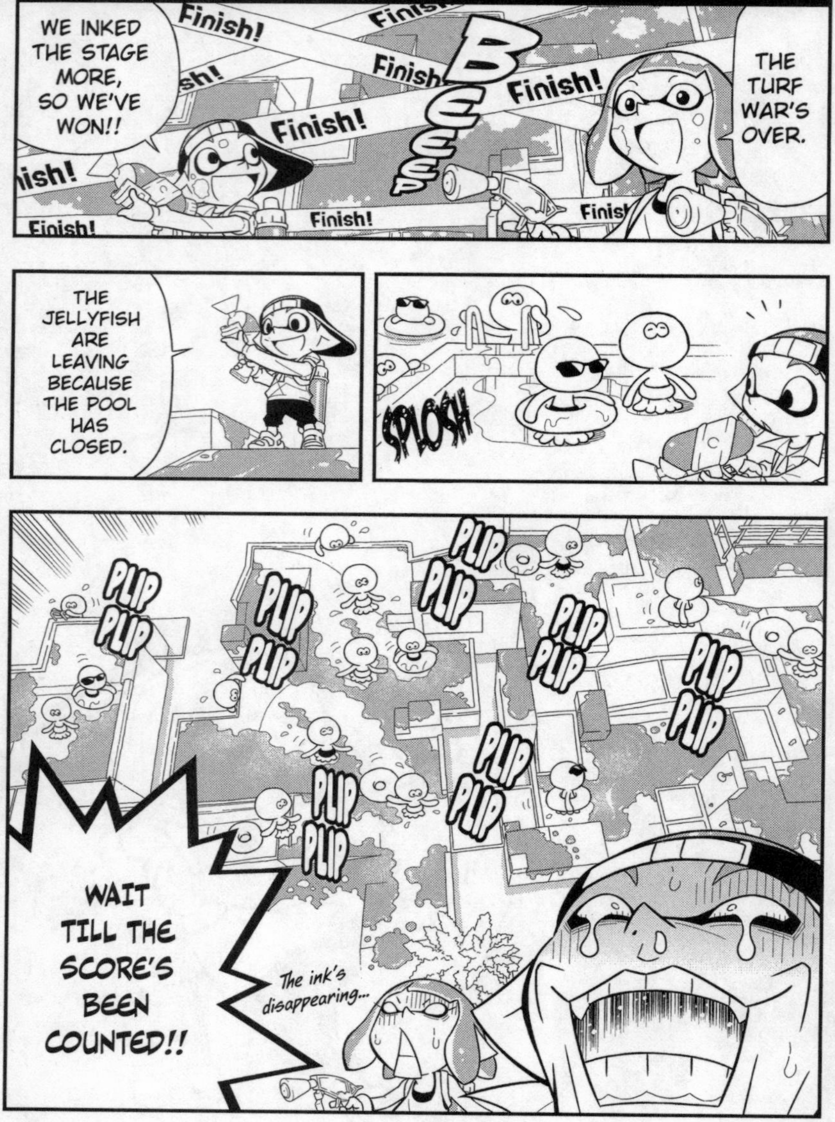
THE TURF WAR'S OVER.
Finish!
BEEEP
Finish!
Finish!
WE INKED THE STAGE MORE, SO WE'VE WON!!
SPLOSH
THE JELLYFISH ARE LEAVING BECAUSE THE POOL HAS CLOSED.
PLIP PLIP
The ink's disappearing...
WAIT TILL THE SCORE'S BEEN COUNTED!!

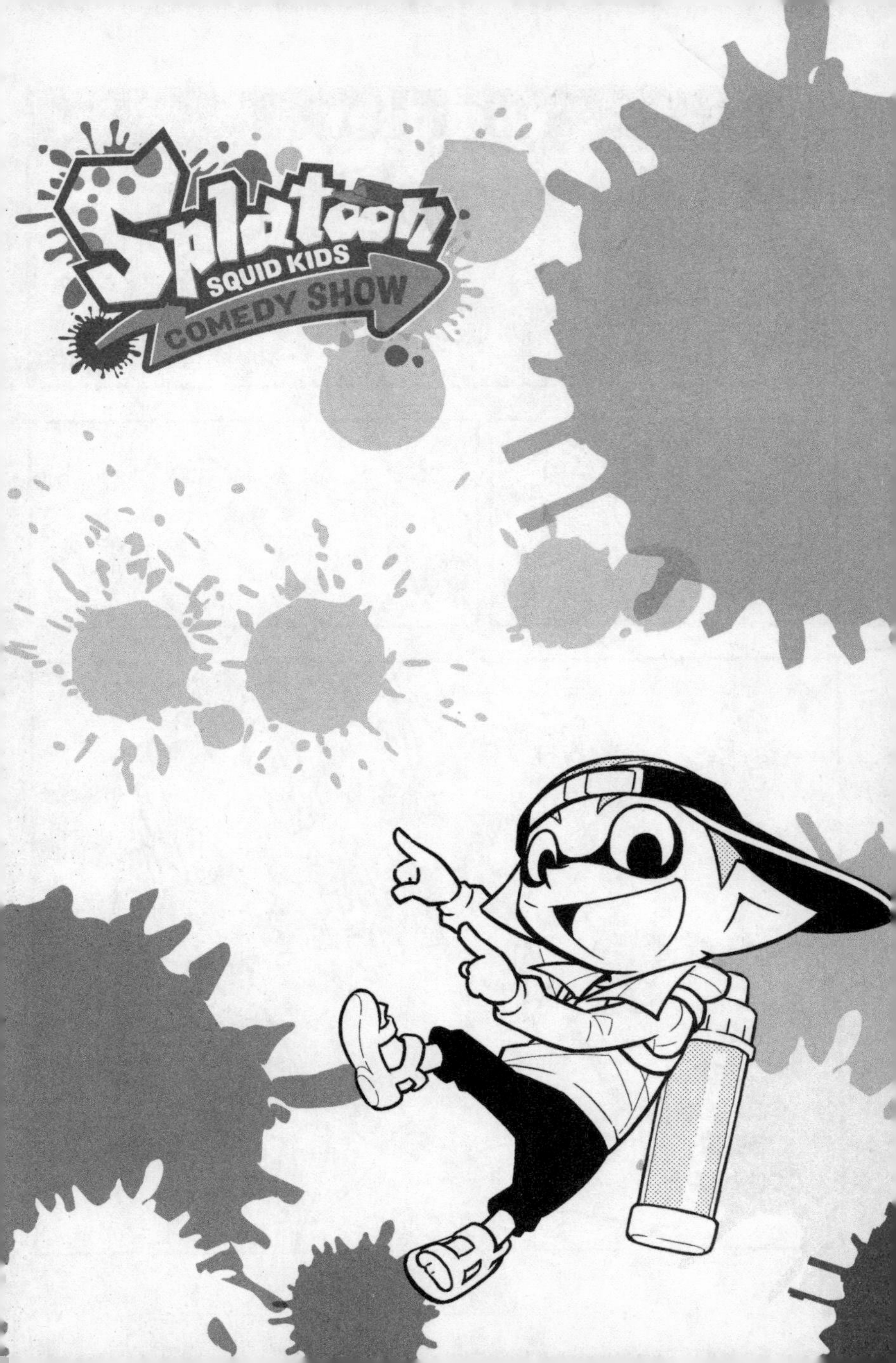
Splatoon
SQUID KIDS
COMEDY SHOW

TIME TO FIGHT WITH A BATHTUB!

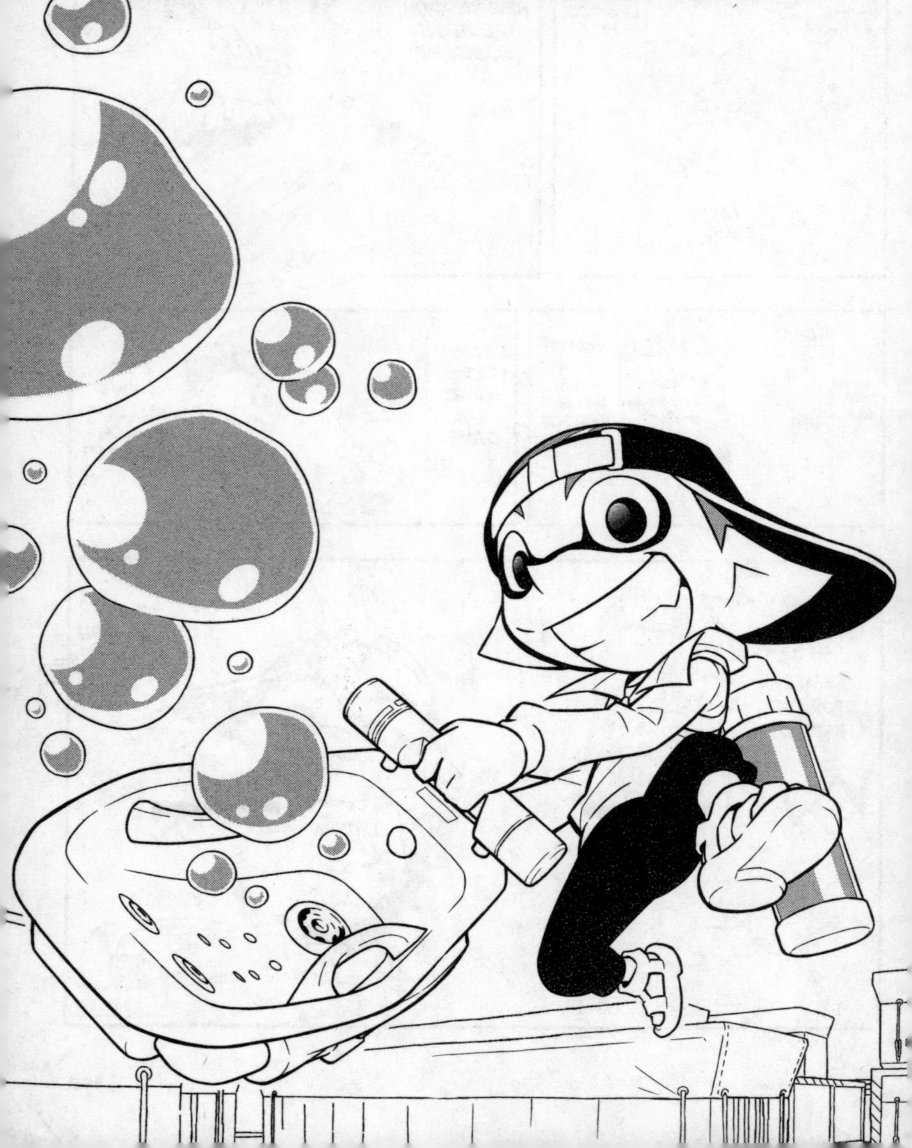

BLOBLOBBER

HI, I'M HIT!!
TODAY, I'M GOING TO BE USING THE NEW WEAPON, THE BLOB-LOBBER!!
YOU BOUGHT ONE TOO, HIT?
I DID! WE'VE ALL GOT A BLOB-LOBBER!!
READY? LET'S START THE GAME.
RUSTL RUSTL
WHAT?! IT'S NOT HERE!! MAYBE I FORGOT IT?
YOUR SUB WEAPON?
MY SHAMPOO!!
SHAMPOO
YOU'RE SUPPOSED TO BE PREPARING FOR THE BATTLE!!

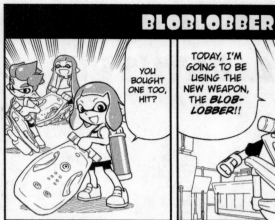

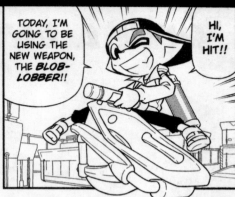

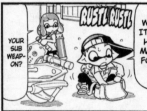

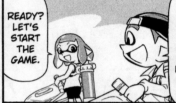

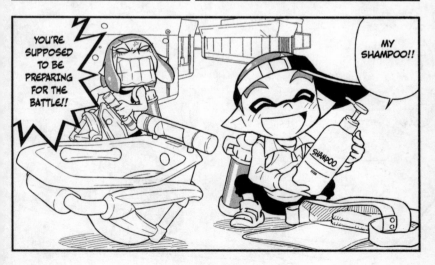

READY MELODY

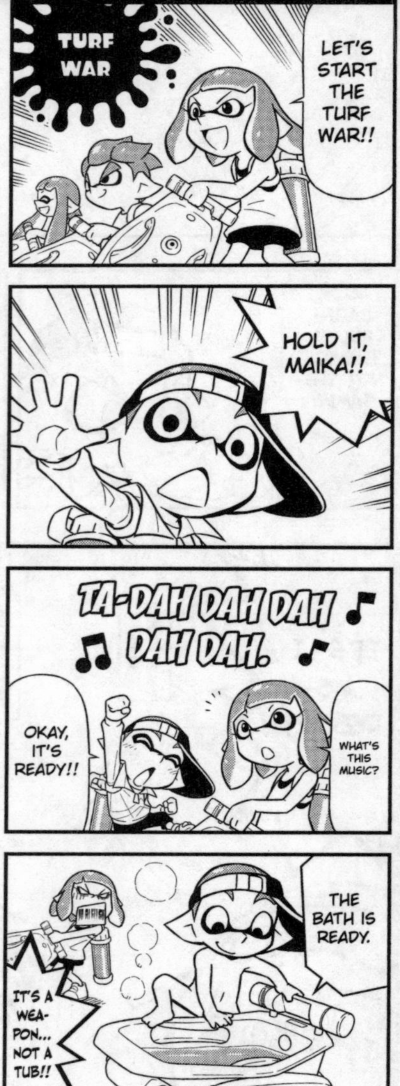
LET'S START THE TURF WAR!!
TURF WAR
HOLD IT, MAIKA!!
TA-DAH DAH DAH DAH DAH.
WHAT'S THIS MUSIC?
OKAY, IT'S READY!!
THE BATH IS READY.
IT'S A WEA-PON... NOT A TUB!!

INK LEAK

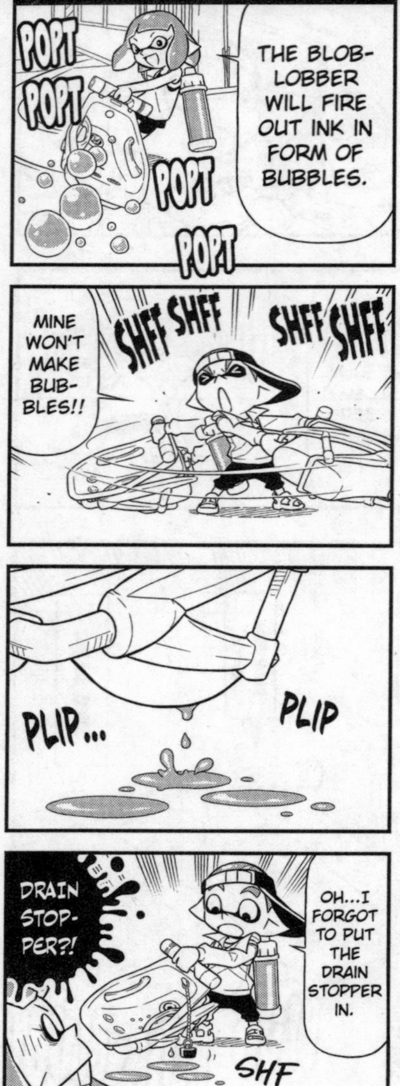
THE BLOB-LOBBER WILL FIRE OUT INK IN FORM OF BUBBLES.
POPT
POPT
POPT
POPT
SHFF SHFF
SHFF SHFF
MINE WON'T MAKE BUB-BLES!!
PLIP
PLIP...
OH...I FORGOT TO PUT THE DRAIN STOPPER IN.
DRAIN STOP-PER?!
SHF

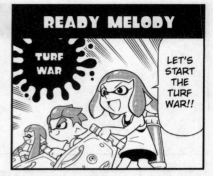

BLOBLOBBER VARIATIONS

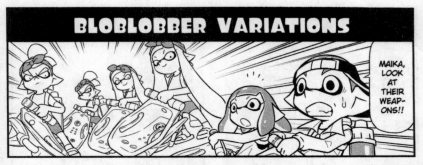

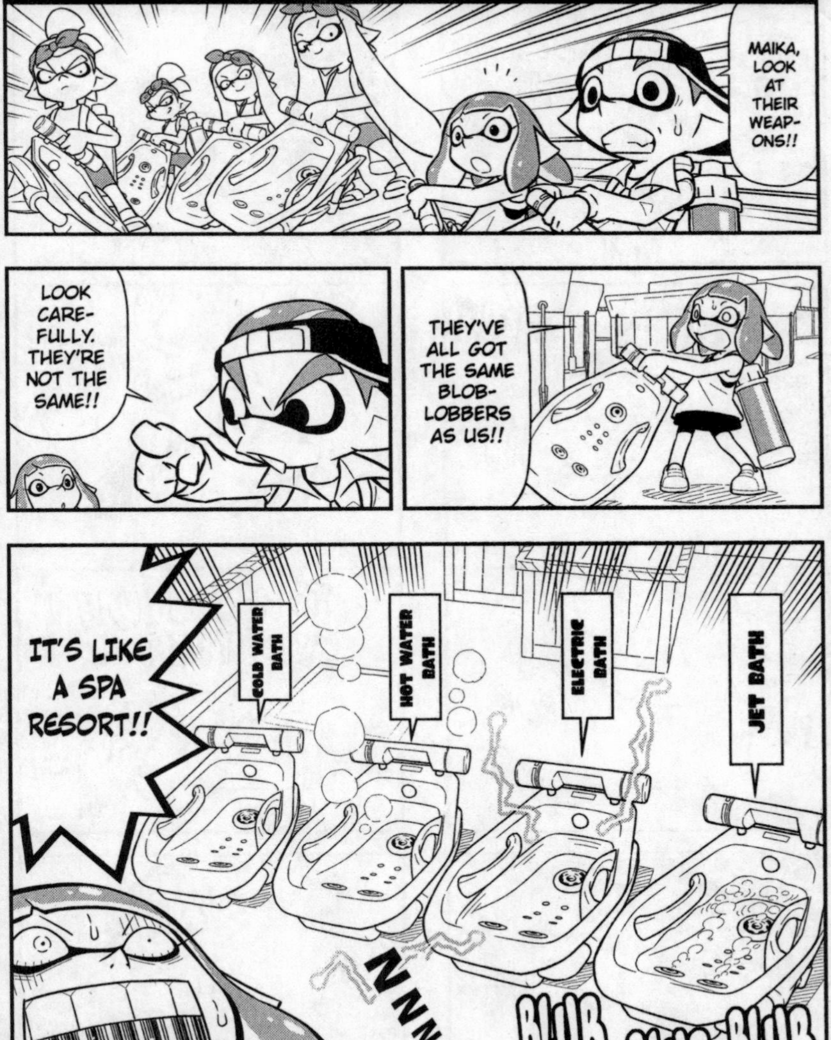
MAIKA, LOOK AT THEIR WEAP-ONS!!
THEY'VE ALL GOT THE SAME BLOB-LOBBERS AS US!!
LOOK CARE-FULLY. THEY'RE NOT THE SAME!!
JET BATH
ELECTRIC BATH
HOT WATER BATH
COLD WATER BATH
IT'S LIKE A SPA RESORT!!
BLUB BLUB BLUB
NNNNT...

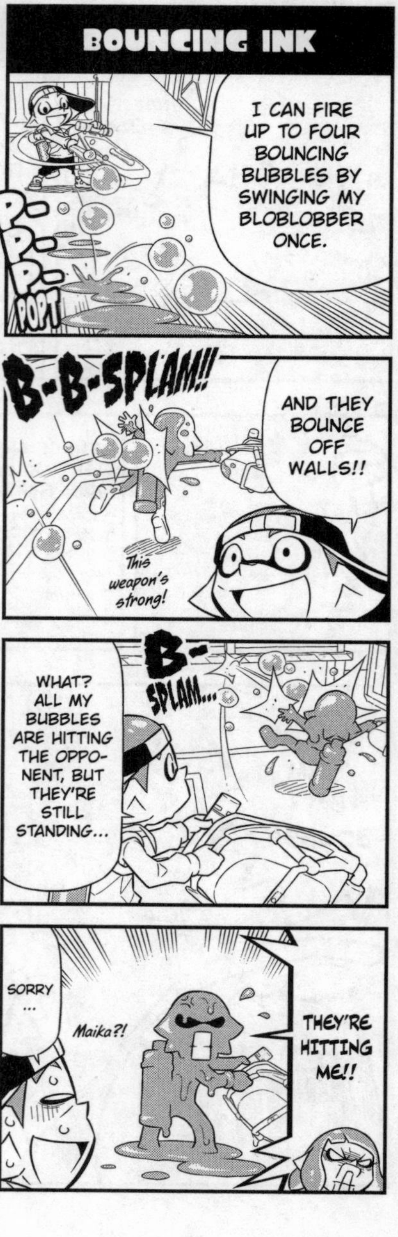
BOUNCING INK
I CAN FIRE UP TO FOUR BOUNCING BUBBLES BY SWINGING MY BLOBLOBBER ONCE.
P-P-P-POPT
AND THEY BOUNCE OFF WALLS!!
B-B-SPLAM!!
This weapon's strong!
WHAT? ALL MY BUBBLES ARE HITTING THE OPPO-NENT, BUT THEY'RE STILL STANDING...
B-SPLAM...
THEY'RE HITTING ME!!
Maika?!
SORRY ...

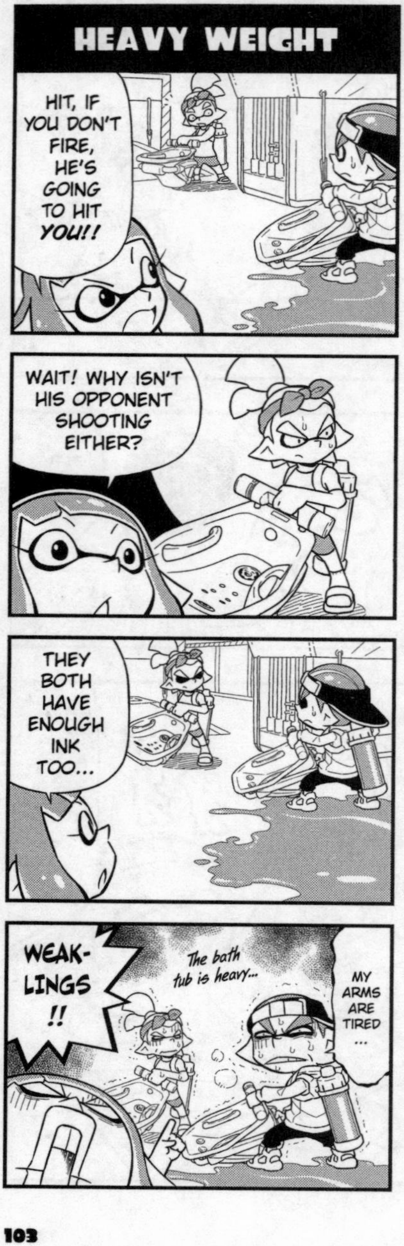
HEAVY WEIGHT
HIT, IF YOU DON'T FIRE, HE'S GOING TO HIT *YOU!!*
WAIT! WHY ISN'T HIS OPPONENT SHOOTING EITHER?
THEY BOTH HAVE ENOUGH INK TOO...
MY ARMS ARE TIRED ...
The bath tub is heavy...
WEAK-LINGS !!

WHEN YOU'RE TIRED

THIS WEAPON IS HEAVY...
PANT
PANT
WHAT? EVERY-ONE'S TIRED?!
USE THIS, EVERYONE !!
SHA
BURST BOMBS!!
THOSE ARE LIGHT, SO YOU CAN THROW THEM EVEN IF YOU'RE TIRED.
SHWAAA...
OOOOOH... THIS IS SO RELAXING. ♪
SHWAA
SHWAA
SHWAA
SHWAA...
SHWAA
SHWAA
YOU GAVE THEM BATH BOMBS!!
SHWAA

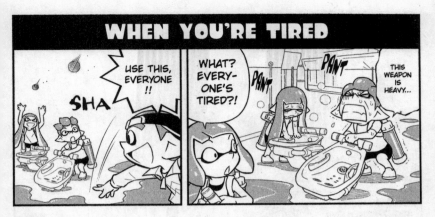

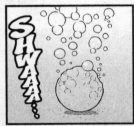

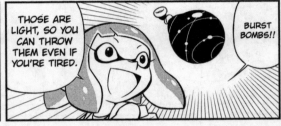

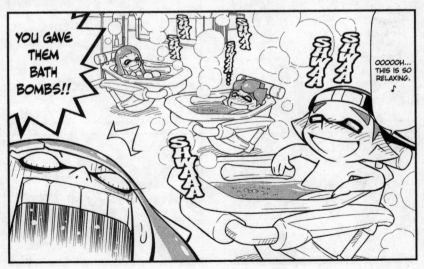

BATH TOGETHER

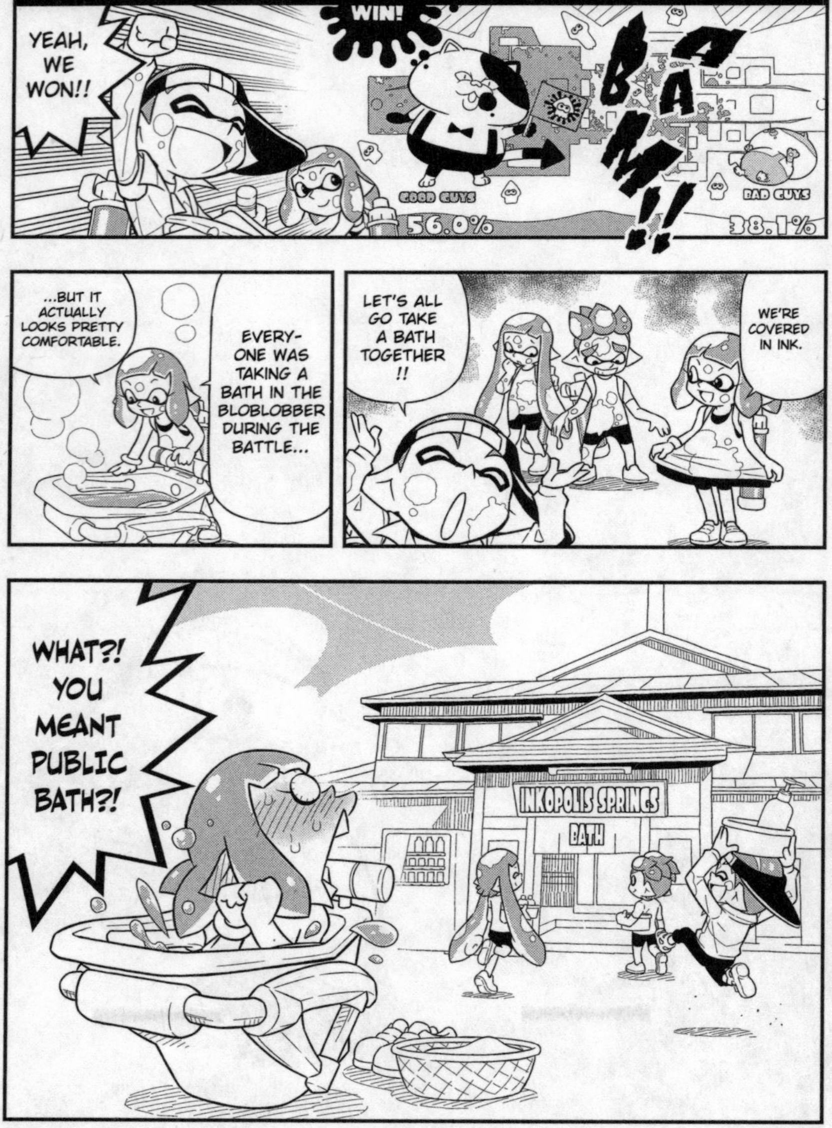
BAAM!!
WIN!
YEAH, WE WON!!
BAD GUYS
38.1%
GOOD GUYS
56.0%
WE'RE COVERED IN INK.
LET'S ALL GO TAKE A BATH TOGETHER !!
EVERY-ONE WAS TAKING A BATH IN THE BLOBLOBBER DURING THE BATTLE...
...BUT IT ACTUALLY LOOKS PRETTY COMFORTABLE.
INKOPOLIS SPRINGS
BATH
WHAT?! YOU MEANT PUBLIC BATH?!

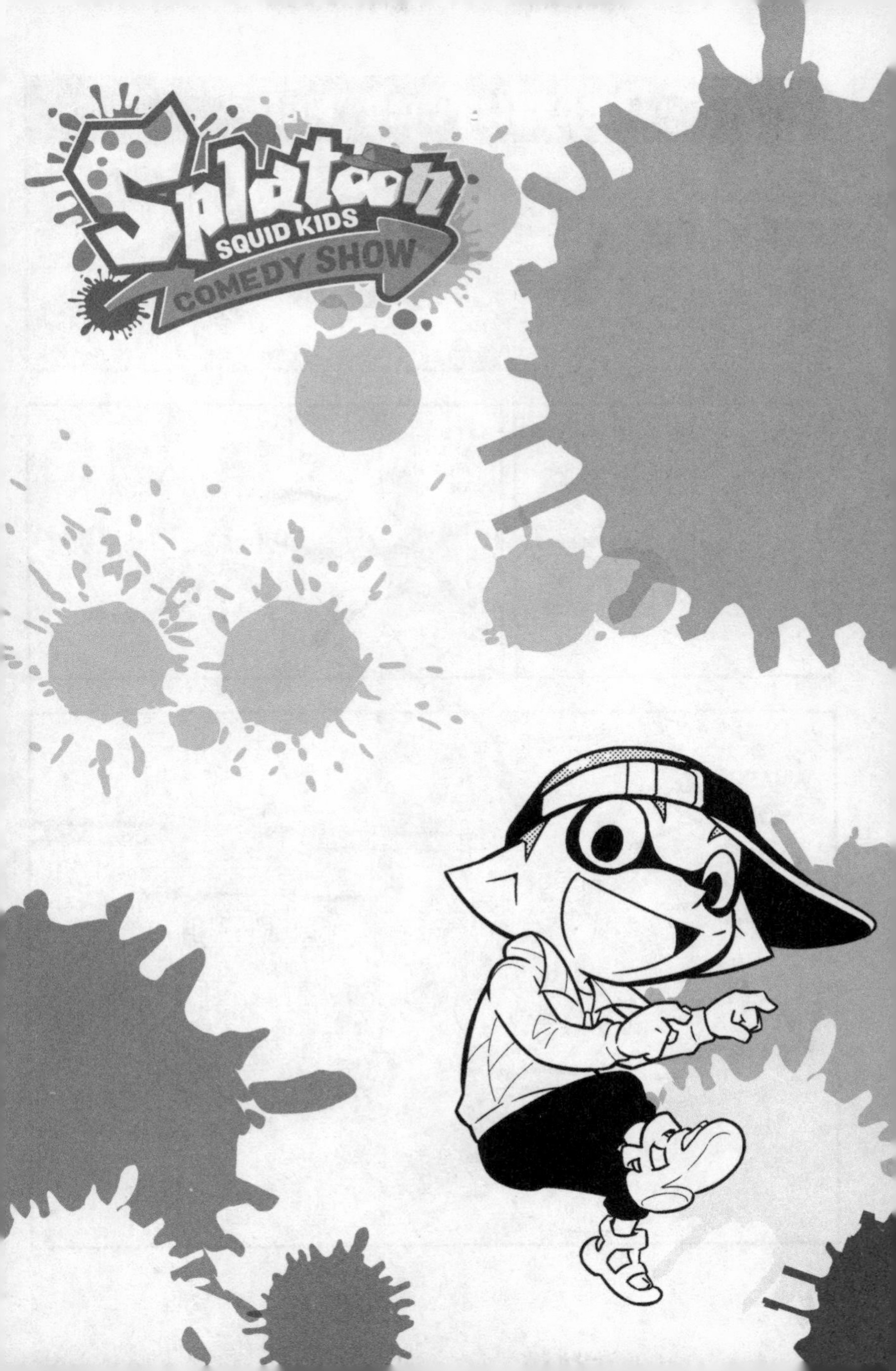
Splatoon
SQUID KIDS
COMEDY SHOW

TIME TO PROTECT THE ZONES!

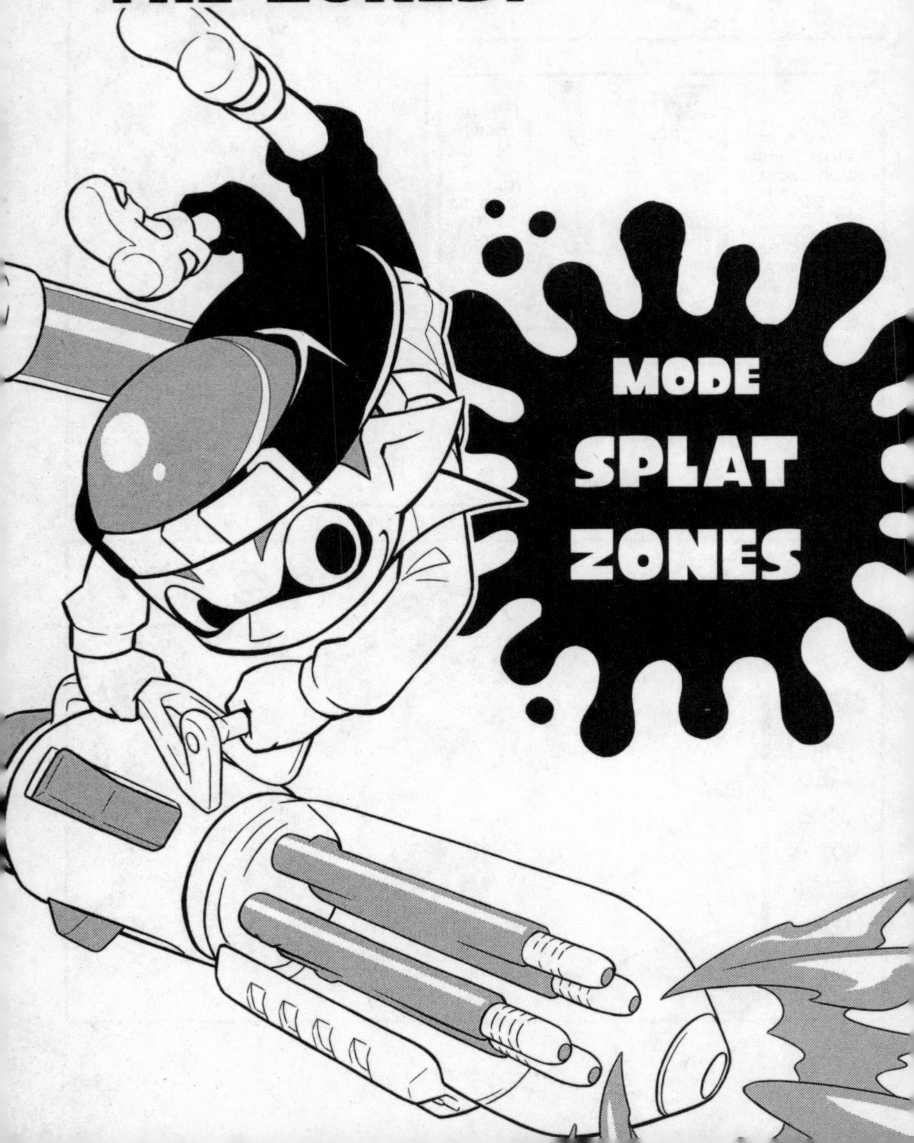
MODE
SPLAT
ZONES

CAPTURING AN AREAZONE

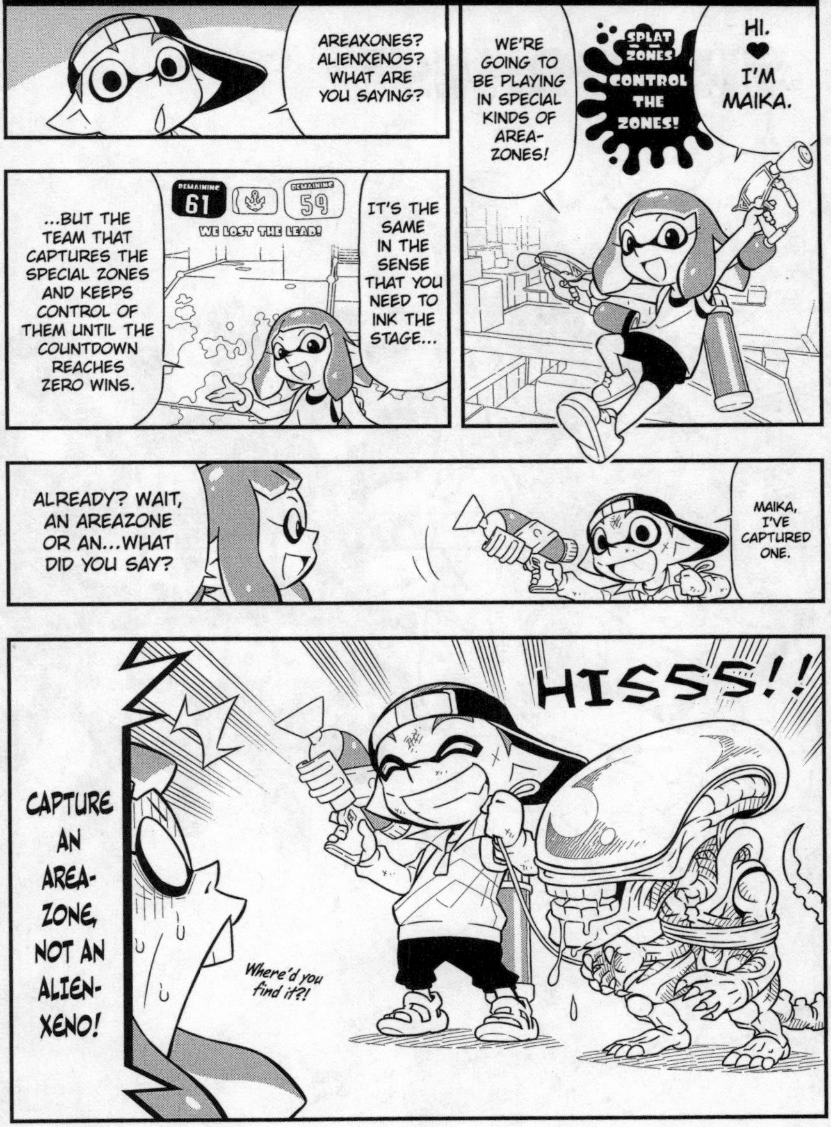
HI. ♥ I'M MAIKA.
SPLAT ZONES
CONTROL THE ZONES!
WE'RE GOING TO BE PLAYING IN SPECIAL KINDS OF AREA-ZONES!
AREAXONES? ALIENXENOS? WHAT ARE YOU SAYING?
REMAINING 61
REMAINING 59
WE LOST THE LEAD!
IT'S THE SAME IN THE SENSE THAT YOU NEED TO INK THE STAGE...
...BUT THE TEAM THAT CAPTURES THE SPECIAL ZONES AND KEEPS CONTROL OF THEM UNTIL THE COUNTDOWN REACHES ZERO WINS.
MAIKA, I'VE CAPTURED ONE.
ALREADY? WAIT, AN AREAZONE OR AN...WHAT DID YOU SAY?
HISSS!!
Where'd you find it?!
CAPTURE AN AREA-ZONE, NOT AN ALIEN-XENO!

BALLPOINT SPLATLING

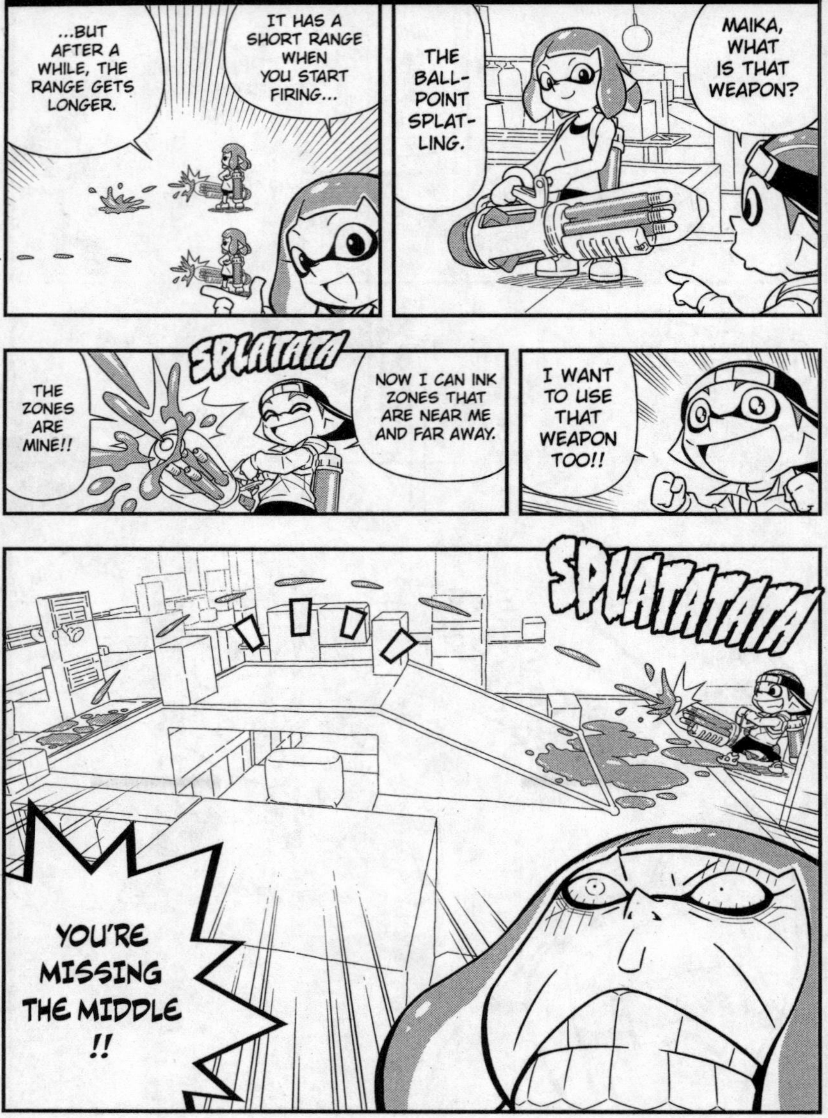
MAIKA, WHAT IS THAT WEAPON?
THE BALLPOINT SPLATLING.
IT HAS A SHORT RANGE WHEN YOU START FIRING...
...BUT AFTER A WHILE, THE RANGE GETS LONGER.
I WANT TO USE THAT WEAPON TOO!!
NOW I CAN INK ZONES THAT ARE NEAR ME AND FAR AWAY.
SPLATATA
THE ZONES ARE MINE!!
SPLATATATATA
YOU'RE MISSING THE MIDDLE!!

SLOW INKING

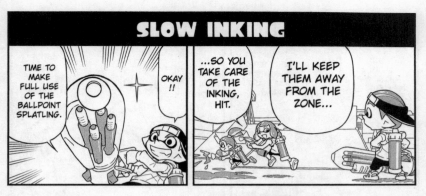

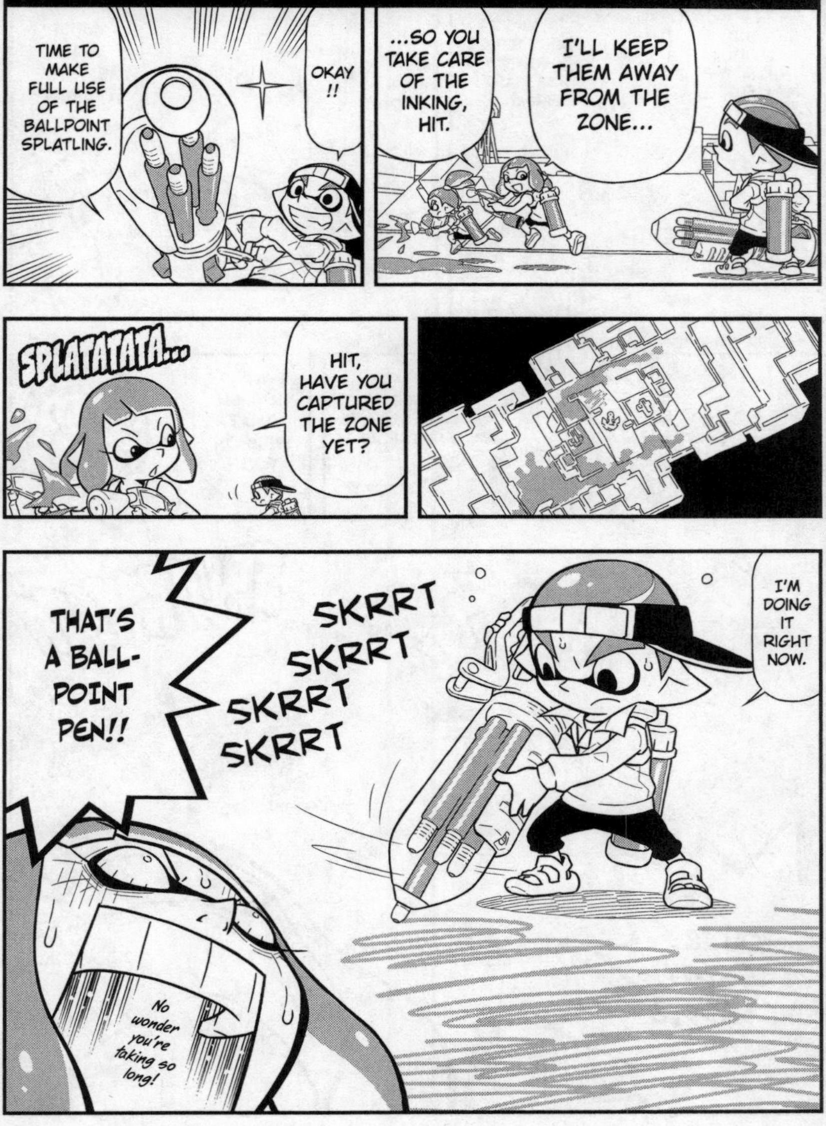
I'LL KEEP THEM AWAY FROM THE ZONE...
...SO YOU TAKE CARE OF THE INKING, HIT.
OKAY!!
TIME TO MAKE FULL USE OF THE BALLPOINT SPLATLING.
HIT, HAVE YOU CAPTURED THE ZONE YET?
SPLATATATA...
I'M DOING IT RIGHT NOW.
SKRRT SKRRT SKRRT SKRRT
THAT'S A BALL-POINT PEN!!
No wonder you're taking so long!

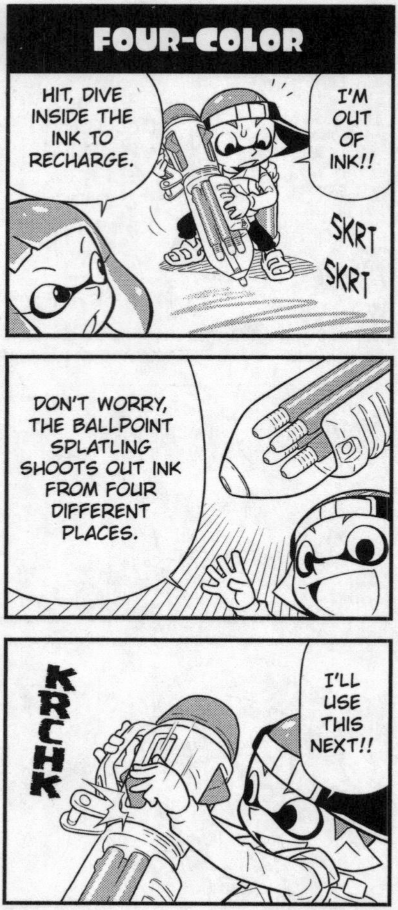
FOUR-COLOR
I'M OUT OF INK!!
HIT, DIVE INSIDE THE INK TO RECHARGE.
SKRT SKRT
DON'T WORRY, THE BALLPOINT SPLATLING SHOOTS OUT INK FROM FOUR DIFFERENT PLACES.
I'LL USE THIS NEXT!!
KRCHK
SKRT
SKRT
WRONG COLOR!!
A four-color ballpoint pen!

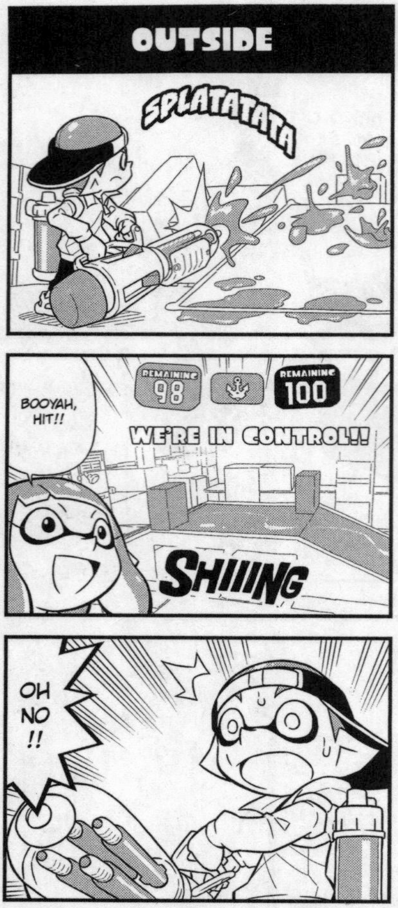
OUTSIDE
SPLATATATA
REMAINING
100
REMAINING
98
BOOYAH, HIT!!
WE'RE IN CONTROL!!
SHIIING
OH NO!!
I INKED OUT-SIDE THE ZONE.
WHITE OUT
PLIP
PLIP
YOU DON'T NEED TO ERASE IT!!

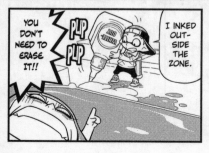

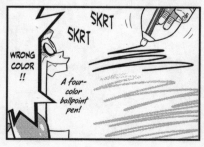

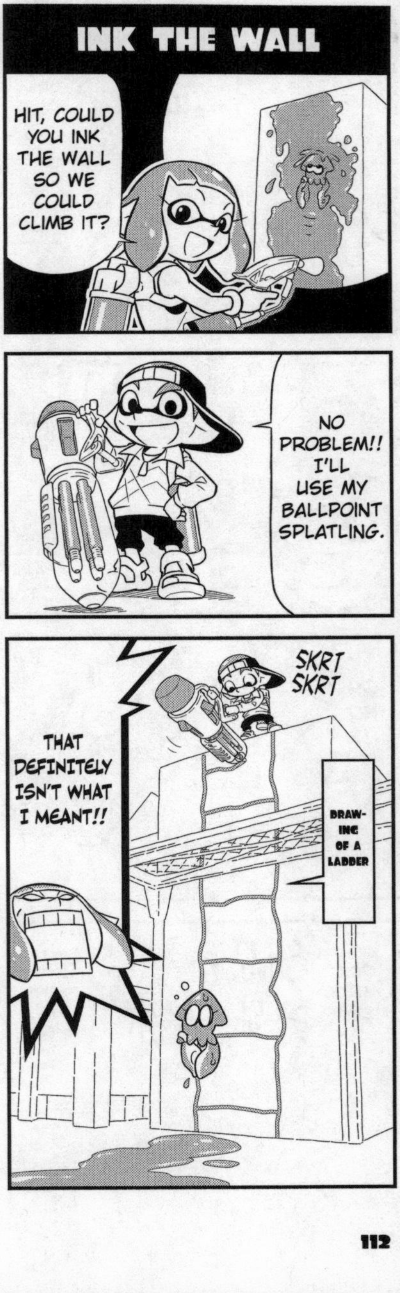
INK THE WALL
HIT, COULD YOU INK THE WALL SO WE COULD CLIMB IT?
NO PROBLEM!! I'LL USE MY BALLPOINT SPLATLING.
SKRT SKRT
DRAW-ING OF A LADDER
THAT DEFINITELY ISN'T WHAT I MEANT!!

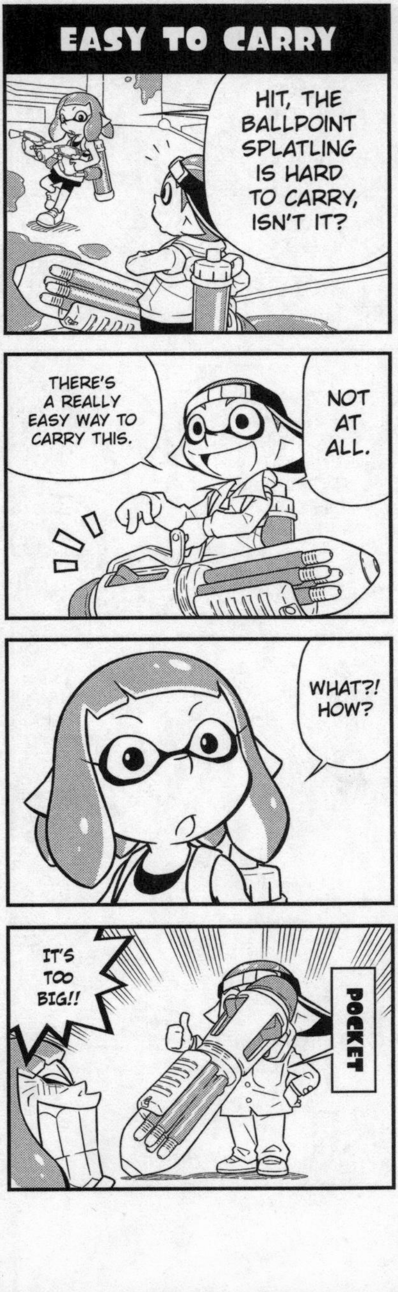
EASY TO CARRY
HIT, THE BALLPOINT SPLATLING IS HARD TO CARRY, ISN'T IT?
NOT AT ALL.
THERE'S A REALLY EASY WAY TO CARRY THIS.
WHAT?! HOW?
POCKET
IT'S TOO BIG!!

STOP

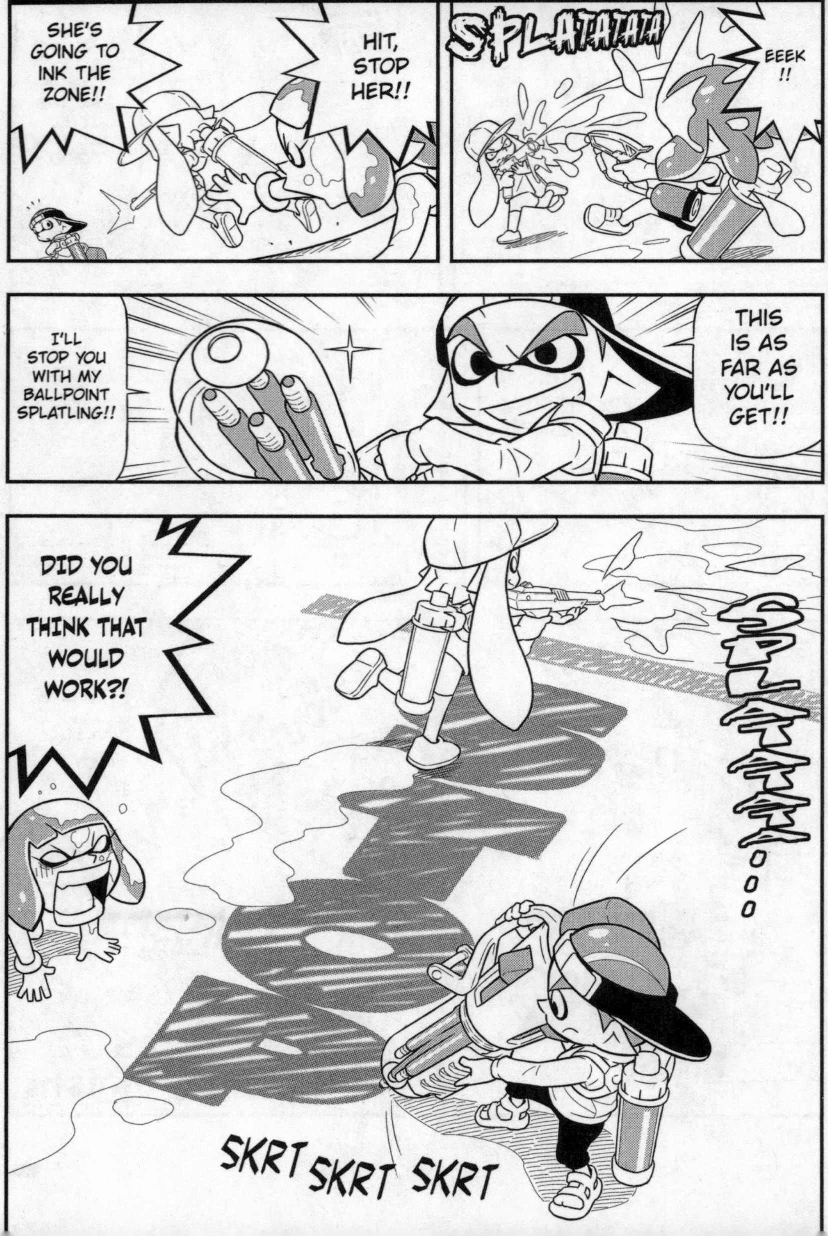
SPLATATATA
EEEK !!
HIT, STOP HER!!
SHE'S GOING TO INK THE ZONE!!
THIS IS AS FAR AS YOU'LL GET!!
I'LL STOP YOU WITH MY BALLPOINT SPLATLING!!
SPLATATATAooo
DID YOU REALLY THINK THAT WOULD WORK?!
SKRT SKRT SKRT

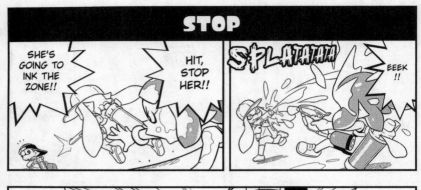

KICKING OUT OF THE ZONE

WE HAVEN'T BEEN ABLE TO RECAPTURE THE ZONE SINCE THEY TOOK IT.
REMAINING 9
REMAINING 25
WE LOST CONTROL!
THE COUNTDOWN HAS BEGUN!!
DASH
REMAINING 8
LEAVE IT TO ME!!
7
REMAINING 6
REMAINING 5
REMAINING 4
WOW, HIT! THE OPPOSING TEAM HAS ALL BACKED AWAY!!
HURRY! INK THE ZONE!!
REMAINING 3
SPLATATATA
HOW DID YOU KICK THEM OUT OF THE ZONE?
REMAINING 2
YOU FARTED?!
REMAINING 1
Finish!
Finish!
Finish!
Finish!
Finish!
Finish!
Finish!
Finish!
Finish!
BEEEEP

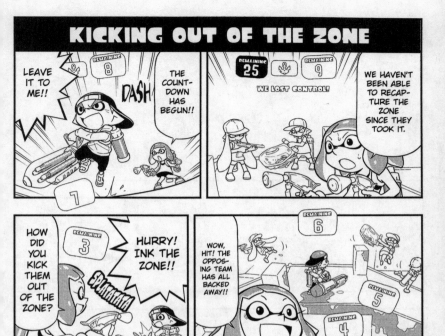

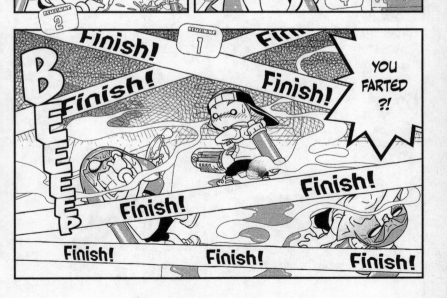

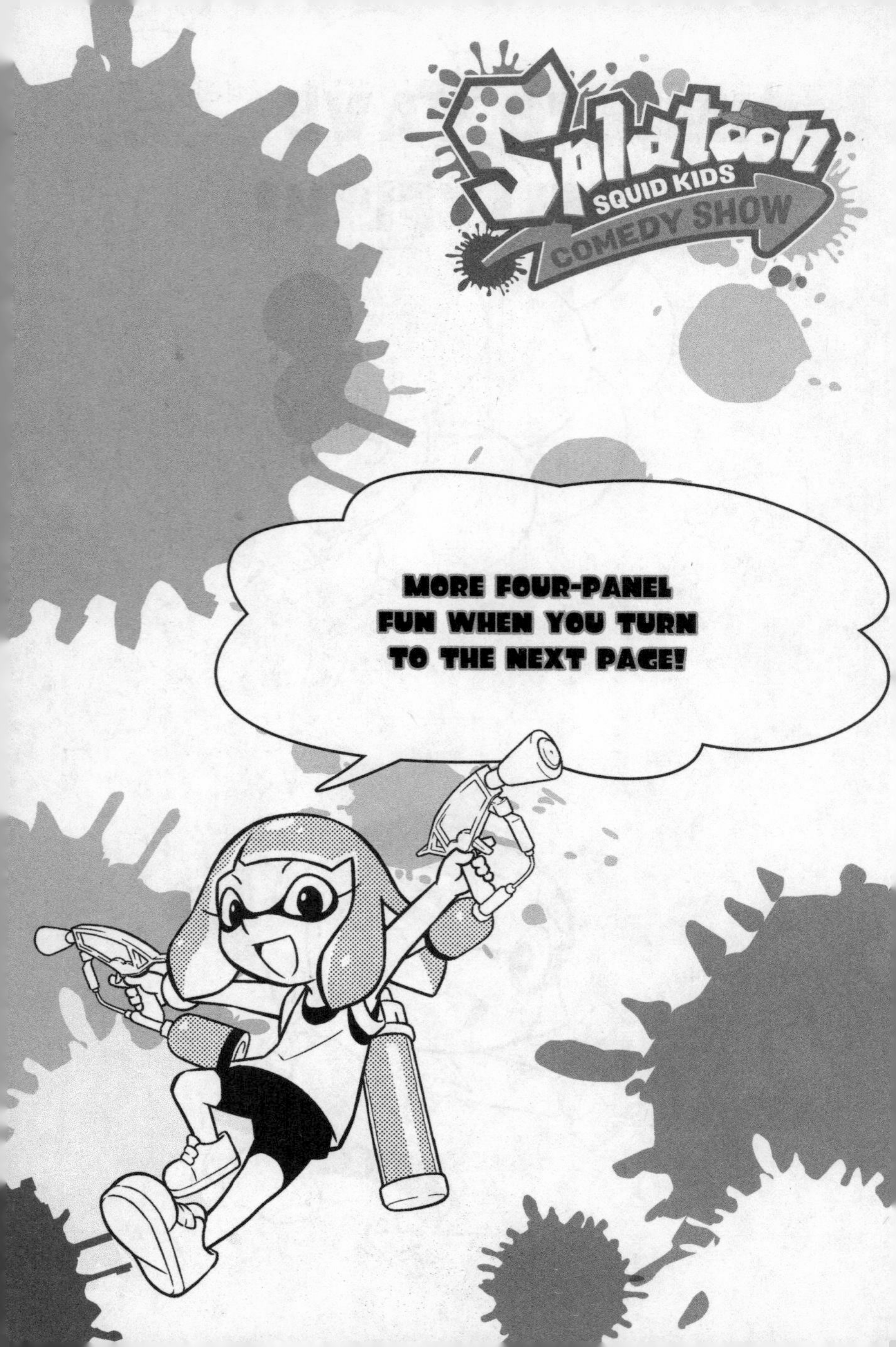
Splatoon
SQUID KIDS
COMEDY SHOW
MORE FOUR-PANEL FUN WHEN YOU TURN TO THE NEXT PAGE!

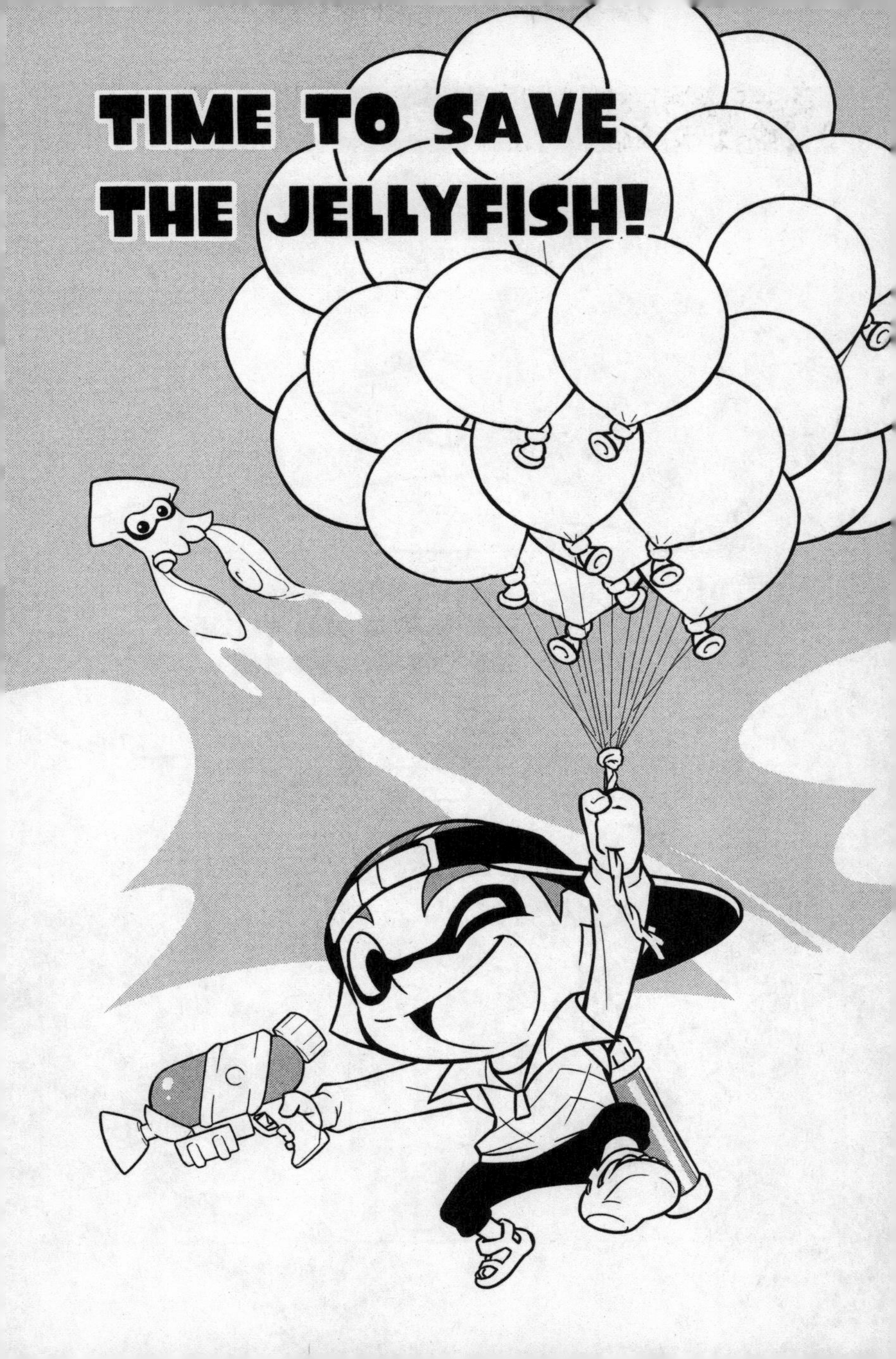
TIME TO SAVE
THE JELLYFISH!

HIT THE BALLOON

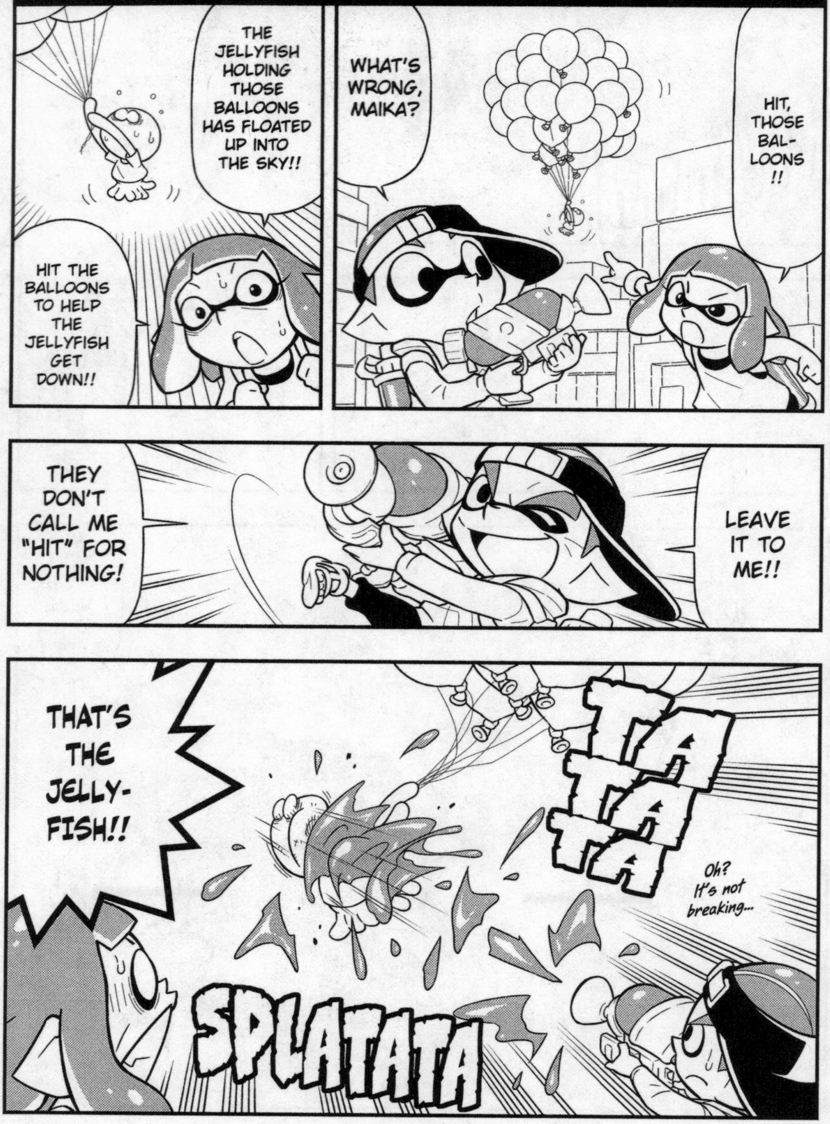
HIT, THOSE BAL-LOONS!!
WHAT'S WRONG, MAIKA?
THE JELLYFISH HOLDING THOSE BALLOONS HAS FLOATED UP INTO THE SKY!!
HIT THE BALLOONS TO HELP THE JELLYFISH GET DOWN!!
LEAVE IT TO ME!!
THEY DON'T CALL ME "HIT" FOR NOTHING!
TA TA TA
Oh? It's not breaking...
THAT'S THE JELLY-FISH!!
SPLATATA

MAZE

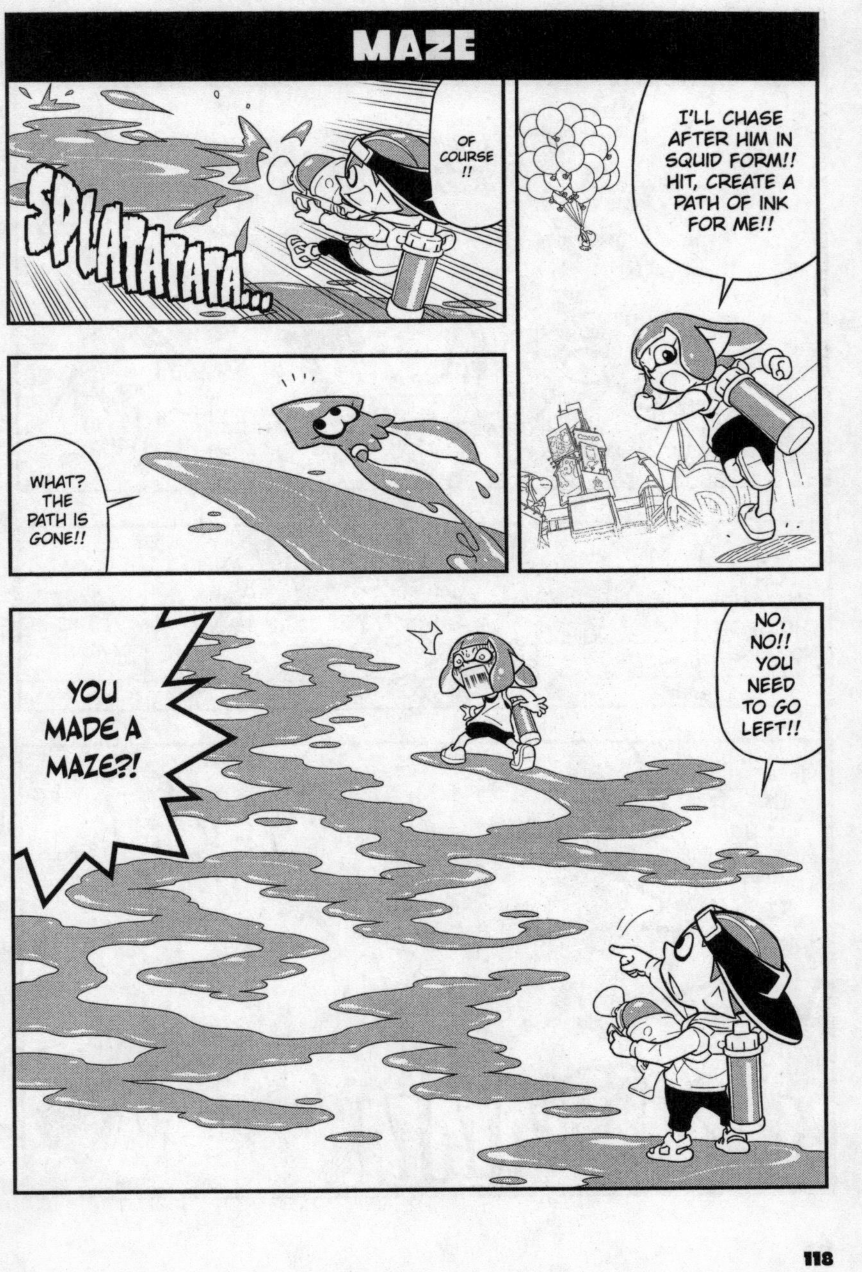
I'LL CHASE AFTER HIM IN SQUID FORM!! HIT, CREATE A PATH OF INK FOR ME!!
OF COURSE!!
SPLATATATA...
WHAT? THE PATH IS GONE!!
NO, NO!! YOU NEED TO GO LEFT!!
YOU MADE A MAZE?!

LOTS OF BALLOONS

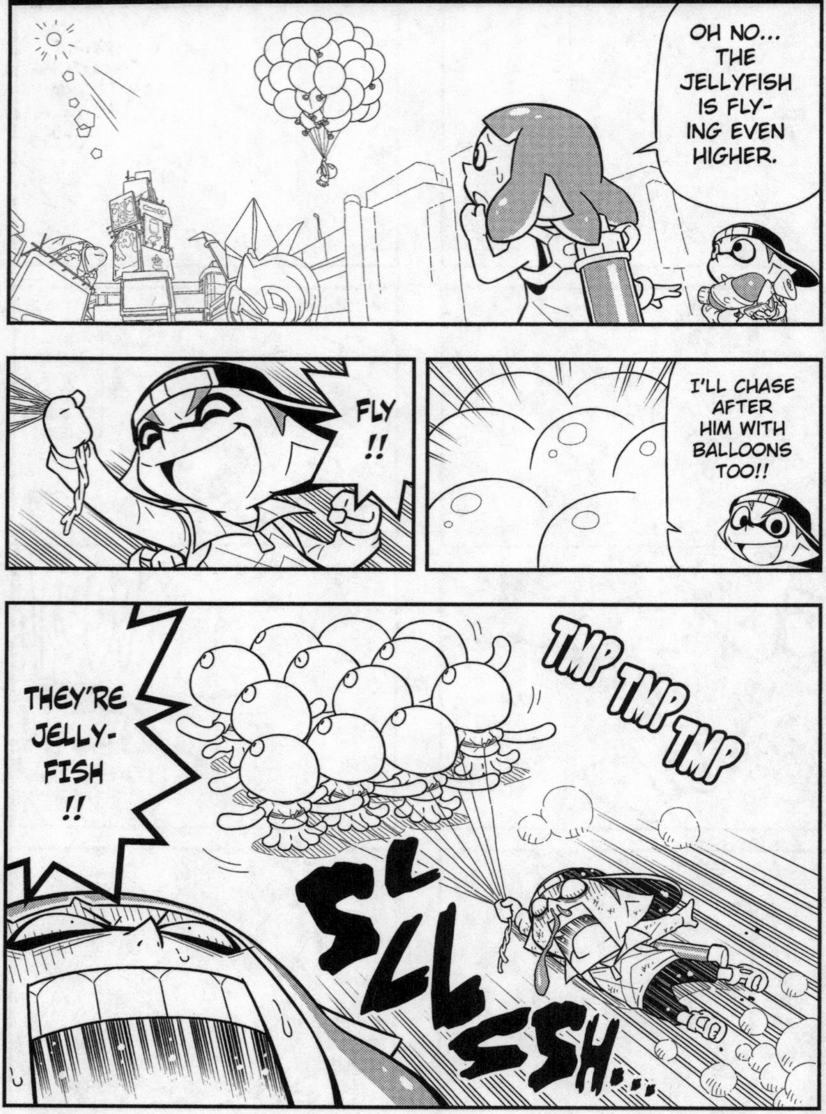
OH NO... THE JELLYFISH IS FLY-ING EVEN HIGHER.
I'LL CHASE AFTER HIM WITH BALLOONS TOO!!
FLY !!
TMP TMP TMP
THEY'RE JELLY-FISH !!
SLLLSSH...

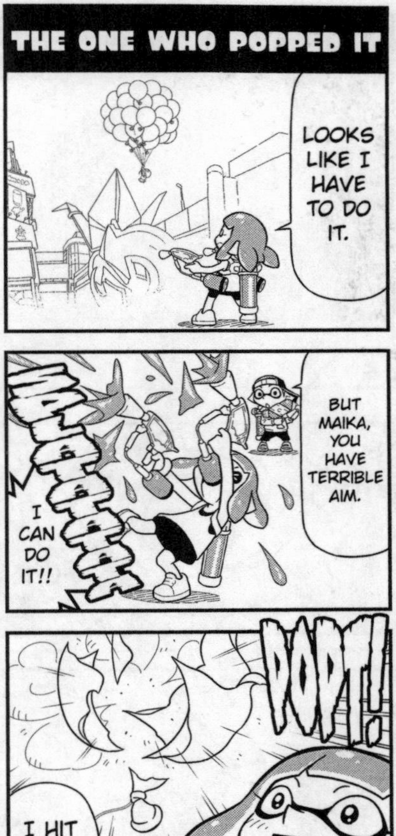
THE ONE WHO POPPED IT
LOOKS LIKE I HAVE TO DO IT.
BUT MAIKA, YOU HAVE TERRIBLE AIM.
I CAN DO IT!!
POPT!
I HIT IT!!
THE BALLOON POPPED BECAUSE IT BUMPED INTO THE CRANE!!

*DID YOU KNOW THERE WAS A STATUE OF A PAPER CRANE IN INKOPOLIS SQUARE?

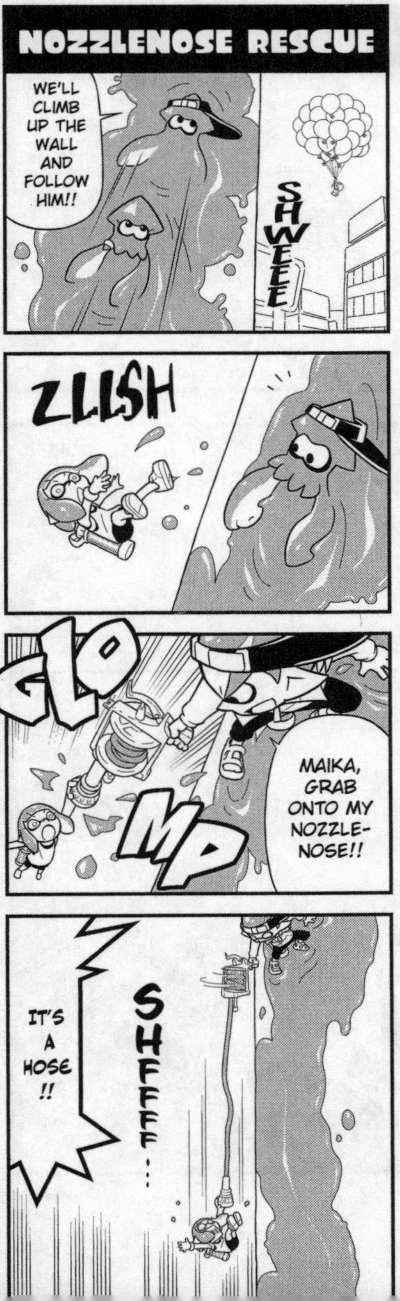
NOZZLENOSE RESCUE
WE'LL CLIMB UP THE WALL AND FOLLOW HIM!!
SHWEEE
ZLLSH
GLOMP
MAIKA, GRAB ONTO MY NOZZLE-NOSE!!
IT'S A HOSE!!
SHFFFF...

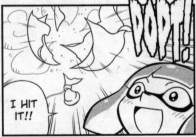

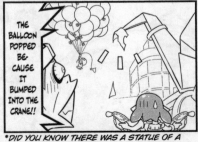

BULL'S-EYE WITH THE STING RAY

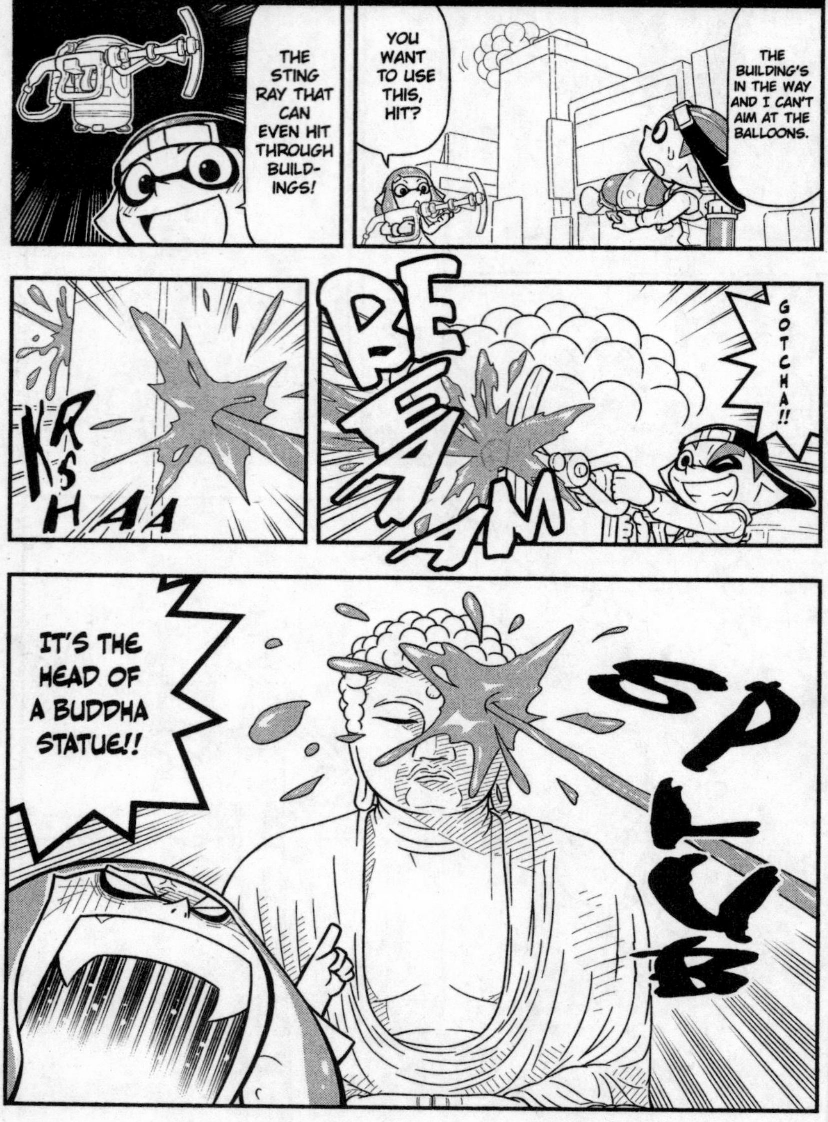
THE BUILDING'S IN THE WAY AND I CAN'T AIM AT THE BALLOONS.
YOU WANT TO USE THIS, HIT?
THE STING RAY THAT CAN EVEN HIT THROUGH BUILD-INGS!
BEEAAM
GOTCHA!!
KRSHAA
SPLUB
IT'S THE HEAD OF A BUDDHA STATUE!!

FLY! INKJET

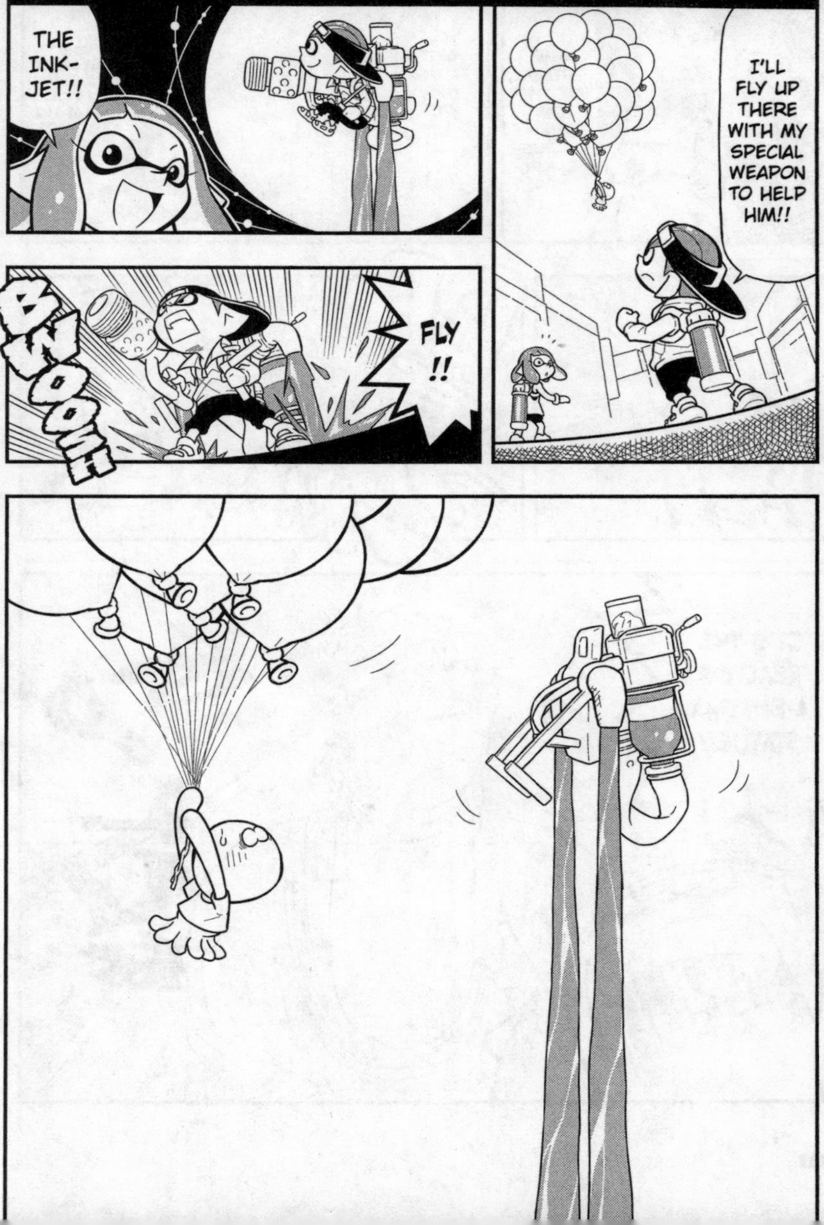
I'LL FLY UP THERE WITH MY SPECIAL WEAPON TO HELP HIM!!
THE INK-JET!!
FLY!!
BOOM

UNSTABLE LOCATION

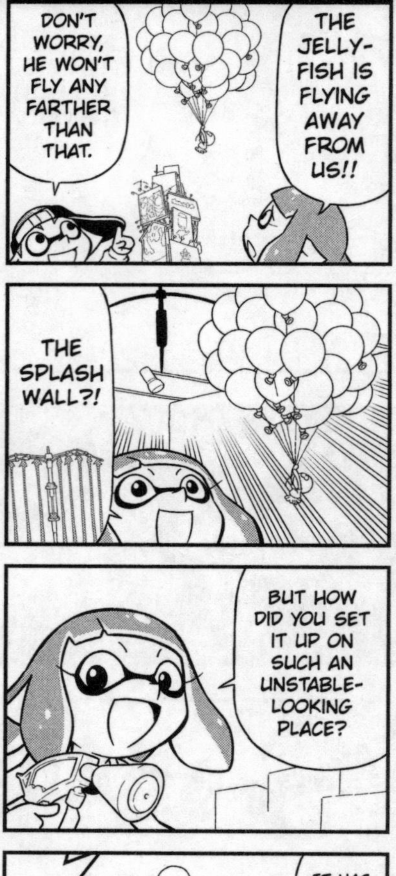
THE JELLY-FISH IS FLYING AWAY FROM US!!
DON'T WORRY, HE WON'T FLY ANY FARTHER THAN THAT.
THE SPLASH WALL?!
BUT HOW DID YOU SET IT UP ON SUCH AN UNSTABLE-LOOKING PLACE?
IT HAS REALLY GOOD BALANCE.
A BALANC-ING TOY?!

SHOCK ABSORBER

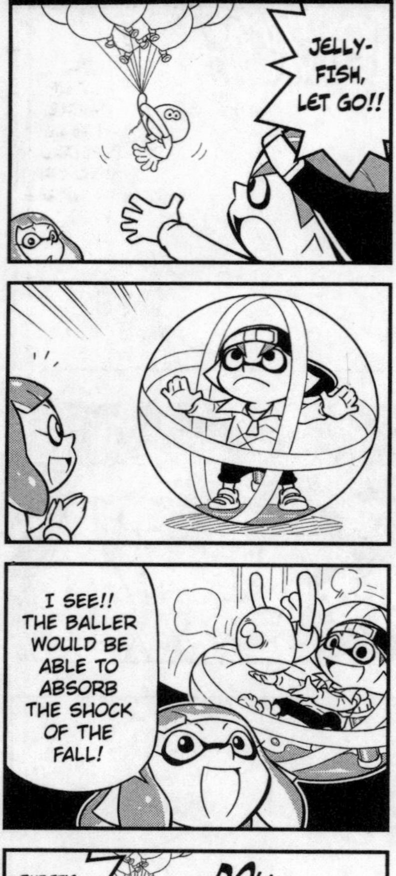
JELLY-FISH, LET GO!!
I SEE!! THE BALLER WOULD BE ABLE TO ABSORB THE SHOCK OF THE FALL!
Ahhhh!!
ROLL
ROLL
ROLL
BUT IT'S NOT GOOD ON SLOPES!!

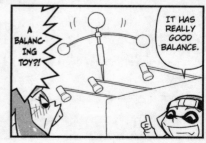

TENT CUSHION

BWOOSH
JELLYFISH, I'LL CATCH YOU WITH THE TENTA BRELLA!!
DON'T WORRY! YOU CAN JUMP DOWN!!
SHOOM
I LAUNCHED IT!!

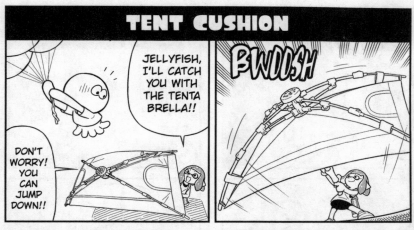

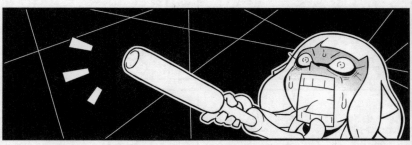

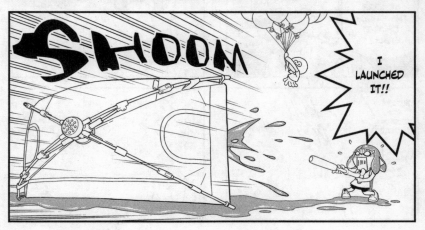

SUPER JUMP?!

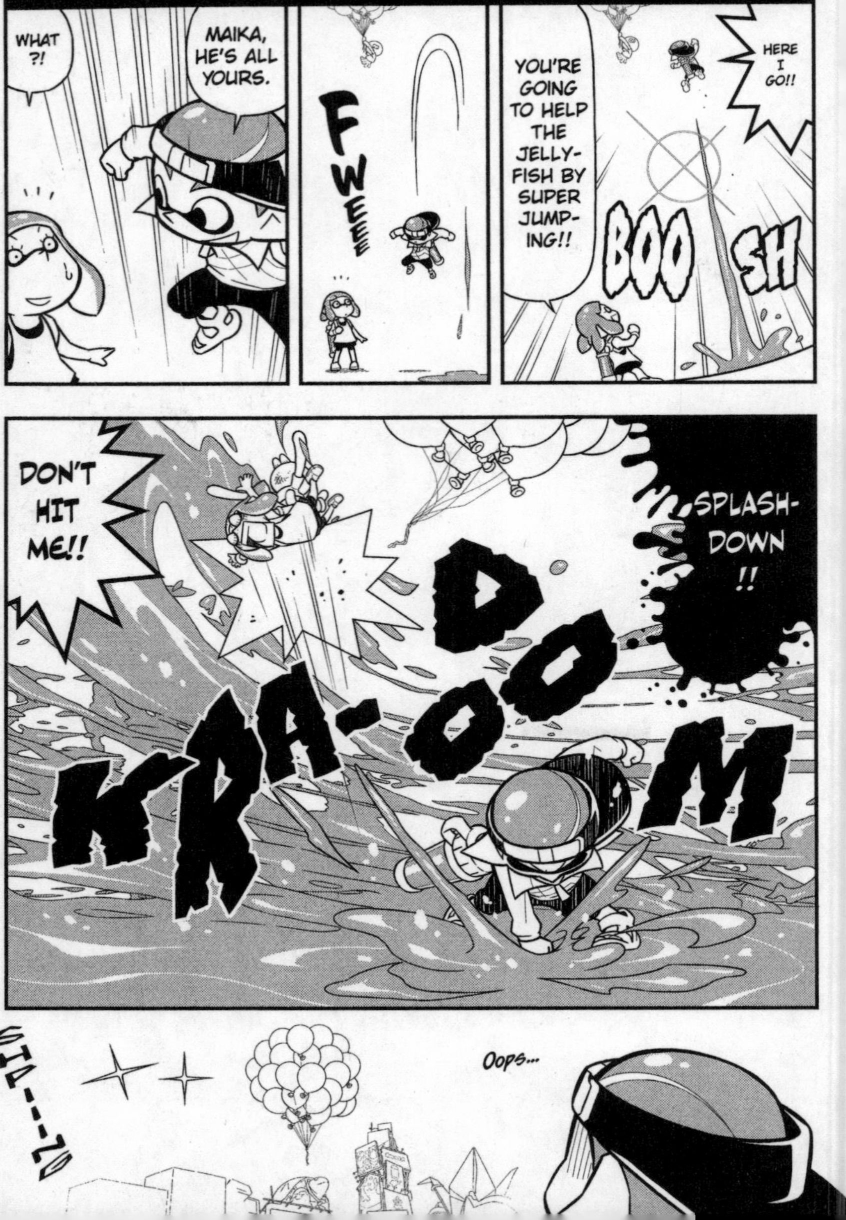
HERE I GO!!
YOU'RE GOING TO HELP THE JELLY-FISH BY SUPER JUMPING!!
BOOSH
FWEEE
MAIKA, HE'S ALL YOURS.
WHAT?!
SPLASH-DOWN!!
DON'T HIT ME!!
KRA-DOOOM
Oops...
SHI---NG

KRRRKT

LOSE...

HIDEKI GOTO

It had been a while since I last played *Splatoon 2* and my rank dropped to B– from S...

Hideki Goto was born in Gifu Prefecture, Japan. He received an honorable mention in the 38th Shogakukan Newcomers' Comic Awards, Kids' Manga Division, in 1996 for his one-shot *Zenryoku Dadada*. His first serialization was *Manga de Hakken Tamagotchi: Bakusho 4-koma Gekijo*, which began in *Monthly Coro Coro Comics* in 1997. *Splatoon: Squid Kids Comedy Show* began its serialization in *Bessatsu Coro Coro Comics* in 2017 and is Goto's first work to be published in English.